THE OPTIMAL PERFORMANCE FORMULA

An Actionable Blueprint for Those Passionate About Achieving the Impossible

Adolfo Gómez Sánchez

Praise for *The Optimal Performance Formula*

"*The Optimal Performance Formula* is an encyclopedia of performance enhancing techniques, based on Adolfo's unique methodology, that's actionable for any CEO or professional athlete that wants to gain separation from the competition."

Tobías Martínez
Founding CEO, Cellnex Telecom
Board member Eutelsat

"In professional tennis, performance training can mark the difference in tough matches. Adolfo brings unique tools to achieve that advantage, and now he's put them all in his new book, *The Optimal Performance Formula*, so anyone willing to do the work can access the secrets he teaches professional athletes."

Guillermo García-López
Top 20 ATP Tennis Pro
Grand Slam finalist (doubles)

"Achieving optimal performance based on Adolfo's book will be life changing for many. There are some lessons that you can only learn from a few. The art of applying the concepts of *The Optimal Performance Formula* is about building the inner strength to overcome struggles and get up once more than the average. That's what makes the outstanding optimal performer with lasting consistency. It can only be transmitted by people who have been through it. Listen to the Master!"

Dirk Wittenborg
CEO Axxola Venture Capital
Chairman Foxxum
Chairman Rlaxx

"The neat thing about Adolfo is not only his innate understanding and expertise in mastery, but that he can teach people how to improve performance to reach their goals through easily executable steps. His book, *The Optimal Performance Formula*, is a master playbook."

Donna Flagg
Faculty Dance Teacher, Joffrey Ballet School
Faculty Dance Teacher, Steps On Broadway
Founder LASTICS Dance Stretch

Acknowledgements

I would firstly like to thank my martial arts teachers. I have had the great fortune of studying under, and training with, true masters in every sense from Japan to North America and Europe in Karate, Tae Kwon Do, Jujutsu, Aikido, and Chi Kung. During the three-plus decades that I have been teaching and training, the philosophies of Budo (Martial Way) and Bujutsu (Martial Science), imbued with Zen teachings have become an integral part of who I am, serving me in every aspect of my life. These teachings have provided the cornerstone for many of the skills and techniques which have helped my clients, both athletes and executives, achieve dramatic improvements in performance, focus, and happiness.

Great masters teach that achieving the level of black belt signifies that you have reached the point where you are ready to start learning the subtle and transformative lessons of the arts, and one must continue to train, meditate, and grow until the belt gets so worn out that it loses all color and becomes white again. The objective is to attain the "beginner's mind" and develop an unquenchable thirst to learn and integrate new information, viewpoints, and nuances into one's training with no concern for the traps set out by the Ego. My belt has begun to fade, and every day I understand a little more of the true, deeper meaning of what these great masters taught me, and as a result, I realize what a long way I have to go. Thank you for teaching me that this is a good sign and that the value is in the journey.

I would like to thank all the great ATP and WTA coaches and players, both active and retired, who contributed in one way or another to this book and to my broader work on optimal performance. Tennis is a wonderful metaphor for business and life, and their profound knowledge of the tactics, strategies, and dynamics of the game have allowed me to include illustrative examples of the application of the elements that drive optimal performance. To include all their wisdom would have required five additional volumes, but even with the little I was able to capture and share, this book has been immeasurably enriched by real experiences from the world of professional sports.

Thank you also goes out to those unique captains of industry that I have been fortunate enough to work with, who have shown that it is possible to be a disruptive, innovative leader, while being a kind and caring human being. You are a living example of how passion, courage, purpose, and compassion are essential qualities for real leaders.

Finally, thank you to my mother, who at the time of publishing this book, has lost herself in her battle with Alzheimer's disease, and so she sadly cannot understand this message. Nonetheless, thank you for having taught me to never give up and to believe that I can achieve anything I set my mind to. That spirit is at the seed of this book and the programs that have converted my company, GOLD Results, into the go-to reference for Optimal Performance.

Table of Contents

Teaching also benefits me personally because the more you need to understand and break down the basics of any craft, the further along it propels you towards mastery. I've always told clients that I am "my own laboratory." Before teaching anyone skills and techniques that help drive performance, I test them on myself and experiment a lot, with the corresponding errors and failures, until I find the essential variables and parameters that drive real improvement.

So it seemed natural when I finally discovered that the area where my mission lay would be the intersection of those passions and skills: *striving for mastery, modeling what drives performance, and teaching others.*

The Optimal Performance Formula detailed in this book is the summary of the fundamental variables, tools, and techniques for driving performance in any field that I've accumulated and refined over the last three decades. It's the marriage of my academic training and research on the science of performance, together with the learnings that the ancient wisdom of the martial arts offers any student willing to embark on a lifelong journey to chase perfection in the hope of reaching one's maximum potential. These concepts have been refined and optimized in my own *internal lab* and battle tested in the trenches with top professional athletes and senior business leaders from leading multinationals whom I've mentored over my career.

What makes it unique?

One of the most essential constraints I set for myself in developing *The Optimal Performance Formula* was to make it practical and easy to understand. Although there's a lot of science behind it, most of my clients neither care nor have the time to spend years studying the research. They want to know "Why should I care? How does this help me achieve my goal of becoming a world class [insert aspiration here]?"

This is one of the key differences I believe *The Optimal Performance Formula* provides. It takes the complex *why* and breaks it down so it's easy to understand, then it links it to the *what* and the *how* you need to do things to benefit from each underlying principle.

I've included in the Appendix a list of some of the best research and books I'd recommend, in case you enjoy that kind of thing and want to get into the details. However, you don't have to read any of that to understand how the variables in *The Optimal Performance Formula* work and how to apply them to your particular mastery journey.

Let me give you a quick example I use often with my ATP players that illustrates how *The Optimal Performance Formula* is such a powerful toolbox to help ambitious top performers effectively integrate scientifically validated techniques to enhance their skill acquisition no matter their craft.

Here's a short teaser of how you'll be presented complex neuroscience and performance concepts in a digestible way that's relevant to your personal goals.

There's a weird phenomenon which occurs when highly skilled players try to overthink. The classic example in tennis is a soft ball at half court that the player shanks outside the court. How can that be? I'll often explain to players, without getting into the detailed neuroscience of learning and skill development, why this happens and how to avoid it. To do that, it helps if I give them a very high level view of how different parts of the brain work and are involved in executing a skill, because then we have a base upon which to start training ways to manage those different interactions.

When you learn a new skill, let's say a simple forehand in tennis, you need to think about each piece of the move: choose the right grip for the stroke, hit the ball in front, follow through over the shoulder, etc. At this point, you're executing with the prefrontal cortex, or the cognitive part of the brain. In other words, you're consciously controlling, or striving to control, each part of the technique. This is part of why it's so clumsy at the beginning.

As you drill thousands and thousands of forehands, and assuming you've gotten proper coaching along the way, you will start to burn the correct movement into your nervous system by generating more and more myelin, an insulator that makes these neural pathways easier and faster to access (we'll learn more about myelin later in the book). Note something important here. If you don't have good coaching, you will still consolidate technique, but it will be bad technique you hardwire into your system. For this example, let's assume you do develop excellent form. Your "skillful" forehand gets stored in the cerebellum located at the back of the brain beneath the occipital lobes. The cerebellum connects the brain to the spinal cord and is responsible for motor skills and controls unconscious activities of various organs like heart, lungs, digestive tract, etc.

Now here's the so what? Once you have a finely tuned process, your cerebellum takes care of that being executed in the way you've programmed. If you try to take control with your prefrontal cortex, i.e. your cognitive or conscious mind, you'll find your technique gets poorer, because in effect you're trying to control it with the same part of the brain that you used when learning the technique as a beginner, and it's not as efficient at executing complex movements with precision. Take walking as an example. If you think too much about how each muscle flexes and extends, you start walking clumsily because you're trying to override the skill you've fine tuned and stored in the cerebellum.

This explains how a player can make tens of shots in a row at fast speed from the baseline, but suddenly misses a short, easy shot. The answer is because he is trying to control a finely tuned motor process with the prefrontal cortex. Once the player understands how this can be negatively impacting his performance, we now have motivation and a base on which I can work with the player on techniques to avoid overthinking and choking like this in other situations.

(Side note: this is why golf is such a difficult sport, because it provides ample time to torture yourself mentally between strokes instead of just letting technique flow.)

So, that's one of the differences of *The Optimal Performance Formula.* It's designed to provide you with clear, simple-to-implement tools and techniques which incorporate the scientific research in a way that helps you understand how to apply, in your own journey, the methods that top performers use to reach such high levels of mastery in their crafts.

What else makes it unique and why should you—as an athlete, performing artist, or ambitious business leader—care?

The best way to answer those questions is by sharing a quick summary of the 11 most common reasons I've identified in my work with clients over the years that cause individuals and teams to fail when they try to implement performance improvements, change, and transformation efforts. *The Optimal Performance Formula* is designed to help avoid these pitfalls.

Mistake 1: Wanting a "quick fix"

One of the biggest challenges we face today is that everyone wants massive results without putting in the time and effort necessary. Let's be clear about this. It's naive to think you can develop world class skill, change a team culture, or address weaknesses in ridiculously short periods of time. It just isn't possible. The result is people "butterflying" from one trend to another, and quickly giving up if they don't get the results they seek in short order.

"If I had an hour to solve a problem, I'd spend 55 minutes thinking about the problem and 5 minutes thinking about solutions."

In other words, make sure you invest enough time in understanding what the REAL problem is, before rushing down the path of solving for the wrong thing. In my experience, even how you phrase the question goes a long way in facilitating innovative thinking. For example, asking, "Why can't I/we beat this competitor?" sends your mind off looking for answers as to *why it is not possible*, without contemplating *if it could be possible*. Instead, try asking, "What would need to be true, and what would I/we need to improve in order to beat this competitor?" This sets your brain on an active search to identify what concrete things you need to improve, and from there you can start exploring how to improve them and designing a plan to get to work on them.

Mistake 11: Not understanding how humans learn, integrate, and master skills

When trying to accomplish something ambitious, be it in business or sports, you will need to have a very high level of cognitive or physical skill, and usually you'll need both. No one ever achieves mastery in a short period of time, and there are specific ways to help drive learning and skill improvement (you'll learn these later in the book).

Although this sounds obvious, I constantly see clients set unrealistic programs and timelines for achieving those skills. All too often in the corporate world, there isn't even a plan beyond *We'll train you in a half hour and then expect you to integrate it seamlessly into your day to day*. Expecting behaviors and skills to evolve overnight only leads to disappointment from another failed change initiative. Likewise, I often find athletes adopt this approach with mental skills training, thinking once you explain it to them, they're done. However, like any skill, it needs to be worked and honed so you can leverage it in pressure situations.

I hope the above gives you a better understanding of what *The Optimal Performance Formula* can provide you and how it can be the missing piece in driving your performance to the next level.

What you won't find here

Let me take a few minutes to also flag what *The Optimal Performance Formula* is NOT, so you don't confuse it with other, very different things you may have seen in the past.

It's NOT:

A series of cute sports stories

Although listening to former athletes and coaches share some inside stories about how they achieved success might give you goosebumps— and may even be entertaining for a while—it's like processed, high-sugar junk food. It tends to leave you hungry again soon after because you realize you've learnt nothing about how to replicate those results in your own craft.

A hack

Although *The Optimal Performance Formula* does give you a significant jump start by distilling and structuring the best techniques and principles I've discovered over my 30 years of working with top performers, it requires a lot of work and is designed around a long-term view. You will be able to achieve improvements in the short- and mid-terms, but the real power lies in it being an integral program that helps you structure your journey to world class. The only hack for that is consistent, focussed work over a significant time period. Remember, no one ever achieves mastery in a week or a month, or even just one year.

A regurgitated compilation of academic literature

Clients want results. To get results, it helps to understand how and why different techniques and methodologies work. To that end, I'll break down into the most simplified terms the neuroscience that explains how your brain and body work. However, I have tried to avoid a trend I've seen in some books that just throw in reference after reference of scientific experiments. Most of my clients neither want (nor need) that level of detail.

Oh, and one more thing: the majority of the underlying concepts have not been invented by me. *Wait, what?* Shouldn't I be telling you I am the Chosen One who has received divine information from the universe that no one else knows? Well, that's not true. Not for me nor anyone else out there. All the basics used in any performance program have been around for a long time, even centuries (I'm sure you've heard someone quote Aristotle's famous line—"We are what we repeatedly do. Excellence, therefore, is not an act, but a habit.").

Now what I **DO** believe I have achieved with *The Optimal Performance Formula* is a significant innovation, and history has shown that innovation is often where you can create incredible jumps in value. Let me break this down in detail for you, because it is an important learning on your journey.

Let's use an example to solidify this concept of creating value via innovating vs inventing. Back in the late 1880s, Thomas Edison discovered electricity and developed direct current (DC), i.e. current that runs continually in a single direction, like in a battery or a fuel cell. That was exciting, but there was one big problem. Direct current is not easily converted to higher or lower voltages, thus the cost of using electricity for many practical ends, like powering homes and businesses, became prohibitive, and it was not widely accepted as the solution for the future.

In came Nikola Tesla, who believed that alternating current (AC) was the solution to this problem. AC reverses direction a certain number of times per second and can be converted to different voltages relatively easily using a transformer. This resulted in driving down the cost of providing electricity, and all of a sudden you could build a competitive business case for electricity in a whole slew of new applications that would not work with direct current.

As a result, General Electric, which had been selling solutions based on Edison's DC, lost out in every major bid to electrify large populations to Westinghouse that was using Tesla's AC and, thus, was able to always come in at a more competitive price. Westinghouse won some first symbolic opportunities such as the Chicago World's Fair in 1893 and, later that same year, sold a solution to the Niagara Falls Power Company that could power not only Buffalo, but also the entire Eastern United States. Soon after, GE jumped on the AC bandwagon.

My point here is that Edison was the inventor, but Tesla was the innovator. And most people would say the value of electricity lies in all the ways it can enhance your life and business. In that same sense, everything in *The Optimal Performance Formula* has been thought up already by great thinkers and visionaries in the past. A fundamental step change is the way I explain the elements that drive performance so they can be easily understood and embedded into your day-to-day to significantly accelerate progress in your quest for mastery.

Just like electrical current is of little value if you can't harness it, the drivers of performance are useless if you only get them cognitively or theoretically, but can't figure out how to integrate them into your training and performances.

Essentially, this is why getting in shape and losing weight is simple in *theory*, but actually *doing* it is really hard. As a result, anyone who can get you results is in high demand (in case you haven't looked lately, the fitness industry is estimated to generate about 87 billion dollars per year for the taking by the best innovators).

The secret sauce

We've talked about how *The Optimal Performance Formula* breaks down and synthesizes the science of performance into actionable steps within a complete, coherent model. We've also seen the common pitfalls it is designed to help avoid, saving you months and even years of marginal progress or plateauing.

However, if I had to choose one thing which I think is the most powerful element of the model, it's the way it breaks apart performance into its component pieces, optimizes each one, then stitches them back together.

Let's face it—if you strive to be the best athlete in your field, you need to master conditioning, technique, and strategy, as well as mental strength. Likewise, in business you need to be able to ensure foundational skills, technical skills, and leadership skills, all the while balancing management (predictable, repeatable outcomes) and innovation (growth mindset) to stay ahead of the competition.

This integrated view is what I find missing in the thinking and development of professional athletes and top executives alike.

One recurring theme I've found over the years and across clients is that people try to silo different pieces of performance training as separate and independent disciplines. In other words, athletes may have physical trainers, technical coaches, nutritionists, and specialized functional experts—such as flexibility coaches, physiotherapists and mental skills mentors—but they view them as separate, and that's where you lose all the synergies.

Many athletes have strong, pre-existing biases that one or two of the disciplines are *the really important ones,* and the others are nice add-ons. Elite performers, on the other hand—like Michael Jordan, Kobe Bryant, Tom Brady, or Novak Djokovic—are famous for seeking out any millimeters of growth and improvement they can find across as many disciplines as possible.

In business, the above mentioned biases manifest as siloed departments trying to effect change alone, while ignoring the fact that true value is created across the value chain. Another common occurrence is managers trying to drive transformational change without developing the necessary foundational capabilities, such as a true understanding of how to create psychological safety for their teams, effective communication skills, and performance coaching training.

As you've probably figured out by now, I have a very strong view on this, and it's the basis of how *The Optimal Performance Formula* is designed. I have discovered from my years in the trenches with highly talented and ambitious performers that, if you really want to fulfill your maximum potential, you need to understand a much broader and more holistic definition of performance, because that's the uncomfortable truth of how human beings work, learn, grow and achieve mastery. In essence:

Performance training impacts not just when you're under the lights on the court, field, boardroom, or stage, but it also deeply influences how you think, learn, practice, and program your road to mastery.

It's about learning how to analyze and understand your craft at such a deep, foundational level that you are working on details that most people don't even know exist. This entails understanding the fundamentals of how humans acquire, develop, and master skill. It also requires understanding how the different pieces or disciplines stack together to drive optimal performance.

No one can walk the road for you, but a battle-tested system can help you design and build the roadmap to understand how you can improve in all dimensions of performance development.

If you burn with passion to see how much better you can get, and you're hungry for new insights and tools, then read on. Your higher performing future self awaits!

The Three Main Blocks of
The Optimal Performance Formula

Knowledge without action is vanity,
but action without knowledge is insanity.

Hafsah Faizal
(NY Times Best Selling Author)

It's time to roll up our sleeves and start getting into the model.

First, let's lay out the overall structure of *The Optimal Performance Formula*. It's based on three fundamental blocks, within each of which are a series of methodologies that serve as levers you can employ to drive performance. Although I often use sports terminology to give each lever an easy-to-remember name, all the variables in all of the blocks have been selected because they are equally applicable and effective for businesses as they are for athletes and sporting organizations.

First, we'll define what's in each of the three fundamental sections. In successive chapters, we will delve into each of the variables within the three blocks. I like to explain them from a birds-eye view, then zoom in, as I find this helps people understand what they are and how each piece is part of a holistic model, not a separate and unrelated concept. The reason this is so important is because the value multiplies when you leverage the synergies across the three big blocks.

To get the most out of the model, I recommend working through it in order, since each block serves as a fundamental cornerstone upon

BLOCK 1:
MINDSET

The mind is the athlete; the body is simply the means it uses to run faster or longer, jump higher, shoot straighter, kick better, swim harder, hit further or box better.

Bryce Courtney
(Best Selling Author)

Batman's Greatest Power
Is Being Batman

Rather than thinking about what we're doing, we need to think about our thinking. Our story. . . will always determine our strategy and . . . our results. If we want better results, we have to tell ourselves better stories. By changing our narratives, we can change our neural patterns. . ."

Michael Hyatt and Megan Hyatt Miller
(From the book *Mind Your Mindset*)

WHAT'S THE BIG DEAL?

Your identity—or your mission if you're a company—defines everything around *how* and *why* you do things, and in fact determines *what* you do. Identity defines what you believe you are capable of, and what you've convinced yourself is impossible (for you). It's the first subject in the *Mindset* block because everything else builds upon identity.

Growing up as a huge comic book fan, I have always pointed out that Batman's greatest power is that, deep down in his soul, he believes that his true identity is not Bruce Wayne, but Batman. As such, he has unwavering faith that he can do things that only Batman can do. In essence, he proves Albert Einstein's famous statement,

Everyone knew it was impossible, until a fool who didn't know came along and did it.

That's how powerful belief is and how important it is to define your identity.

One of the first things I evaluate when I start working with a new client—either a professional athlete, a performance artist, or a business—is whether they have a clear identity. Identity gives us parameters to define what makes sense, what we should do, and what we shouldn't do. It really is one of the most powerful tools you must understand and use if you aspire to reach your maximum performance potential.

Let's start by taking a look at how identity can work for you or against you, then I'll share how I've used identity to drive impactful performance improvements with some professional athletes. Finally, we'll see how this lesson has also been of paramount importance to companies trying to optimize performance.

Choose who you want to be (or you'll be told who you are)

Identity (or self-image) is actually an incredibly powerful concept and pays huge dividends if you do the work. We all have a self-image or identity,—in other words, a perception of who we are and what makes us uniquely, well, *us*. We are wired to conform to what is coherent with our self-image or who we believe ourselves to be. If we deviate from there, we experience what psychologists call *cognitive dissonance*, which is basically the disconnect you feel when you act in a way that you don't believe is aligned with who you are. For example, if your identity is that you are a fair and kind person, and you find yourself having to do things you consider unethical, you'll be hindered and won't perform well.

Since the mind doesn't like the feeling of cognitive dissonance, it will drive you to behave in a way that is aligned with your self-image. That's great, if you have consciously designed and decided your identity, but for most people, it's something that is developed subconsciously since childhood, based on the experiences you live, the meaning you give them, and the influences of the people around you.

So, keeping in mind the impact of cognitive dissonance, you can start to understand the importance of aligning who you are with the type of person you believe you need to be to achieve your goals. This is where so many people become frustrated trying to change their results, just to find that they keep sabotaging themselves. Your brain is stubborn and, if it feels you're experiencing something which is not coherent with your identity, it will do everything possible to eliminate the disconnect by aligning reality with identity. So, if you haven't worked on defining the identity you want, you'll be fighting against the *de facto* identity planted in your subconscious.

I've seen this many times with players who believe they can't beat a given rival. They may be ahead during a match, then the brain says, *hey, we can't beat this guy*, and they will find amazing ways to lose. I worked with one very talented player who was in the top 20 ATP ranking. He could hold his own against almost any player, having even beaten several of the top 5 players in the past. However, there was one player on tour who was what we'd call a *black beast* for him—a player who was living in his head rent-free and whom my client believed he couldn't beat. We had faced him (and lost) in a recent Masters 1000 tournament, then a few weeks later, the draw matched them together again in another Masters 1000 during the clay season.

My client lost the first set, then he found his groove and won the second set 6-2. He maintained a high level of play and managed to gain a 4-0 lead in the third. In other words, he had won 10 of the last 12 games and clearly had the momentum in his favor. Despite all the objective evidence that he could, and should, beat this rival, his identity had not yet accepted it, and he found a way to lose the match. The belief in his subconscious became a self-fulfilling prophecy, and he dropped six straight games to lose 6-4 in the third. That's a powerful example of why identity is so important for performance.

This is not something rare. I've seen many similar occurrences in the ATP. In the Madrid Masters about 10 years ago, I saw Fernando Verdasco leading Rafael Nadal in the third set, then all of a sudden, it appeared as if he'd *remembered* that he wasn't supposed to win, and he gave up a 5-1 lead and lost the match.

There are also classic examples of this in other sports. For example, in Super Bowl LI, the New England Patriots were down 28-3 at halftime vs an Atlanta Falcons team that had been dominant in the first half. However, in the second half, the Patriots leveraged their belief in their core identity that they could always come back, no matter how steep the deficit, and the Falcons suffered imposter syndrome, doubting what they had achieved in the first half, resulting in one of the greatest comebacks ever, with New England winning by a final score of 34-28.

From the above examples, it should be clear that who you are and who you want to become serve as a guidance system for every part of your mastery journey. The evolution of Rafael Nadal is another epic example. Back around 2007, Nadal had just won his third French Open title in a row. He was already being hailed as the *King of Clay*, the best clay court player of all time. He could have stayed with that identity, comfortably dominating the clay court tournaments for another decade but not being dominant on other surfaces. However, Nadal had other plans. He had decided he wanted to be the best he could possibly be, and his identity was that of a tough, battling competitor on all surfaces.

Remember, we mentioned that how you train and compete changes depending on how you see yourself. Since Nadal believed he could be a top competitor on all surfaces, not just a clay court specialist, he started focussing on areas like his serve and his volley skills that were much more relevant for hard courts and grass courts than on clay. He started changing his style of play and flattening out strokes at times to finish points more quickly. If he'd been content to be *just* the best player on clay, he would not have trained the same way. He would have focused more on stamina and ability to get the ball back, because clay is not fertile ground for racking up aces with big serves or hitting tons of flat winners.

Not having your core identity clear can lead to catastrophic mistakes in business also. Look at the example of Smith Corona! One hundred years of success made them lose perspective and ultimately led to bankruptcy. Just in case you don't know who they were, Smith Corona was market leader for many years in the typewriter manufacturing business. They released many innovative products over the years, including the following list of milestones:

1886: First machine to write in upper and lower case letters
1906: First portable typewriter
1957: First electric portable typewriter
1960: First automatic return
1973: First replaceable cartridge
1984: First word eraser
1985: First electronic dictionary
1989: First portable word processor
1989: They declared over $500 million in revenue

Despite all the innovative products Smith Corona had launched, they forgot their identity and suffered what I call *boiling frog syndrome*. When frogs are put in very hot water, they will try to jump out, but if you place them in water at room temperature and heat it slowly, the frogs will not identify the change in temperature fast enough and will not try to escape, boiling to death. In essence, this is what happened to Smith Corona. They failed to react to the changes in their environment because they forgot their core identity.

Smith Corona saw themselves as a typewriter company, and that was their downfall. They forgot that all their innovations had been around tools to capture and share human thought. During a period, the best vehicle for that were typewriters, but as technology evolved, other tools would supplant typewriters. As a result, instead of signing an agreement with ACER to build computers when they had the chance, Smith Corona decided to invest in Mexico in a new plant to make typewriters at 12% less cost. Three years later, they went bankrupt.

The good news is, you can work on modifying and defining your identity, and it all starts with defining your future self. That person you need to be in order for your mission to become a reality. Although it sounds simple enough, it's actually very difficult, because we are complex creatures and are often wed to the images and behaviors we were brought up with. Even when we rationally see they are not productive, at a subconscious level, we identify with them as a safety mechanism or protective layer. If you're interested in this, I recommend reading the work of Kegan and Lahey on *hidden commitments* that's included in the list of recommended reading at the end of this book.

"Michael's Secret Stuff"

They say that what makes jokes funny is that, behind all humor, there is some truth. I believe that, and it's what helped create one of the most iconic scenes in the 1996 movie *Space Jam*, where Michael Jordan plays basketball with the Looney Toons.

At one point, the Toons team is getting beaten badly, and they've given up. Jordan gives a passionate speech in the locker room to no avail. The team feels defeated. Then Bugs Bunny fills a water bottle with tap water and hand writes a label that says *Michael's Secret Stuff*. Bugs then storms in and says,

"Hey Mike, stop holding out on us!"

Bugs passes the bottle around to the other Toons, who transform into stronger, more athletic versions of themselves as they drink the magical potion. Of course, they then go out and kick alien butt.

I love that scene because it is so true and highlights a key principle. You need to purposefully craft your identity, examine, and then define beliefs and expectations coherent with that identity, because this will define the limit you believe you can or cannot reach.

We'll explore the science that confirms this is a real and powerful phenomenon, but first let me share how I lay this out for my clients, as it will help you understand how it relates to your daily choices.

It's a given that everyone *wants* to win a Gold Medal at the Olympics, but only a select few athletes actually *believe* they can win a medal or *expect* to win one. That may sound like semantics, but it's a crucially important distinction if you want to achieve optimal performance for yourself and your team. Here's the link with identity. Batman *believes* he can do amazing feats and *expects* to defeat criminals when he clashes with them, because that's who he is. Likewise, an Olympic athlete who has carefully curated an identity as a top medal contender, will have a strong belief that they can win a medal, and will sincerely expect to do so. Do you think you would approach training, scheduling of qualifying competitions, and all other aspects of preparation over the four years leading up to the Olympics in the same manner if you expected to win a medal vs if you'd already met your objective by just making your national team? The answer is a resounding *NO!* It's just human nature.

The point you need to grasp firmly here as a cornerstone for building your mastery journey is that your *actions* come from your *identity*. This is one reason that change and creating new habits is so difficult and often fails. Your identity is what you're most committed to. Your actions come from your identity, and consistency only comes if those actions are natural for *someone like you*. The ultimate form of intrinsic motivation is when a habit becomes part of your identity. It's one thing to say "I'm the type of person who *wants* this." It's a whole different ball game to say "I'm the type of person who *is* this."

The magic occurs when you achieve a virtuous circle between identity, beliefs, expectations, and actions. You act based on who you are and what you expect from yourself, given your identity. The synergies occur when your actions provide positive feedback and proof to your brain that you are, in fact, the type of person who acts like that, thus reinforcing your identity. The identity itself then reinforces the beliefs and actions. You do it because it's who you are, so your performance habits become the norm and your expectations and belief grow stronger.

I hope you begin to really understand the importance of this, because so many people underestimate the impact it has on their journey. The same principle is applicable to corporations. I see so many large multinationals that launch transformation initiative after transformation initiative, and yet 90% fail. The reasons are varied, but one of the major ones is that they don't do the work to ensure the entire team believes the change will happen and that the organization is capable of implementing the vision.

Furthermore, it's common to fail when communicating how the initiative ties in to driving the mission. This is why there are so many team members suffering from *change fatigue*. They feel they are being asked to take on someone's political agenda and don't *believe* they will be actually leading a legendary change, thus they just suffer through a plethora of corporate initiatives, some of which seem contradictory.

Belief is the secret sauce in visualization

Visualization is gaining popularity in all fields, but athletes have been using it for many years to see themselves as already having achieved their goals before they actually do. Accounts such as that of Andre Agassi, who reported that he had seen himself winning Wimbledon thousands of times in his mind before he actually won it, are common in sports lore. However, many people, especially those in the corporate world, still feel that visualization is some New Age, intangible technique because it hasn't worked for them.

Here is one of the best-kept secrets about how to make visualization work. You need to not only envision how that future moment will look, but you need to *feel* it as if it's really happening, and then take the absolute conviction that comes from having lived that experience and know that you can reproduce it at any time. Again, it's the same difference as *hoping* to win a medal vs *believing and expecting* you will win a medal. Visualization without the feeling and conviction that it is real, is just daydreaming. However, when you actually experience the vision as if you are living it, then you're much closer to a night time dream during REM sleep. Research shows that the brain and the body do not know the difference between a dream and reality. However, you do know that your daydreams are not really occurring. That's the key difference, and it is what allows your mind and body to process proper visualization as real-life experience.

The reason this works is because one of the biggest sources of confidence that mental skills coaches teach is to leverage your past successes as proof to convince yourself that you can do what you are aspiring to achieve. Here's the catch that perplexes so many athletes and ambitious performers in other fields who try to tap into the power of visualization: How do you leverage the confidence from having done something if you still haven't done it even once? That's where the power of belief and expectations, combined with proper, full-sensory visualization help elite performers create separation from the rest.

The absolute G.O.A.T. at using this superpower was NBA legend Larry Bird. Despite his non-athletic appearance and average speed, Bird is universally admired and recognized by other NBA legends as one of the greatest players of all time, bar none. Known for his prolific trash talking, Bird was actually using his own *secret stuff* to not only visualize how he was going to dominate opponents, but actually tell them about it beforehand, to further cement his conviction that his prophecies would become reality. You could write an entire book just about Larry Bird's mental skills, but let me share a few short stories, told by other NBA legends and media experts that give you a flavor of how much of a Jedi Mind Master Larry Bird really was, and how he used his belief to create his identity as unstoppable.

Nike Talk reported the following story:

"On a West Coast trip in 1986, Bird told the entire Dallas Mavericks bench that after the time out, Ainge would inbound the pass to DJ, who would hit Bird in the corner where Bird would step back and take a three. Bird then asked the Mavericks bench, 'So you got that? I'm gonna stand right here. I'm not going to move. They'll pass me the ball, and the next sound you hear will be the ball hitting the bottom of the net.' And that's exactly what happened. Bird winked at the Maverick bench before heading back down to the other end of the court."

Former NBA player and coach Michael Cooper shared this story about the 3-point contest at the NBA All-Star Game:

"Larry walks in and says 'I hope all you guys in here are thinking about second place, because I'm winning this'... and he started shooting and he just didn't miss. Of course, he won, lifting his finger in the air before the final shot went in, and not even removing his warm up jacket."

Former Boston Celtics player and General Manager Danny Ainge on what Bird would do when playing in opponents' stadiums:

"Larry used to come in the locker rooms, he'd be getting his ankles taped and he would say: 'Hey mop boy, go run and find the scoring record in this building'– he needed those kind of challenges."

NBA legend Dennis Rodman recounts the following about playing Bird:

"I would be all over him, trying to deny him the ball, and all Larry was doing was yelling at his teammates, 'I'm open! Hurry up before they notice nobody is guarding me!' ... then he would stick an elbow in my jaw and stick the jumper in my face, then he would start in on my coach 'Coach you better get this guy out and send in somebody who's going to D me up, because it's too easy when I'm wide open like this."

The takeaway here is that Bird wasn't shooting off at the mouth. He had visualized—and internally lived and felt—the situation and used the trash talking to cement that feeling and consolidate his confidence, almost as if he was hypnotizing himself into believing everything he said was 100% true.

Preparation bolsters belief and sets expectations

Visualization, as we've seen, powered by belief and expectations, is very powerful for driving performance. The question now is: how do we bolster belief?

One of the secrets that elite performers use is putting preparation very high on their priority list, because they understand that the confidence they get from knowing that they have trained and prepared at world class levels, is a game changer when it comes time to perform. The work they put in also provides their minds with confirmation of their identity, and feeds the loop of expectations and belief.

Preparation trumps pressure and fuels confidence. Preparation is the unseen grind that generates belief in your abilities when you're under the lights. A great example is NBA pro Ray Allen who practiced to simulate game situations so when the time came, he would know he was capable of performing. He would practice shots from the spots he expected to be taking those shots from in the game, at game speed and simulating game tension and fatigue by doing pushups to tire his arms and still be able to make the shots.

As Kevin Eastman says, preparation allows you to"be there before you get there." In other words, it bolsters confidence and expectations, just like Larry Bird's visualization techniques. And here's the link to your future self: *Who is the person you want to become?* Your answer should extend beyond your current context. Imagination is more important than knowledge, and having a clear view of who you have to become and how you need to perform to achieve what you want to achieve is essential.

Another example comes from the winner of 28 Olympic medals, swimmer Michael Phelps. Phelps tells the story of how visualization of all possible scenarios built his mental strength and was a key factor in his victory in the Beijing Olympics in 2008. Here's an extract from an interview where Phelps tells the story in his own words:

> "So for me, like when I would visualize. . . I mean getting up to a meet, and I would visualize probably a month or so in advance just of what could happen, what I want to happen and what I don't want to happen because when it happened I was prepared for it.
>
> So you know, when I go into 2008 and in the 200 fly, my goggles fill up with water the first 25. And I am blind for 175 meters. I revert back to what I did in training and counted my strokes. And I knew how many strokes I take the first, second, third, and fourth 50 of all of my best 200 flies. So I reverted back to that and I was ready for that because I was mentally prepared for it."

Again, notice how the quality of the visualization was key so Phelps could feel like he's done it before and reverted to counting strokes and feeling his motion to produce a world class performance. He didn't *hope* he would work it out; he *believed* he could do it, because he'd done it a thousand times in his mind and in practice.

Many people get tripped up or trapped in a continuous loop of believing they can only do what they've managed to achieve in the past. This is where belief is so powerful. Who you want to become should be irrespective of your current situation and irrespective of your past. Since you may not have historical data, such as experiences that validate that you can achieve that level of performance, you need to tap into your belief and *live* the experiences before they occur by full-sensory visualization. Since your brain generates the same signals and sensations when you vividly visualize as when you physically perform an action—be it physical or cognitive—you are essentially living those experiences before you live them. Your brain leverages the confidence of having *been there, done that* to boost your belief that you can do it again.

The alternative is to simply be content consolidating the skill level you are currently at. In this case, you'll likely slide backwards, and you definitely won't be realizing your full potential. Rather than having goals that are reactive to their current context, top performers create the vision they want, which is way beyond their current skill level, and use that vision to drive their actions and choices in the present. Once you believe you are the best in the world at your craft, you start acting the way the best in the world would act.

The Pygmalion effect

In case you're wondering if all this is just based on opinions, it's not. This principle is actually a real, scientifically studied and proven phenomenon called the **Pygmalion effect**, or **Rosenthal effect.** In summary, the Pygmalion effect occurs when people's performance conforms to the expectations in their environment, resulting in self-fulfilling prophecies. In other words, high expectations lead to improved performance in a given area and low expectations lead to worse performance.

The alternative name, the Rosenthal effect, comes from the work of psychologists Robert Rosenthal and Lenore Jacobson which famously showed that teachers' expectations of their students affect the students' performance. The experiment was run in a California elementary school where students were given a disguised IQ test but did not disclose the results to teachers. Teachers were told that about 20% of their students, selected at random, could be expected to be "intellectual bloomers" that year, doing better than expected in comparison to their classmates. The names were made known to the teachers. At the end of the study, all students were again tested and first- and second-graders showed statistically significant gains favoring the experimental group of "intellectual bloomers." This led to the conclusion that teacher expectations can influence student achievement. Rosenthal believed that even attitude or mood could positively affect the students and that the teacher may pay closer attention to—and treat the child differently—in times of difficulty.

The Pygmalion study is fascinating, but there is a much larger body of scientific trials that you've probably heard of that confirms the power of belief. I'm referring to the power of placebos.

A placebo is a medicine or procedure prescribed for the psychological benefit to the patient rather than for any physiological effect. The substance has no therapeutic effect and is used as a control in testing new drugs. The beneficial effect produced by a placebo drug or treatment cannot be attributed to the properties of the placebo itself, and must therefore be due to the patient's *belief* in that treatment.

The volume and clarity of research results into the effect of place-bos is unquestionable, and it's the same mechanism that we've been discussing here and that proves Steven Covey's assertion:

"Mental creation always precedes physical creation."

Coaching Case File: How an ATP player leveraged identity to reach the top ten

One player I worked with was in the top 50 in the ATP ranking at the time we began working together. He was one of the hardest working players and one of the most rigorous, disciplined professionals I've ever encountered (besides being an exceptionally nice guy). One of the things we spoke about was that he was playing in a manner that did not leverage his strengths, and thus he lost games against rivals he could have beaten if he'd focussed on developing his game and strategy around his strengths and unique identity. So, the first order of business was to clearly define that identity and what it implied in terms of how he would train and compete.

As you saw above, your identity is crucial, because it impacts your performance so significantly, and this is what I explained to this player. He was a very solid base-liner and didn't have super powerful shots to blow opponents off court, but he was very consistent and exceptionally fit. So we worked on pinpointing where he felt most confident and ended up defining his identity as a *Gladiator*. His style would be to wear down opponents with long, physically draining points. He stopped trying to hit a high number of winners, which led him to many errors and points given away to rivals, and focussed on getting the ball over to the opponent a ridiculously high number of times, wearing rivals down and generating pressure for them to not miss a shot during long rallies. Generally, as a rally gets longer, players tend to get more anxious about missing a shot, and this is where my client found his sweet spot. The longer the rally wore on, the more in command he felt.

We started leveraging that new identity to gain mental advantage over his rivals at the US Open. This was the first Grand Slam since we'd started working together. He had a first round match against a veteran who was very talented, but physically weaker and less fit. So my advice was:

> "Make every game, every set as long as possible. And even if you lose the first set, as long as it was drawn out and exhausting, it is a WIN for you. I want you to smile at the rival on changeover to show him you're comfortable doing this for five sets."

And that's exactly how it went down. The first set went to a tie break that the opponent won, but it was a long, hard-fought battle and after just one set, he was clearly thinking that he couldn't play at this pace too much longer. On the changeover, my player looked at his rival, smiled and said,

> "I can do this all day long,"

The opponent's body language immediately showed a rise in tension, and he began taking unadvisable risks in the second set to try and finish the match quickly. My player kept to his identity, fiercely defending the backcourt and returning everything, forcing his rival to make 10 or 15 great shots to win one point. The opponent began committing more and more unforced errors, and lost the second set.

On the changeover, my player didn't even sit to recover; he kept bouncing, showing he was ready. It seemed like he was getting stronger. From there, the opponent mentally gave up. My player won the third and fourth sets with much less resistance and moved on to the next round.

After the match, as we discussed the results together, my client began to understand the power of his unique identity. He no longer worried about not having *Federer-esque* shots, and committed to wearing down his opponents and making them beat him. In other words, to beat him, they would have to hit winners; he was not going to miss shots and give away free points. This generated tremendous pressure on his rivals when they were facing what seemed like a brick wall that returned everything shot.

The interesting part is that, because of clarity on his new identity, my client also began transforming his training, to focus more on turning his strengths into superpowers. He upped his physical conditioning even more, until he was considered one of the fittest players on tour, and every rival knew any match would be a long struggle. The result was that, over the next months, he climbed steadily and eventually broke into the top ten, which is a significant achievement and marks becoming one of the best.

Coaching Case File: Leveraging identity to unblock resistance to change in organizations

As we've seen, changing long-term paradigms and identity can be very complex to unwind, and it can sabotage your growth and improvement initiatives if you don't address the underlying resistance. I have seen this problem many times in business settings with large, successful multinationals struggling to drive cultural change. Here's one example of how this played out in a client of mine.

We've all seen the problem of the micromanaging supervisor in companies. Many of these managers have gone through training about empowering employees and delegating tasks, yet they can't seem to implement the behavior. One common cause is that the controlling behavior, in some previous point in their career or broader lives, served to *protect* them. I had a client who had this exact problem. He was now the GM of a division of his company, but still tortured his team by getting into every little detail, and consequently, slowing down the pace of everything because he was a bottleneck.

After working together for some time, it became apparent that, when he started in the company, 20 years before, his manager was one of a group of highly political characters who would search for tiny events or details and then use them against the team, saying that they did not have control over the business. For example, this toxic manager would find someone on the team who had not followed up on a given topic (even if it was not something important), then would go to my client and say,

> "Did you know Tom did not follow up on topic X? You have no control over what's going on."

As a defensive mechanism, my client began overworking himself to make sure he reviewed every detail of everyone's work so he would never get caught in that situation. However, 20 years later, he continued to act in the same way, although the toxic manager was gone, and he was now a senior executive with a thousand employees in his division. I shared with them the metaphor of when I returned to visit my kindergarten class as an adult. Everything seemed so much smaller than I remembered it. Obviously, I had grown and my perspective had changed. That, I explained, is what happens with beliefs and paradigms that we formed earlier in life when we revisit and examine them once we've grown and matured. I invited him to look at the reasons behind his behavior and evaluate if who he was now was a person who needed to act this way.

It was only when we redefined what his identity should look like that he was able to stop the behavior. His identity as the leader of a division should not include checking cells on an Excel sheet unless he viewed himself as a small time manager, not a visionary leader. As my client began to envision who he should be to carry out his current role, he was able to step away from the unconscious behaviors.

Players Only Beyond This Point

The process is the most beautiful part
of the journey because that's where
you figure out who you are.

Kobe Bryant
(NBA Legend)

WHAT'S THE BIG DEAL?

I believe that the best way to introduce this variable of *The Optimal Performance Formula* is by reproducing the conversations I have with most CEOs when they invite me in to evaluate if they should hire our services. The first meeting usually goes something like this:

The CEO and/or his team introduce the company, explain all the great success they've had, then they eventually segue into what's not working. Usually, the frustration of not getting the level of performance they want, need or expect from the organization is palpable, but they haven't been able to move the dial up until now.

After having listened for a while, I usually drop what I refer to as *The Question:*

> "Before we explore the team further, what is your personal 5-year plan to be a better CEO?"
>
> *[Incredulous looks from all present. Sometimes a small gasp escapes the mouth of a member of the leadership team. Then silence for a long, long minute.]*

The truth is most senior executives think I'm joking, but nothing could be further from the truth. The answer to this question, or the habitual lack of answers, give me the information I need to evaluate this second element of the *Mindset* block.

Here's how I explain it to clients like the ones in the scenario above. *The Optimal Performance Formula* is built to model common elements across top performers so you can apply these principles to your own mastery journey. Keeping that in mind, if you look at Kobe Bryant, Tom Brady, Michael Jordan, Rafael Nadal, Novak Djokovic, Tiger Woods, and a long list of other legendary athletes, you'll find that their approach to improvement was, simply put, obsessive and unwavering. Moreover, as these superstars got more and more famous and made it *to the top*, the focus and intensity with which they pursued new knowledge—and the fervor with which they approached their growth—actually *increased* over time.

This may sound logical and natural, but after working with dozens of professional athletes and top executives, I can tell you that it's the exception, more than the rule. The vast majority of performers get to a certain level, and feel that they have acquired all the skills they need. Their training then focusses on maintaining that level of skill, instead of consistently increasing it over their entire careers, or even their entire lives. A good example for most people is learning to drive. Once you stop crashing into things and running over people, most drivers stop even thinking about how they could improve. As a result of not trying to improve, skill levels actually go down, because you pay less attention than you did at the beginning, leading to more mistakes and potential problems.

That kind of mindset is a trap, because if you think success is a destination, you'll never get there. The magic is in the eternal chase to become better—in the never ending pursuit of perfection, knowing you can never reach it, but hoping you manage to achieve excellence along the way. Moreover, I believe human beings are wired to crave growth. It's what makes us feel alive.

You must be a player, not a fan

Everything we've been discussing is encapsulated in a phrase I picked up from former NFL player Bo Eason and is the embryo of the title of this chapter. When you enter the dressing rooms in professional sports stadiums, you'll see a sign that says something along the lines of *Players Only Beyond This Point.* Eason explains the difference between being a professional athlete,—a *player* in his language—and being just a fan. He explains that choosing the path to mastery requires understanding the following...

> "From this day forward, you are no longer a spectator. You are no longer a fan. You are a player. Players play. They don't critique, and they don't have commentary. They play. . . . As a player, you don't have time to complain. You have time to practice, and you have time to perform. . . Our culture is fan culture, not a player culture."

I think that is a brilliant summary of one of the biggest problems most teams and individuals trip over on their journey. Choosing to be a player is an essential basic component, which is why it is considered "raw material" in the *Mindset* block. If you start without having this clear, you will struggle mightily to optimize your personal performance or that of your team or organization.

The pervading paradigm that causes so much damage is the belief that, once you reach a certain level,—be that a C-Suite role in a company, or playing in the highest category league or competition environment in your sport (eg NFL, NBA, MLB, ATP, Olympics, etc.)—then it is an embarrassment to admit that you need to improve. For most CEOs, when I pose the question about their improvement program to be better at their jobs, it feels like an insult. Likewise, when I ask professional athletes where they need to improve, they struggle to mention technical skill. Reading this, I'm sure you can think of many people who would react in a similar way, but here's the point: it's incredibly naive and ignorant. I know that sounds aggressive, and it is, as it's meant to shake your ego out of its lethargy, but let's look at this objectively and logically.

To better understand this, let me cite again the work of Dr. Anders Ericsson on *Deliberate Practice*. In the *Mojo* section we'll delve deep into the details and protocols of *Deliberate Practice*, but for the moment, let's stay with a few high-level concepts. Dr. Ericsson's work was made known to the broader public outside the world of performance science geeks, such as yours truly, when Malcolm Gladwell published his best seller, *Outliers*.

In summarizing the findings of Dr. Ericsson's research, Gladwell simplified, and slightly misrepresented, the conclusions in what is now known as the *10,000 hour rule*, that basically states that it takes 10,000 hours of *Deliberate Practice* to achieve mastery in any subject. Again, that's not exactly right, but it's close enough. The point is that becoming great at any skill requires years and years of focussed practice that meets a series of criteria in order to be classified as *Deliberate Practice*, such as pushing you just beyond your current level of skill, breaking performance down into smaller component pieces, and receiving feedback, among others. In other words, no one becomes a world class violinist in a week, nor an NBA All Star after three months of taking up basketball, nor a ballet dancer after six months. It's ridiculous to even think any of these is possible, yet people think they need to be master practitioners in their first year in a given role.

Again, this is where the mindset of the best of the best creates separation from the rest. The greatest performers in any field detest the concept of "good enough." They know they can continue to improve and believe that they set their own limits. As a result, they often shatter limits that others thought were impossible. As that famous Apple commercial in 1997 called *The Crazy Ones* stated:

> "...because the people who are crazy enough to think they can change the world are the ones who do."

As a result of this obsession to realize their full potential, top performers tend to focus their time and energy differently than most other people. Most markedly, while the majority focus mainly on the moments they will perform or compete, top performers consider practice as a sacred requirement. Whether you look at Steve Jobs spending hundreds of hours designing, writing, practicing, and refining his product presentations, or take stock of the thousands of hours of extra practice that Kobe Bryant invested in mastering the most fundamental skills of basketball on his own time, the pattern is the same. Those who perform at elite levels make practice the center of their universe. They see it not as a chore to be endured, but as an opportunity to passionately attack their weaknesses and intensely work on unlocking a 1% increase in their optimal performance level.

Today's standards shape your tomorrow

The Optimal Performance Formula is meant for people whose burning desire is to achieve just that: Optimal Performance. It's not *The Acceptable Performance Formula* nor *The Pretty Decent Performance*

Formula. That's the difference that underlies the main concepts in this book.

Take note, because this is a game changer:

> *The single most impactful factor that will determine what your future looks like is the quality of the standards you demand and uphold on a consistent, daily basis!*

This is what trips up so many people who aspire to reach the top of their field. If you remember, we talked about the importance of having a clear identity and mission. The reason this is so important is because your daily standards absolutely need to be designed and upheld based on the future you are working towards. This may sound so obvious that you're thinking *duh, of course.* However, very few people actually have the drive, passion, and discipline to do it over a sustained period of time, which is why they derail from their path and never optimize their performances.

Top performers understand that hard work is just the price of admission. It doesn't guarantee anything. It just allows you a chance to try for your dream. What separates the elite few that develop their full potential from the masses is their willingness to do what, in performance circles, is often referred to as *the unrequired.*

The concept of doing *the unrequired* is a consistent factor across exceptional performers in any field. The best of the best always do a little bit more—not because anyone makes them, but because they can't stand knowing there may be an additional activity or effort they can work on that *may* help them get one percent better. Note that there is no guarantee that *the unrequired* will produce a result, but for those chasing optimal performance, the mere possibility that it *might* help separate them from their peers and rivals is enough to make it worth the time and effort.

Jerry Rice, the greatest receiver in NFL history, was a role model for doing *the unrequired*. His reasoning was evident:

> "Today I will do what others won't, so tomorrow I can accomplish what others can't."

Doing *the unrequired* is about working harder and more often than anyone could reasonably demand of you, motivated by the burning desire to deliver more than you could yesterday. This last nuance is very important. Actually, it's essential for your mastery journey. What drives the optimal performer to do *the unrequired* is not to be *more* than anyone else or beat anyone. It's not about the trophy or the money or the prestige. The driver is a mindset of, as Jim Murphy calls it, *"inner excellence"* where the prize you are after is to discover how far you can grow. It's about reaching and stretching the absolute limits of your potential. What the rest of the world does, or doesn't do, ceases to be of interest to you.

When Kobe Bryant put in all those extra workout sessions which he was famous for, over his entire life, or when Jerry Rice exemplified the work ethic summarized in the above quote on a daily basis, it wasn't about being better than the rest; it was about seeing who they could become in the process.

When Rafael Nadal would finish a match where he felt he wasn't performing up to the standard he demanded of himself—even if he had won—he could often be seen going immediately to a practice court, drilling with his hitting partner the strokes that he wasn't satisfied with that day, until they *felt* right. That's what *unrequired* work is all about. No one would expect a tennis legend to put in another hour on a practice court *after* having just won his match. Fortunately, he never did it for anyone else. He did it because it was the internal standard which he demanded of himself.

What all top performers have clear is that standards challenge you to play up to the level of your talent and potential. They prevent you from dropping down to the level of your opponent or allowing any exogenous circumstances to distract your focus away from realizing your true potential.

Your standards reflect if your actions are coherent with your ambitions

When I work with clients—even those who are successful professional athletes or accomplished C-suite executives—I always try to establish what their goals are and make sure they have coherence of ambition and actions. What do I mean by this? We've talked about how top performers have a burning desire and a clear vision. And that's really valuable, but none of it will move the needle if you're not willing to make the investments in time, energy, emotions, and focus that are required to reach the level of goal you are committing to.

When I say "coherence," I'm not judging their talent. Although it's true that current skill level and potential may make the journey easier, the key element I'm looking for is whether my clients are mentally ready for the work and sacrifices that their goals or dreams entail. Spoiler alert: most people are *not*.

Let's face it—aspiring to become the best at what you do, or achieve mastery, requires that you dedicate yourself mind, body, and soul, to achieving that goal. No one—and I mean *no one*—has ever achieved a very ambitious dream without putting in extraordinary amounts of work. Real work goes beyond just showing up when you train or compete. It's the work that goes on in the dark, when no one is watching, when you have doubts and pains, and your body and mind are screaming for you to stop, but your soul refuses to give up on the dream, even though it may be far away. I'm referring to doing *the unrequired*, because truly becoming the best you can become requires seeing every tiny step, every extra effort, every ounce of work as a part of the overall recipe that will get you as far as you can possibly go.

Now here's the thing. It's hard! By definition, pushing your limits is very hard. Speaking colloquially, it sucks a lot of the time. It requires you to maintain a furious level of focus, intensity, and dedication, regardless of your feelings. Kobe Bryant spoke often about this. In one interview, Kobe explained how he designed his off-season training plan and signed it so that the days he didn't feel like giving everything that ambitious plan required, he would remind himself of his commitment to the most important person in his career: himself. In his own words, whenever he found himself trying to modify the plan, he'd give himself this speech:

> "I'm not negotiating with myself. The deal was already made. I said this is the training plan I'm doing, I signed that contract with myself. I'm doing it. This is non-negotiable."

That's the power of standards. You hold yourself to your standards, every day, regardless of how you feel.

That's a truth few people understand. But whether you want to be a standout in your sport, or you're an entrepreneur trying to build a disruptive company, you must realize that, to have a minimal chance of getting there (and remember, nothing is guaranteed), you need to place the work of chasing your dream ahead of almost anything else.

It doesn't matter if you don't feel like it—you do it. You take time from other things, especially things that don't directly contribute to your mission. When you're not training, competing, or working on your dream, you're thinking about how to get better and what you will implement when you get back to the field or the office, whatever your battlefield may be.

Steve Jobs was notorious for placing the pursuit of his vision above all else. That pattern is common with the extreme 1% who aspire to be the best in the world. Great athletes make strict choices on nutrition and social life and make many other sacrifices in order to chase their goals, because they know that, if they don't do it, someone else will. They understand that they may be outplayed, but they refuse to be outworked.

Again, let me just highlight that you don't have to aim to be the world number one in your craft for this philosophy to be useful, but you need to be driven to be the best you can be. If you're chasing mastery, in fact, you shouldn't be looking at the competition, except to see what you can learn. Your focus should be on *you* and how you can consistently gain those millimeters of advantage that drive you closer to your full potential.

So the first thing you need to be clear on is if it's worth it for you to do all that. By the way, there's nothing wrong if the answer is no. This *obsession* that elite performers have with their missions does not make them better as humans; it just makes them different, and is often necessary to compete in that particular space at that level. So ask yourself right now:

> *Am I willing to do the extra work, beyond what's required by my coaches, teammates, or clients?*

If so, then I have another question for you:

Are you ready to do that unrequired work and effort over a very long, sustained period of time?

If one thing has become clear from all my years of working with elite performers and studying the sea of excellent and insightful research done by leading practitioners and academics in the field of performance science, it's that consistency trumps intensity. Ideally, you want consistent intensity, of course. As we've seen, focussed practice requires you to push beyond your current skill level, and that, by definition, demands focus and intensity. However, knowing that you won't be perfect, on those rare days when you're not feeling 100%, you'll get more out of doing your workout (consistency) at a lower level of intensity than you would by skipping the workout. Of course, there are exceptions, such as injuries and illness, but we're talking about common sense criteria to apply to 98% of your days.

We'll discuss grit and consistency in more detail in a later chapter, but for now, just realize that they are key variables for top performers, and nowhere is that more obvious than when you're chasing an *impossible* dream. It's about focussing 100% on the present, while knowing that reaching your goal will only occur in the long term, so you need to get motivation from doing the hard work and maintaining your standards every single day.

We've said it before, but it's worth repeating because you should burn this into your nervous system so it's automatic. Great things take enormous effort!

You don't become a world class pianist or a martial arts grandmaster or an industry-disrupting entrepreneur in a month or even a year. It takes many years of *Deliberate Practice* to begin to approach mastery in any area.

The key, though, is the compounding effect of continuous effort and work on a specific goal. One reason this is so important is that, as you get better, you start to understand things at a deeper level. You see nuances and small details in the basics of your craft that you never even noticed, and then you obsessively work to perfect them. You then test and innovate to see if you can squeeze out another one or two percent. By repeating this cycle again and again—making seemingly marginal gains—over time, those gains, that understanding, and that mastery compound and set you apart. Again, Kobe Bryant talked about how he'd train three or four times a day, starting at 4:00am, while others trained once or twice a day. That extra session or two, compounded over months and years, put him so far ahead of his competition that no one could catch him.

The same principles apply to business. Entrepreneur Brandon Arvanaghi wrote about how the real differentiating factor for start-ups is the compound effect of extraordinary execution. He argues that the majority of the value is not in the *idea*, but in the long-term *execution* of that idea at a world class level. And founders need to be the ones who drive this, he says.

The examples are endless, but the principle is the same. Striving for Optimal Performance requires unwavering commitment to upholding your standards. It's not something you do part time or when you feel like it. It's not something you do during a short period of time until you hit a milestone. It's something top performers do every day, every week of every year.

You need to commit to upholding your standards—and holding everyone around you to a higher standard—even when you are struggling. You hold fast even when the people around you are criticizing or doubting you. You don't ever drop your standards, even when your goal seems so far off that you start to doubt if you can reach it, because you hold a strong belief in what you are doing and you never forget that your *why* is non-negotiable.

Standards allow you to look yourself in the eye

Ultimately, top performers believe that the pain of upholding their standards is less than the pain of not respecting who they see in the mirror. If you aspire to realize your maximum potential, then accountability is of paramount importance. Above all else, elite performers place a premium on being accountable to themselves.

Accountability is an inward-first evaluation, where you look at your role and performance when things don't work out as you had hoped. Annie Duke, former World Champion of Poker and PhD in Cognitive Psychology, laid out a painful truth in her fascinating book, *Thinking in Bets*. Duke's research and experience in the world of professional betters shows that, on average, people tend to heavily *overestimate* their own merit when things work out well. Conversely, when it comes to loss or failure, most people *underestimate* their responsibility and attribute much more weight to exogenous circumstances such as luck or the environment.

That's a key differentiator of elite performers. They always look at themselves first and ask what they could have done better. This focus isn't a self-flagellation exercise, rather it's about being brutally honest on what doesn't work and what they need to work harder on in order to perform at the level they aspire to. Most importantly, they never portray themselves as victims. Even if there are factors that were objectively out of their control, the best of the best focus on how they can turn the situation around and improve for next time. They know that life isn't always fair. So what! Wallowing in a pity-pool won't fix anything, so why spend any energy on it? Which brings us to another important point: saying no!

If it doesn't take you closer to your goal, eliminate it

Champions focus exclusively on what drives them closer to their goals, and they say no to the rest. They make sure to exercise their freedom to set strict boundaries and say no to anything that isn't contributing to building their dream. The top performer valuation criteria is binary: either you're building or you're not building. It's that simple. And since energy, time, and focus are finite resources, anything that isn't contributing to the dream gets cut out. Top performers ruthlessly choose what gets their energy and what is a clear *NO* based on their mission and identity.

Stated simply, it's a brutal application of *second order thinking*, which is based on looking past the immediate results and considering the long-term impact. So essentially, you are either training, performing/competing, or recovering from performing and analyzing/learning from your performance. Anything that doesn't meet these criteria is seen as a distraction, and distractions are considered kryptonite by elite performers.

When top performers make certain choices—like training even when they don't feel like it, or adhering to their diet, or not going to that party everyone else is going to—they are putting their long-term mission ahead of their short-term pleasure. If those short-term pleasures don't help get them closer to their goals, then they are distractions and go on the *never do that again list.*

Kevin Eastman, in his book, *Why The Best Are the Best,* shares a list of "No's" that helped shape the standards for Doc Rivers' Boston Celtics *[I've summarized the list below, adding explanations where convenient to facilitate understanding of the core message]:*

No Settling for anything less than best effort.
No Stopping when you fail. You overcome it.
No Procrastination.
No Excuses, only solutions.
No Regrets. Give it all.
No "Me Firsts." It's always about the team.

One of the most important areas where you need to eliminate what doesn't help drive your mission is in your environment. This refers to more than just your physical surroundings; it's the people you give your energy to and those whom you allow to share their opinions with you. It includes the information you process, the culture you work in, the foods you eat, the music you listen to, and a long list of etceteras.

Your environment will impact you, so if you don't choose to shape it, you're leaving to chance an important variable that can later deter your progress and performance. Elite performers are so protective of their dreams that anyone who brings doubt or pessimism is shown the door. Normally, negativity comes from people because they are projecting their limitations, not judging *your* true potential. It's important to make sure that your environment supports you, instead of being something you have to fight against or overcome on your journey towards optimal performance.

Working on yourself needs to be a core principle

Daniel Coyle, author of the best-selling book, *The Talent Code,* says that:

> "For them [top performers], practice is the big game."

This is true whether you are a C-suite executive or an Olympic athlete. Your performance under the lights will be enabled or limited by how you train and work on improving yourself when you're not performing. What the rest of the world sees is just the result of how well you have prepared.

Keep in mind that, in any craft, you're only performing 5% to 10% of the time. The rest is preparation or training. Top sales experts dedicate significant time to researching, tailoring the storyline, and practicing their sales pitches for each and every client. Mediocre sales reps believe they are sufficiently experienced and they don't need to prepare. My answer to those whose ego leads them to believe that their experience excuses them from the need to prepare is the following example. Lionel Messi is a pretty experienced, highly-skilled soccer player, but he still practices before each game. Why? Because he understands that preparing for the unique strengths of each rival, and running through different scenarios he may encounter in a specific game, will allow him to perform better than if he does not prepare. And, on the pitch, Messi is all about being the best player to ever grace the game. In fact, if Messi refused to practice because he's "got enough experience," his fans and the media would universally roast him. Yet, most companies think it's okay for their highest ranking team members to skip preparation and practice. Is this happening in your environment? Do you see the double standard there?

Likewise, I've seen professional athletes across many sports train at half speed and effort. Of course, you'll never see the best do that. Receiver Jerry Rice's training standards were legendary. Every time he would catch a pass in training, he would sprint to the end zone. His explanation was clear. He wanted to burn into his nervous system the belief that, in his own words:

"Every time these hands touch a ball, it ends up in the end zone."

Greats in every sport are known for never coasting. Michael Jordan and Kobe Bryant were feared by teammates who did not give every ounce of their soul in practice. Hockey legend Bobby Orr was famous for staring down teammates in the locker room between periods when he felt they were not performing up to standard. Reporter Ross Atkin recounted the phenomenon:

"Orr was disappointed when either he or a teammate didn't maintain it. And while Orr was not verbally confrontational, teammate Derek Sanderson remembers that he would stare daggers at any player in the locker room who he felt was mailing it in."

The key is understanding what drives value, and top performers know that the measure of success is whether they can unleash their best performances when it counts most. And that is contingent upon consistently pushing themselves beyond any reasonable expectation.

Prerequisite: a beginner's mindset

If you aspire to reach your maximum performance potential, your desire to improve must be much stronger than your ego's need to look good. Great performers are constantly pushing themselves outside their current level of skill, whether that be trying to improve a core skill they already possess or developing a complementary skill that will drive performance. They understand that they will, and *should*, fail more than anyone else because they are trying harder than the rest.

One of the most essential elements that separate world class performers in any field is that they have a *beginner's mindset*. This sounds easy, but the more accomplished you are in your field, the harder it becomes for people to forget about ego and value learning and growth above all. Being considered good at what you do by peers and competitors is like a drug, and it requires a fierce will to unlock your maximum potential in order to willingly push yourself to work on new skills where you feel clumsy and unsure. The results, however, are spectacular.

A beginner's mindset is something I've worked on and cultivated over years and, as I have matured, I've actually started to enjoy the feeling of being a beginner. Despite the frustration of the ego, a beginner's mindset has so many fantastic benefits. First off, it's healthy to level up and admit to yourself: *In this specific subject matter, I'm not the super expert. I have so much to learn.* We all tend to take our foot off the accelerator when we feel we're pretty good at something, and that's how top performers use the beginner's mindset. They continually ask: *What else am I not aware of that would drive my performance if I became better at it?*

Another powerful benefit of a beginner's mindset is that, since, by definition, you don't feel fully confident or competent in this new arena, you need to *focus* much more intensely, so you get closer to a state of complete immersion in what you're doing, and this is a fundamental component of achieving the flow state. As you'll learn in the chapter where we deep dive on *Deliberate Practice*, training beyond your current skill level is essential to improving performance. Why?

Because it requires such extreme focus, which ends up improving the benefits of the training.

Finally, exploring areas where you are not an expert—even if, at first glance, they don't appear to be related to your craft—can be a source of incredible learnings that you can apply to improve performance in your craft. One example very near my heart is my company, *GOLD Results*. We specialize in taking lessons from the science of performance in the world of professional sports and applying them to help businesses improve their performance,—and with amazing results. However, *cross fertilization*, as I call it, isn't new. So many people have applied learnings from seemingly unrelated areas or sectors to create tremendous improvements in their industry. One very significant example is how healthcare professionals in hospitals adopted the methodology of checklists from the airline industry to standardize protocols in operating rooms, resulting in a drastic decrease in the rate of post-intervention infections.

Coaching Case File: How an ATP pro improved performance by incrementally raising his standards in different areas

One of my players on the ATP circuit was doing relatively well, but was frustrated because of the lack of titles he'd won. He was looking for an epiphany to reveal the one big thing he was missing. I told him that the big thing was the sum of a ton of small things, and that's why he was missing them. And what was his response?

"Small things won't make the difference I'm looking for."

I figured the best way to get him to really understand this was with an exercise. I picked up a 1.5 liter water bottle and asked him if he thought holding this bottle could challenge his strength. Of course not, he said. So we made a bet. If I could create the conditions whereby he could no longer hold that water bottle, he would commit to implementing a series of small changes over 60 days. He took the bet with no doubt that he'd win.

I walked him to the baseline and had him hold the bottle straight out in front of him, as if it were a tennis ball he was about to toss. Arm fully extended at shoulder level. No cheating. He obliged and told me it would be a "piece of cake."

My response:

"Super. Now hold it there for the next hour."

He still thought this was a waste of time, but he wasn't about to lose the bet that easily. Over the ensuing minutes, his face changed from annoyed to strained to worried as the weight of the bottle seemed to grow heavier by the minute until his shoulder began to burn and eventually his arm began to shake. Before we hit the 20-minute mark, he dropped his arm. While he was shaking his arm out and rubbing his shoulder, I asked him if he thought that doing that every day for 30 minutes would make his shoulder stronger. That's when he understood that small efforts, sustained over time, can generate significant results.

That was the lesson, but since I'd won the bet, we now had the chance to implement specific things I wanted to improve. One of them was his focus and concentration when he trained. Here's the scene! Whenever he would walk into the club to train, he'd arrive 15 minutes late, annoying his coach to no end. Then, with a relaxed gait, he'd meander towards the practice court, bag half-open, stopping to chat with several club members along the way, since he was a bit of a celebrity in the club. They'd joke and comment on who would win the next Champions League soccer match, then eventually he'd make it to the practice court where his physical trainer tried to warm him up. The player would do a few light movements, then say he was ready, all the while being oblivious to the grimacing face of the frustrated trainer who wondered why he worked with an athlete who didn't follow his advice. Not to mention his worry about the player getting hurt because he was not properly warmed up.

The whole two-hour practice would evolve in the same way—relaxed, chatting to bystanders, checking his phone for messages every time he went for water, etc.

So now that I'd won the bet, I redesigned his arrival ritual. Sounds silly and insignificant, right? Well, it wasn't. The first change was he had to be at the court five minutes before his coach, fully laced up and ready to go. He had to walk to the court without speaking to anyone. When people would approach him, he was to say,

> "I'm sorry, I'm in training now and can't speak. Business is business. I'll catch you later."

On the court, he had to follow his PT's warm-up routine. No complaining, no changes, and no talking. During the warm-up, he had to repeat the three process cues we'd developed that identified when he played best. This way, by the time he stepped on the court, he'd told himself about 50 times the key things he had to ensure he was executing properly. This focussed his attention on the performance coming up.

Then I really challenged him by having him play a practice set with a lower-ranked tour pro who trained at the club. Meanwhile, I brought all the young children who had classes to watch the match and told them to yell and make as much noise as they wanted. The exercise was to help my player learn to block out external distractions and focus on the match. Often during real match play, this player struggled with distractions from the crowd or the opponent's coaches who could sometimes act in a less-than-ideal way.

At first, it was incredibly difficult for him to follow, but over the weeks, he started to realize how the sum of the little things resulted in better practice sessions that improved his confidence, and ultimately it had a tremendous positive impact on his focus and performance in matches.

Coaching Case File: How making senior sales reps prepare "like players" drove performance

My client was a leading multinational that had grown incredibly quickly since IPO. As a result, the business portfolio had evolved and the sales force was being asked to generate new business, both in terms of selling to clients in sectors where they previously did not have a strong presence, as well as in terms of selling new services that the company had developed.

The reps were all experienced, with over 15 years tenure on average. Egos ran rampant and, when I suggested that they practice role-playing before going on sales calls, the reactions ranged from being offended to directly dismissing the idea. The level of resistance to change was so intense that you could feel the tension the moment you walked in the room, and it skyrocketed when I began challenging their current beliefs.

The wildcard I had was the Managing Director of the division who firmly believed they needed to change something, and the CEO of the group, who had been the one who brought me in. So, reluctantly, the group crossed their arms as if that could protect them from the ideas we were discussing, and we began to explore why they were having so much trouble opening up new clients. I asked the team to present to me as I roleplayed a new client. It became immediately evident that their pitch was what I call *belly button focussed*. In other words, their entire strategy was based on the technical traits of the services and the experience of their team. In their traditional market, that worked, because the buyers had a similar technical profile and generally knew what they wanted. However, these new markets presented a challenge the reps hadn't faced before. They now had to sell to clients who didn't understand the technology and had never thought about how it could be applied in their businesses.

After having the reps do research on a series of selected clients in different industries, I had them run roleplays with me and with other reps acting as clients. It took them a while to get over the feeling of awkwardness, then something amazing happened. They started getting into their roles, and the rest of the group started sharing experiences and techniques that had worked for them. Although many of them had worked together for years, it became clear that they'd never spoken and shared insights. The room was soon filled with comments like *I had that problem once, and this approach worked like a charm.* We closed the session and assigned them a series of real life sales calls to do over the next 15 days.

The real breakthrough came when we had the next session two weeks later. The energy was very different in the room and what had been a collection of reluctant employees forced to go to a performance improvement program had become a team of optimistic and rejuvenated professionals anxious to share their experiences over the last two weeks and get more insights. The most common benefit most reps reported was that the prospects they had visited actually presented a lot of the concerns, objections, or questions that had come up in the interactive roleplay, and they felt much more equipped to answer and keep the process moving in a positive direction.

I've been doing this for over 30 years, and the pattern is always the same. At first, there is strong resistance, then once you get a team of senior executives to try the technique, they see how it benefits them, and it becomes a required activity for everyone. Executive board members who have gone through this process have called me and asked:

> "Can I run this important presentation past you and you roleplay [as person X] so I can be prepared and not get sideswiped by this person?"

Do you find this surprising? You shouldn't unless you think NFL, NBA and other professional sports teams just show up to games without practicing and preparing for the strategies they will see from their opponents. Having been through the situation—even if it's a simulation—will always improve your performance when it's time for the real thing.

Masters of Meaning

*There is nothing either good or bad
but thinking makes it so.*

Shakespeare

(from Hamlet)

WHAT'S THE BIG DEAL?

Imagine that you had the power to make any situation work in your favor. Would you be interested in learning how to flow with any circumstance so that it contributes to helping you instead of being a hindrance or a mortal blow to your dreams? Do you believe that superpower would help you on the path to achieving your most treasured goals? Well, that's what this variable of *The Optimal Performance Formula* is all about.

Top performers in any field are like Aikido masters. They take whatever comes their way and use the force to their advantage. Confused? Stay with me for a few minutes and it will all become clear. It's much less esoteric than it sounds, but you need to understand the fundamentals first.

Aikido is a martial art developed by Morihei Ueshiba, referred to amongst Aikido students as *Ōsensei* or *Great Teacher*. I had the great privilege of training in Japan under the lineage of Rinjiro Shirata Sensei, one of the original students of Ōsensei. Ueshiba believed that the objective of the true martial artist is to achieve a level of mastery that allows them to manage all attacks with harmony and love, not violence and destruction.

Few people ever advance enough in Aikido to understand it fully, and this is due to the fact that it requires a much higher level of skill to apply it effectively than other martial arts. It is more attractive for most students to study the more commercially popular mixed martial arts and, after a few weeks, they can kick and punch, albeit with much less skill than they believe they possess. For this reason, Aikido is less popular and much less understood. However, if you meet—and can learn—from a true master, you will understand the immense power it can teach you to unleash. I was already a black belt in Karate, Tae Kwon Do, and Japanese Jujutsu when I started studying Aikido, and I had never seen the level of power and presence I encountered in training with the masters I met in Japan. The extra bonus I never expected is that the learnings of Aikido go far beyond the physical application of technique and provide invaluable lessons to drive performance in any craft you are trying to master.

The main idea of Aikido, known as the art of peace, is to blend with the energy of the opponent's attack while staying centered and redirecting it towards resolution. I have used this little known concept to help professional athletes and large corporations turn challenges into opportunities, flowing to the next level of performance instead of struggling against their particular circumstance.

Masters of Meaning

One of the key tools I teach professional athletes and business leaders is something I call becoming *Masters of Meaning*. You can think of it as *mental Aikido*. This is such an essential skill that, in my opinion, it should be taught in schools, because it is a powerful lever to manage your internal state and make it the most conducive to optimal performance. Also, mastering this variable is invaluable in driving meaningful connection and relationships between team members.

When I do live events, I usually introduce this concept with a roleplay right off the bat. I will choose one person from the audience, usually a female (why will become evident in a moment), and ask her to participate in a little roleplay/simulation with me. The conversation almost always goes as follows:

> **Me**: "First, I'll set the scene. Let's imagine it's late at night, you're on a bus or a train or a subway car. There are very few people on the bus or train at this hour. Now imagine you've never met me, but you see me sitting a few seats over, and staring at you. It's very obvious I'm looking at you. How do you feel?"
>
> **Her**: "I feel uncomfortable, nervous, uneasy."
>
> **Me**: "Why? What makes you feel uncomfortable?"
>
> **Her**: "I'm unsure what you want, what your intentions are."
>
> **Me**: "Great, so now imagine you, all of a sudden, think that you know me from somewhere. Maybe a work event. You can't quite place me, but you think I may be staring because we've met and I want to say hi. How do you feel now?"
>
> **Her** [visibly relaxing]: "I now feel curious and more relaxed."
>
> **Me**: "Okay, one final thought. Now imagine that, all of a sudden you realize where you recognize my face from. You saw me on a news segment that said I was being sought out by the police for multiple homicides. How do you feel NOW?"
>
> **Her**: *"I feel panicked, scared, looking for an escape strategy."*

At this point, I'll thank my partner for participating in the simulation and point out that, over the course of a few minutes, she went through a rollercoaster of different emotions, but I was doing *the exact same thing* in the roleplay. I was just looking at her. What changed was the *meaning* she gave to that look, and it changed her entire outlook and her list of possible reactions.

The reality is, we do this hundreds of times a day, albeit in less dramatic fashion. We give a *meaning* to what occurs to us or around us, and it changes how we feel about the situation and about other people who might be involved. Now, the powerful part of this is that we are in *full control* of what meaning we give a situation—and the corresponding reaction we have—but we so often give up this power because we haven't been trained to use it.

It is said, "You don't see the world as it is, you see the world as YOU are," and I believe that is very true. If you seek out data points to prove that the world is full of bad people, you'll find data to support that. Likewise, if you try to prove that the world is full of kind, loving people, you can also find examples to confirm that view. You tend to bias the data you process, and the *meaning* you give it, based on what your core beliefs are. The problem is, no one teaches us to be aware of what those beliefs are or if they are even based on any objective proof. So, in a sense, you're running on autopilot but you're not the one who plotted the course or programmed the computer.

I often refer to the process of how we automatically attribute meaning to an event as our *deep rules*. We all have a series of automated associations we probably have never thought about. If you explore them, you'll find that they are your view of the world, although not necessarily a universal truth. And, when you realize you can give a different meaning to events, you gain an incredible superpower!

Let me give you another example of how *meaning* can play out in your life. I heard a story years ago that I've never forgotten. It was about a distinguished and well-known university professor, who was riding home on the subway, or Metro, and was indulging in his usual ritual of reading a book of his interest during the commute. On this occasion, however, there was a father with three small children in the same wagon, and the kids were just all over the place. They were running and screaming, and one was crying. The professor got increasingly annoyed as the scene unfolded, thinking to himself how rude some people are. Finally, he could take it no more, and he stood up and said to the father,

> "Hey, we all pay to ride this train and you should get control of your kids because it's really annoying for the rest of us."

The father looked sheepishly up at him, and choked out the following confession:

> "You're right. I'm sorry. We just came from the hospital and their mother just died and they don't know how to handle it, and to be honest, neither do I."

Of course, the professor's rage and anger instantly disappeared and was replaced with empathy for the family and shame for his own behavior.

What changed for the professor? The *facts* were the same, but once he understood what was behind the behaviors, his emotions changed, and he gave the scene a whole different *meaning*. As a result, he acted differently, thought differently, and was in a completely different physiological state.

If we're honest, we all do that hundreds of times a day. If someone cuts you off in traffic, you feel anger and attribute it to an irresponsible individual. If a coworker doesn't say hello in the morning, you may start feeling concerned and wonder if there is a problem or if it's linked to the disagreement you had with that person last week. The fundamental error in all these examples is that you are making interpretations without enough information. Moreover, you are violating one of the cardinal rules of powerful and constructive communication: you are making judgement about *intention*, instead of focussing on behaviors.

When you judge *intention*, you give yourself *false proof* to vilify the other person. You move from condemning a behavior or a concrete action to discrediting the ethical fibre of the person in front of you. That can take you down a very slippery slope, because, in reality, you *don't know* the truth. You think you do, but you usually don't have any concrete evidence. The moment you realize that, you begin to understand that *maybe*, just maybe, your conclusion, i.e, your *truth*, is nothing more than an *opinion*. That realization can change how you feel about events and how you react.

So, how is this relevant to optimal performance in sports and business? Here's where the best of the best excel. They understand that nothing really has any *absolute* meaning; it merely has the meaning you choose to give it. So, given that realization, they know how to give events an empowering meaning, even when most people would only see problems. And by doing so, they can change everything from their physical state to their mental outlook and generate exceptional levels of grit and staying power, even in the face of seemingly insurmountable odds.

A great example was Rafa Nadal's epic victory over Daniil Medvedev in the 2022 Australian Open. Down two sets against a rival ten years younger, Nadal battled back against all odds to win the title. When interviewed, he said something that, to me, showed his amazing mindset and mental strength:

> "I committed to myself to play 100%. Even if the most probable outcome is that I will lose, because the situation is very difficult, but I will not leave the court without trying 100% on every point."

In essence, Nadal changed the *meaning* from what most players would have thought:

> "I'm done. There's no way to come back against this younger opponent from 2 sets down."

to something more that gave him a reason to continue fighting:

> "Whether I win or lose, my goal is to fight each and every point to the death. If I do that, then I've done my best."

By changing the *meaning*, the scoreboard no longer generated anxiety and stress. He was able to focus exclusively on the current point, then the next, and then the next, and so on. If this sounds like a small or subtle difference, you should understand that it is one of the key elements that distinguishes top performers and allows them to achieve seemingly impossible outcomes.

Kobe Bryant had a similar outlook. In an interview he said the following:

> "Doubt is such a strange thing. There will be times when you succeed and times when you fail. So wasting your time doubting if you'll be successful or not, is pointless. Just put one foot in

front of the other, control what you can control, and then see what the outcome is. If you win, great, you're going to have to wake up the next day and do the journey all over again. If you lose, it sucks, but you'll have to wake up the next day and do the journey all over again anyway."

Kobe was a *master of meaning*, and that quote illustrates it. Outcomes did not change his belief in himself or his identity. Win or lose, it was just data. He would analyze what he had to improve, and get to work the next day. Contrast that with so many athletes who lose one match or have a lower-performing game and start doubting themselves. The difference is the *meaning* you give to the event, so why would you want to give up the power to choose a *meaning* that empowers you?

In the corporate world, I've met many senior executives who are too scared of losing pace in their careers. They believe that, if they have a bad year, or spend too much time between jobs, they are automatically seen as less valuable and will struggle to find a job they consider ideal—or at least equivalent to their current or previous roles. The funny thing is, no one's career progression is a straight line upwards. No matter what field you're in, you may have a period of meteoric rise, but you will eventually flatline or take a step back, at least temporarily. The difference between the legendary leaders and the rest is that those steps backwards—or challenges along the way—serve as learning situations and never put in doubt their self-worth or belief of what they can achieve.

Just look at Steve Jobs, who got kicked out of Apple, the company *he created*, by John Scully, the CEO *he brought in*. However, you can guess by how the story ended with Jobs coming back to become the savior of Apple, that he never doubted himself. He learnt, he adapted and adjusted, but he always mastered the *meaning* of events and never let anyone else determine what these events meant for *his* life.

There's one more aspect I'd like to highlight. Since very few people are even aware of the power of *mastering meaning* of what occurs during their journey, the common evolution is that people "stack meanings," (which I'll explain in a minute) and this leads to what I call *hemor-rhaging*. Let me explain what this looks like. I've had clients who knew they were meant for more or were passionate about following a different path or just believed they could make a positive impact in their companies if they were given the chance. Yet, they were afraid to take a risk, and the stories they told themselves were elaborately structured to keep them frozen in fear. A typical conversation with a client like this starts with them saying how speaking out to upper management about what they believe should change could get them fired. When I challenge them, suggesting that even if that were the case, it might be a good thing to leave a company that was that far removed from their values, they start to stack meanings. One senior manager went down this path:

> " *If I get fired, at my age, I will have a lot of trouble finding a job at the same pay grade and seniority level. So I could then spend months unemployed, which would doom my career. I'd eat through our savings and then we'd have to sell the house because I couldn't pay for it. My wife and kids would hate me, and they might even leave me...."*

That's how you can *hemorrhage* or *bleed out* by stacking meanings. You start with one fatalistic *meaning*, which is just fear of a possible outcome, but you turn it into a certain fate in your mind. This leads you to another possible event,—that you also believe with the faith of a devout cult follower listening to their supposed illuminated leader— and soon you believe you've lost it all and are living under a bridge.

I can't over-stress how powerful *meaning* can be, and how it can empower you or destroy your dreams and ambitions. And it's 100% in your own hands.

Coaching Case File: How an ATP pro used meaning to improve play in high-pressure moments

All too often, especially when an athlete is under pressure, if something does not go as expected or as they believe it should, the athlete can be thrust into a whirlwind of negative emotions and doubts. I had a client who fell into this trap often. When we discussed it, I told him jokingly that the best summary of his problem was given by Captain Jack Sparrow when he said:

> "The problem is not the problem. The problem is your attitude about the problem."

In other words, the problem was the *meaning* the player would give to what happened.

This client was an ATP pro who felt extreme pressure when he had a break point opportunity in his favor. In other words, it was the other player who was serving and whose serve was at risk of being broken. Normally, in that situation, you would expect the player serving to feel more pressure, but what happened to my client is actually quite common. I asked him why, if it was the opponent's serve that was in danger of being broken, he felt pressure. In other words, what *meaning* did he attribute to the situation and what outcome was he worried about? He answered without hesitation:

> *"If I don't convert the break point, I'm basically a poor player, not one of the best players on tour. "*

I now understood the meaning he was attributing, and I was able to challenge him and help him change it. I asked:

> "Do you know what conversion rate the best in the world will usually achieve when they have a chance to break the opponent's serve? I mean guys like Djokovic, Federer and Nadal."

He admitted he'd never thought of it. When I told him it was 30% to 35% on average, he couldn't believe it. So we went to the box scores of tournaments over the last few months and did the math. His eyes opened wide when he verified that I was in the right range. With this data, based on cold hard facts—not the opinion of his over-critical inner voice—he was open to being challenged.

We agreed and wrote in his notebook that, from now on, he would change his habitual inner dialogue that went something like the following:

> "If I don't convert one break point, everyone will know I don't belong here. What's worse is that the rival will grow more confident, knowing I am crap and did not take advantage of my opportunity. I will have lost all momentum."

Instead, we agreed that it was more than fair for him to have the following conversation with himself:

> "If I don't convert this break point, it's no big deal. As long as I'm converting about three out of ten, then I'm at world class level. The outcome of this break point alone means nothing. Just having a break point works in my favor because my opponent knows he won't win his serve easily, and he will get tense because he'll feel that he either serves perfectly or I'll eventually break him."

With this new perspective, he was able to greatly eliminate the nerves he felt in those situations and play the point more confidently and aggressively, allowing him to convert more break point opportunities and place more pressure on his rivals. Even his change in body language—from tense to more confident—helped to pressure opponents slightly.

As a side benefit, he began developing a longer time horizon over which he would rate his performance in the match. In other words, he began seeing individual break point opportunities as part of a larger strategy during the match. The more break points he played—even if he didn't manage to convert them—the more he reinforced the *meaning* he was giving the other player serious problems with on his serve, because he kept creating opportunities to break. He then believed that it was just a matter of time before he managed to break, and he would seize the momentum.

As we saw when we discussed identity, belief is a very powerful force. When this player began seeing himself as someone who would break his opponent's serve at some point, he actually began playing like someone who knew he would eventually get the break.

Do you see how simple and powerful that is? By being able to give the same scenario a different *meaning*, you can go from feeling pressured and unsure, to feeling confident and taking control of the situation.

Coaching Case File:
How a star sales leader regained confidence and drove performance through mastering meaning

My client had been a very successful sales executive in a large company that was market leader in the healthcare sector. When she left the company to start her own entrepreneurial venture, she still held the record for most sales in a month—and in a given year—at her previous company.

Life as an entrepreneur, she quickly learnt, was different from having a large, established brand behind you with significant financial resources. Her company had experienced a successful launch and first six months of operations, then the business began to decline as a result of a weak economic cycle and the news that one of the leading competitors in the industry had declared bankruptcy after being investigated for fraud. Both factors combined to make consumers wary of investing in the higher end services my client's business offered.

All areas of the company—from production excellence to sales to employee morale—dropped below previous levels. The founder was perplexed at the turn of events and utterly frustrated because she believed they had a very competitive position in the market, offering excellent service at disruptive pricing and a clean brand image.

After an initial diagnostic, I realized that one of the big issues holding the team and the business back was the doubts about whether they were actually as good as they had believed. What if their previous success had been a stroke of luck that was unrepresentative of their true potential as a business? My client, the head of the entire business, had a knack for sales and a very deep industry and product expertise that she had historically leveraged exceptionally well to close even the toughest sales when no one else could. She also came across as extremely self-confident and having palpable gravitas. Basically, she had all the traits of a classical super star, but now she wondered if she was really just an imposter and began doubting her own potential.

Led by her passion to make a difference in her industry, she had designed the vision for the company over several years, then had convinced banks and venture investors to back her project. Her business plan was very bullish, and she forecasted running at operationally break-even after a few months. The most amazing part was that she actually *achieved* all this. She had been on point and continuing her exponential trajectory—until she stumbled.

The bad press from the competitor that was investigated and declared bankruptcy, together with the weak economic outlook, produced a revenue dip for my client's young business and a significant cash crunch in the business. As they passed through the turbulence, the team began to turn against each other, criticizing one another in a search for someone to blame for their fall from glory of the early days of unprecedented success.

The founder could not understand what had happened and began to lose confidence in her ability to close the big deals, when she used to be the definitive closer. She even began to doubt the concept and the positioning. That's when we began to discuss the *meaning* she was giving to the events of the last few months. I have come across so many talented people like her, both in sports and business. As Manolo Sanchís, former captain of the Real Madrid soccer team, once told me,

> "Talent can often be a curse, because when things have always come easy for you and you are accustomed to winning with relative ease, you don't develop your full potential and, more importantly, the day you stumble or face a challenge at the limit of your abilities, you are completely shocked and start telling yourself negative stories about who you really are."

This was exactly where my client was at the moment we began working together.

We invested time in exploring how some start-ups had stumbled and *failed forward* or had aggressively changed or adapted their initial positioning or business model as they got data on what worked and what didn't. We looked at Amazon, which moved from an online bookstore to a real-time portal offering whatever you need in any category, as well as generating constantly updated customized suggestions based on highly-advanced, multivariable predictive algorithms. The key is that Jeff Bezos, Amazon's founder, had used the early stumbles as data to refine and improve the business. Most importantly, he gave each failure an empowering *meaning*, feeling more and more confident that Amazon was learning and becoming more competitive, instead of falling apart.

Likewise, Facebook began as a project focussed on university students and soon found a much greater market. No one would consider Facebook or Amazon as failures, yet they went through tough times, redesigned their models, and made mistakes. Lots of mistakes—wonderful, information-providing mistakes.

My client began to accept that she needed to take control of the *meaning* she had attributed to the events, and each market-leading entrepreneur's story we reviewed opened her a little more to the possibility that maybe things *could* be different.

Elon Musk, founder of Tesla, PayPal and SpaceX and dubbed as *The real-life Tony Stark* (in reference to the billionaire genius secret identity of the Iron Man comic character), said it well when he spoke of the meaning of innovating:

"If things are not failing, you are not innovating enough."

Basically Musk is illustrating what we have been discussing in this chapter. When you want to do something really challenging—something really great, something that pushes your limits—you will fail, and that's a sign that you're being sufficiently ambitious. You rarely, if ever, show up and, on your first try, become the most influential CEO in your industry or win that prized championship. When you're going through this process, it can feel frustrating because you believe you can do better; you believe you can achieve something really special, but you're not seeing the results (yet). That's where the difference between driving forward to success and quitting can often be the *meaning* you give to your experiences and the challenges you face along the way.

After reviewing these famous companies that struggled mightily, my client was able to admit that she felt like a failure. She felt guilty for having brought in family and friends as investors, for not meeting her own sales targets, and even for struggling and not giving the employees a stable place to work. Essentially, she was scared and, for the first time, she had received a jarring blow instead of scoring an easy knock-out. Her big problem had been accepting that reality and admitting that she was unsure for once in her life. She believed that her recent stumble meant she was finished and could not recover.

We explored how great boxers take tremendous hits and, despite feeling groggy for a minute, they dig deep and find a way to win. Building on the boxing metaphor, I suggested that, instead of telling herself a story about being finished, she could change the meaning and use the blows she'd received as motivation, instead of nails in her coffin. I asked her if she could evolve her identity to include the toughness of a championship boxer. She smiled and seemed to like this, as she had always thought of herself as a self-made person and a fighter.

I showed her a one-minute clip from the Rocky III movie, where Sylvester Stallone's character is absorbing blow after blow from his rival (played by Mr T.), and his trainer in the fight, Apollo Creed (played by the late, great Carl Weathers) says:

"He's getting killed."

Rocky's brother-in-law (played by Burt Young) emphatically responds:

"No, no, he's not getting killed. He's getting MAD!"

Rocky then goes on to get increasingly stronger and more determined with every blow he receives, until he turns the tide and wins the fight. I challenged my client to simply get *mad* at the events of the last months, and be more determined to come back.

My client admitted that the events had damaged her confidence and changed the way she was approaching her job. She was shying away, changing her style, and trying to avoid taking another *hit*. Essentially, I told her that her *talent* had given up control and her *ego* was running the show and making her play small. Before the business had hit rough sailing, whenever she had a big deal to close, failure was *never* an option. Since she believed she would close the vast majority of big deals, she always did. I told her that she had stopped believing she would win the battle because of the *meaning* she'd given to the challenges they'd faced.

I made her write out an ambitious sales target and place it on her desk and read it over and over with conviction. Underneath the target number, she wrote: *I'm getting mad.*

She was skeptical, but decided to give it a month, and if it didn't work, then she would give up and shut the business. Conviction was hard to find at the beginning, so I told her to coach herself by telling everyone she met a different story of what had happened. Instead of bowing her head, she would boldly tell people how the business had grown stronger because they had survived the difficult market situation, and now she knew they would be amongst the few survivors who came out stronger on the other side. Eventually, her subconscious started to believe this new narrative and, by the end of that month, sales were up to pre-crisis level and more importantly, the funnel of potential clients was filling up more than had occurred in the previous months. It's amazing what can happen when you give an empowering *meaning* to events, don't you think?

See Dick Run;
Be Like Dick

Don't stop when you're tired.
Stop when you're done!

David Goggins
(Navy SEAL)

WHAT'S THE BIG DEAL?

What if you could discover the secret to being unstoppable? Imagine that nothing and no one could stop you from fighting for your goals. How much confidence would you gain in achieving your mission if you found a source of energy and strength that would allow you to never give up as long as you still had breath in your body and a heartbeat?

Elite performers tap a similar source of perpetual fuel and become forces of nature in pursuit of their dreams. What is this magical lever? I call it *CAGE-mode*.

I developed the term *CAGE-mode* because there is no one single word that captures everything I believe is essential in this unique lever. The term is an acronym for *Consistently Accurate, Gritty and Enduring*. Also, since I started using it many years ago with fighters, the term *CAGE* reminds them of the environment where their skill is put to the maximum test. However, make no mistake, this is not something useful only for contact sports. The most elite performers in any sport or business all operate in *CAGE-mode*.

Before I break down *CAGE-mode* in greater detail, let me share a short story to help you *feel* it, then we'll delve into what it is and how to develop it.

Rick Hoyt was born in 1962 and he was diagnosed with paraplegia with brain dysfunction. Doctors sentenced Rick to a life as a vegetable, but his parents, Dick and Judy, refused to accept that death sentence for their son. They knew that trapped within that body, there was a world full of emotion and an exceptional human being. The only difference in Rick's case was that his interface with the outside world was faulty and did not allow him to share everything he had within. Dick and Judy kept looking until they found the Tufts University medical team. There they found a way to put Rick in contact with the outside world by means of a special helmet that allowed him to write with his head. From that moment on, Rick was able to communicate with his parents, although he still felt different from other kids. His parents, however, wanted to give their child the most normal life possible.

For several years, Dick and Judy suffered in silence, until the day Rick, then 17 years old, told them he wanted to compete in a race that was being organized in his school. Dick tried to explain to his son that he wouldn't be able to run a race since he was in a wheelchair, but Rick, more creative than any of them, told his father he could push the chair. Dick agreed to his son's request, thinking it would give his son a small measure of joy, but he discovered something much more powerful. Dick discovered the magic potion to help Rick feel more alive and connected. After that first race, Rick put on his special writing hat and composed a message that would forever change his world and that of his father:

"When I run, I do not feel disabled."

At that precise moment, Dick Hoyt discovered how the unstoppable power of a true mission of love can infuse a mere mortal with infinite grit and consistency to fight against all odds during an entire lifetime. Dick realized that he had discovered the key to giving his son what he desired most: *the power to feel normal.* He decided that he would dedicate his life, up to his last breath, to giving his son that feeling as often as possible.

At the time of Dick's death on March 17th, 2021, Team Hoyt, as the father and son duo were known, had finished over 1000 marathons and triathlons, including the legendary Boston Marathon and Iron Man triathlon.

Dick Hoyt personified *CAGE-mode.* Let's take a look at the elements that make it up and how to achieve it.

CAGE: Consistently Accurate, Gritty and Enduring

I made up the acronym CAGE, because consistency is so important, but that word falls short and misses several essential elements of what I've observed makes top performers so driven.

The definition of consistency is "the state or condition of always happening or behaving in the same way." Thus, being consistent, in terms of *The Optimal Performance Formula*, is not enough because you can be consistently stupid or perform consistently at a suboptimal level.

For this reason, the first add-on in the *CAGE-mode* model is *Accuracy.* One of the key learnings from my years of working with top performers is that, whether you're practicing a cognitive skill or a physical skill, you're always reinforcing a pattern or a given performance level. In other words, the old adage that *practice makes perfect* would be more accurate if we said *practice makes permanent.* The question is whether you are burning good or bad form and habits into your nervous system. You want to be consistent, specifically regarding *correct technique.* Top athletes know the limit of their performance is set by the intensity and quality of their technique and training. The same is true in business. *What* you practice and *how* you practice is what you reinforce. When I train martial artists I always caution them about sparring at half speed or with no contact if their goal is to enter full-contact or UFC-type events. The reason, again, is that you compete the way you train, so if you're not used to executing at full speed and power, you'll find yourself subconsciously fighting at the lighter training pace, and the dynamic of the match will quickly overwhelm you.

The third and fourth variables that differentiate the *CAGE-mode* model can be found in the definition of *Grit*, as laid out by Angela Duckworth in her best-selling book with the same title:

> "Grit is not just having resilience in the face of failure, but also having deep commitments that you remain loyal to over many years."

In other words, it's not just about being able to work hard in the moment, or overcome adversity, but it's also about always linking that resilience to the passion that fuels your mission. German philosopher Friedrich Nietzsche famously captured this idea in the nineteenth century when he wrote:

> "He who has a why to live for can bear almost any how."

A very interesting observation from Duckworth's research is that people get grittier as they age. I fully believe this, and I think it's linked to the fact that, as people mature, they get clearer on what they want and more committed to fighting for their dreams.

In summary, operating in *CAGE-mode,* as I've seen modeled in elite performers, represents:

> The virtue of **CONSISTENTLY** giving your maximum effort, focussed on flawless and **ACCURATE** execution of technique, while personifying **GRIT** in overcoming challenges and resistance, allowing you to fuel your **ENDURING** commitment to never giving up on achieving your ambitious mission and audacious goals.

Why is this concept so important? It's the essence of how top performers keep going through good days and bad—when they feel like it and when they don't—to consistently advance along their mastery journey. I believe that one of the most prominent reasons that people fall short of fulfilling their maximum potential is that they approach their goals without all the necessary *CAGE-mode variables.* Let's be honest—motivation is like a shower. It can refresh you today, but tomorrow you need to shower again, or you start to stink. So you need to rely on something much more stable and powerful than just motivation in order to ensure you walk the path to mastery.

You need to be in *CAGE-mode.*

To see the effect of lacking these four variables, just look all around you for everyday examples. Think of the vast majority of people who fail to meet their fitness goals, be it to lose weight, gain muscle, or improve cardiovascular health. The main cause is that they don't stick to things long enough to acquire the necessary skills and get results, preferring overnight shortcuts like pills, performance-enhancing drugs, or surgery. In addition, people cheat themselves. They deviate from their diets, skip workout days, or mail it in when they train, failing to bring the focus and intensity necessary. There's nothing wrong with targeting simpler goals, but you can't expect results for the work you didn't put in. Long-term focus is a superpower because so few people have it in our current culture. Everyone wants a quick hack, but there's no substitute for hard, consistent, focussed practice over the long term to drive you along the road to mastery.

Likewise, many companies test out new strategies, or give executives a chance to run a company or a division of a company, but all too often it's a short leash. If you don't get great results in a quarter or two, then change is imposed. This mindset is insane, because companies that have managed to dominate a niche have invested in the mid-term, understanding that it takes time to start seeing the results.

The secret all great performers share is unrelenting use of *CAGE-mode* in practicing their craft and improving themselves. Most great performers are *works in progress* and consistently work harder and smarter to improve during their entire careers.

There's a common acknowledgment amongst top competitors that it's what you do in the dark, when no one's watching, that defines how you will shine in the light. There have been many versions of this, one of the most well-known in Michael Phelps' Under Armour commercial from a few years back titled *Rule Yourself.*

Authors Joshua Medcalf and Lucas Jadin wrote a few wonderful passages that I think capture the true essence of *CAGE-mode* (although they don't call it that, of course):

> "The bright lights only reveal your work in the dark. . . .
>
> When I say 'the dark,' I'm talking about the countless hours of gut-wrenching, exhausting, tedious work you do while nobody's watching. . .

It's the time you put in day after day that goes unnoticed and unthanked, when everyone else has gone home but you remain on the field, practicing until you simply can't anymore. . .

In fact, it's when the rest of the world is at rest that we make our greatest progress. . .

Talent is only the starting line. . . it's overrated... it is NEVER enough...

The dark is where you realize that confidence is fleeting and shifts with the wind—but that conviction, authentic conviction, is forged through fire.

The dark is where you hone your skills so sharply that even the intensity of the bright lights can't dull them.

The dark is where you forge the conviction that you can do hard things.

The dark is where you transform into a version of yourself you never dreamed possible."

I love that extract because it covers all the elements of *CAGE-mode:*

CONSISTENTLY giving your maximum effort, focussed on flawless and ACCURATE execution of technique, while personifying GRIT in overcoming challenges and resistance, allowing you to fuel your ENDURING commitment to never giving up on achieving your ambitious mission and audacious goals.

Notice Medcalf and Jadin say that there are no shortcuts. The road to mastery passes through many hours of focussed practice, over many years, where you're pushing beyond your limits, breaking down every component of performance, trying to optimize it, and stitching it back together seamlessly.

Another key aspect I want you to understand is that *CAGE-mode* has a multiplier effect because of the principle of compounding. This is like compound interest, where your money makes money, that then makes more money. In other words, you're getting interest on the principal you invested PLUS you make interest on the interest you've made before. Likewise, when you consistently put in the work, the focus, and the intensity, your baseline rises, and any work you do generates greater returns because you have a bigger base of skill to build upon.

So, when people see so-called *gifted* performers in any field, what they're actually seeing is someone who has been constantly busting their ass for a decade or two. What they're seeing are the results of operating in *CAGE-mode* while refining the small details that are almost invisible to the untrained eye, but that make all the difference.

Performance Cyriax

One of the reasons *CAGE-mode* is so important on your journey towards mastery is that it is the consistent willingness to do the hard, focussed work—in order to improve even 1%—that fuels the unending search to identify and fill the *gaps* between where we are today and where we want to go. It's worth noting that, when most people are watching an elite performer, they are not even aware of these gaps. All they see is an exceptional, powerful ability to perform masterfully. However, the serious student on the road to mastery not only sees these gaps in themselves, but is haunted by them and will not rest until they have been improved. Often the gaps are not things that are missing totally, but things that the performer currently does below the level of proficiency required for the performance they want to achieve. This can cover a wide range of areas, but some examples could be the following:

Technique improvement gaps

Tiger Woods changed his swing at the midpoint of his career, seemingly risking losing his elite status, but he became even better as a result.

Physical gaps: compensations or injuries

Often athletes lean too much on a stronger part of the body due to a limitation they have never addressed in another part. A classic example would be athletes who do not have the necessary mobility in their deep hip muscles, then overcompensate with hamstrings or knees and end up with injuries.

Knowledge gaps

Tom Brady is famous for his work ethic in the film room. Brady had the fortune of having Bill Belichick, considered one of the greatest football strategists ever, as his head coach. To his credit, Brady leveraged the wisdom of his mentor, as well as seeking out other experts, such as (then) rival Peyton Manning, in order to understand the intricacies of the game in terms of formations, play calling, reading defenses, and calling audibles. Brady's ability to operate in *CAGE-mode* in this subject, over many years, helped forge his legacy as the winningest quarterback in NFL history.

All of the above examples of how elite performers work to fill gaps is a concept I call *Performance Cyriax*. The name comes from an advanced technique used by physiotherapists called *deep friction massage (DFM)* that was developed by James Cyriax, thus the name. The Cyriax technique is most often used after an injury to mobilize ligaments, tendons, and muscles that have been damaged and prevent adherent scars from forming. In situations where adhesions are already formed, the technique breaks them, helping to mobilize the scar tissue and break the cross linkages between the connective tissues and the surrounding structures and allows for remodeling and reorientation of the collagen fibers in a longitudinal (correct) manner.

This metaphor is exactly how great companies and athletes improve. They are not afraid to break and rebuild systematically in order to fill gaps that are limiting their performance. The key is that top performers are not afraid to feel like beginners or feel clumsy by making a change, as long as it will help them catapult past their current abilities in the future.

This trait is a sharp contrast to how most people and organizations operate. All too often, we get to a certain point, and it seems like the learning and improvement are done. Most people finish their studies and start a job, in a certain area and, 30 years later, they are either in the same job, or doing that job in a similar company elsewhere.

Either way, I find individuals and companies are slow to take into account all the relevant factors that can change in that time, such as technological innovations, cultural changes, and personal evolution. Let's face it—when you finish your degree or start working, you are usually in your twenties. How can you think that you will be the same person for the next 40 years? What you considered a stretch challenge at 25 may be boring and easy 15 years later. Or maybe the world has evolved and you need to question how you are doing things. Imagine if tennis pros refused to move away from wooden rackets. They would be at a tremendous disadvantage. Yet that's how most people and organizations approach their entire professional journey.

CAGE-mode helps turn challenges into growth opportunities

Let me share another learning around *Performance Cyriax* that has great value for anyone aspiring to achieve optimal performance: my own flexibility journey.

As a reminder, I've been practicing, teaching, and competing in various martial arts for over 35 years. When I was younger, I competed successfully in various styles and types of contact tournaments (this was before UFC and the like). I could kick high, and with power, but had not mastered true deep hip and core flexibility (no one taught me back then and few people really get this). As a result, I did what most companies and athletes with under-developed areas do, I compensated with my strengths.

Athletes are master compensators, and this is true for top performers in every field, because what they are focussed on is producing the result, often at a high cost. Ask 10 former dancers and you'll probably get a similar story. Also, when I was on the ATP tour with my clients, I often heard statements like *professional tennis is terrible for your health and joints.*

You can see the same imbalances in any large corporation. How often have you seen someone in business who is functionally solid, but has the emotional intelligence of a doorknob? How many managers have you seen that don't know how to give or receive feedback? All these shortcomings hobble a company's potential and lead to performance issues in the mid and long term.

Back to my case. I compensated with my hamstrings for years, demanding they stretch more than they should to overcome limitations in deep hip/sacroiliac joints. This worked for a long time, until

I had an emergency operation for a hernia in my groin area. The surgeon sewed me up with little care, creating a mess in my fascia and joint alignment, ultimately limiting my hip movement even more, and that just increased the stress on the rest of my body. The fact that I was 20 years older than when I started the martial arts also factored into making the recovery more complicated.

While rehabbing, I was training on a cold day, and I was more tired than usual. My hamstring ripped and my femoral bicep tendon was also injured. The whole back of my leg filled with a huge pool of internal bleeding within minutes. My body had drawn the line and said I wasn't getting away with cheating any more. That's when I decided to take advantage of the setback to rebuild properly, from the ground up (well, from the core out actually).

I started down the rabbit hole of mobility training and sought out the best mentors I could find. The great thing about the era we live in is that you can work with the best professionals, no matter where they are located. That is such a competitive advantage vs how things were when I was growing up, where you might never even know that many of these experts existed unless you happened to live near them (for you younger readers: there was no Internet).

Over time I began to see my own body with a new, more informed perspective, and I realized how poor some of my basic mobility patterns were. For example, my ability to move my hips into anterior pelvic tilt to make more room for the femur in leg split movements and high kicks was almost non-existent. People have no idea how limited their mobility is in areas like hip rotators, hip flexors, and the spinal column, but these are often the cause of back pain and sciatica.

Over years of research and working with experts, I've undone the pieces of the compensation puzzle. It's usually a complex puzzle of interactions between body parts, and as you start to compensate in one area, you start getting negative effects up your *muscle chains.* Muscle chains are groups of muscles that cross several joints but work synergistically for certain movements and depend on the health and mobility of each part of the chain. For example, a poor gait or misaligned leg posture can result in tightness and pain in the neck.

As I learnt more, I felt at times like I was going backward because I was learning to do things in a new way and engaging new muscles I had not learnt to access. However, I knew I had to get comfortable with feeling clumsy and uncoordinated in the short term, because I needed to change the way I moved to be able to improve radically in the long run. It's the same process Tiger Woods went through when he changed his swing or Kobe Bryant when he changed his shot technique after an injury. I knew that I not only wanted to regain the mobility I had lost, but I aspired to build greater flexibility with increased strength and, as a consequence, greater speed and power. I can now say that, after many years, I've finally achieved an advanced level of active and passive flexibility beyond what I had when I was much younger.

Using *Performance Cyriax* to break things down and rebuild them better is hard—physically and mentally—but it's actually a pretty healthy habit. It's not pleasant, and it's emotionally trying, but as I always tell my clients when they have lofty goals, if it were easy, everyone would be doing it. Embracing challenges is required when you want to be exceptional, and *CAGE-mode* is essential for turning them into greater strength and skill.

Coaching Case File: How a professional motor racer personified *CAGE-mode* to thrive after a crippling accident

Toñejo Rodríguez is an absolute titan of a human being and a world class example of how to turn challenges into growth opportunities. I've had the privilege to call him a friend for many years and to present together on performance to some of my clients.

Toñejo is, from a mental standpoint, probably the strongest human being I've ever met, and a spectacular, kind, and generous person to boot. A former motocross and quad champion with 60 first place finishes, and over a hundred more in the top three, Toñejo is the epitome of mental strength and resilience.

Toñejo suffered an accident while competing that left him with a spinal injury and in a wheelchair, but instead of giving up, he found a way to drive himself further and grow with every challenge. His story should be required study material for anyone aspiring to optimize their performance.

After the accident, while still in the hospital, Toñejo processed what had happened to him and decided that it was not going to kill his spirit. He told his doctor that, since he couldn't use his legs to stay on a motorcycle, he wanted to begin racing jet skis as he could tie himself to the jet ski and needed just his arms to accelerate and brake. The doctor told him he was delirious and did not realize what had happened to him. Toñejo responded that he knew exactly what had happened to him, but it didn't mean he had to give up what he loves most: racing. He just had to adapt the modality. He spent the many months in the hospital visualizing every single detail of how he could race jet skis, what team he would need, and even how he would leverage his racing background to beat other competitors. He had not dreamt about it; he had seen the future.

Toñejo's belief that he could compete was so strong and unwavering that he went on to win the Iberian Jet Ski Championships and recorded the pole position at the World Championships. Every other competitor could walk, so he tells the story of being on the podium and looking left and right and seeing people standing while he was in his wheelchair. He called his dad to share the news. When his father asked,

"How many disabled people were in the race?"

Toñejo answered without a second's hesitation,

"None. I was on that podium and I'm not disabled. I'm the same guy I used to be, just sitting down."

That's the power of belief, of visualization, and of self-talk. Toñejo has never stopped believing that he is, in fact, the same racing champion, just sitting down.

This is just one of a million stories Toñejo could share. He is the personification of the principle that it's not what happens to you that defines you, but the *meaning* you give it—and your belief of what is possible—that sets your limits. Toñejo proves mindset is the greatest limiting factor that humans impose upon themselves.

Whenever I have the privilege to spend time with Toñejo, he always finds a moment to be grateful. He says he considers himself to be privileged because he has a great family, amazing friends, and has been able to do everything he's challenged himself to do. He even tells me he's grateful because I convinced him to start speaking and sharing his story when, in fact, I am the grateful one to be able to know and learn from such a giant of a human being.

Toñejo has gone on to win multiple international jet ski championships, complete the *Dakar* in a specially-adapted truck, and be the first Spaniard to drive an F1 ocean racer. He has also advised professional racers, including serving as Sports Director Moto3 for Maverick Viñale's team in 2016.

Notice how Toñejo's process captures all aspects of *CAGE-mode*:

1. **CONSISTENT**: Despite a traumatic setback, he quickly focussed and continued to chase his dream of racing. He never wavered from who he is nor what he was born to do.
2. **ACCURATE**: While in the hospital, he began planning and designing every detail of how he would adapt to jet ski racing and his new condition. Every new challenge, such as the Dakar or the F1, has forced him to grow and improve some aspect of himself. He never stops improving his racing skills.
3. **GRIT**: No additional comment needed here. His story speaks for itself.
4. **ENDURING**: His commitment to never give up his love of racing has been unshakable, and he has gone on to achieve amazing feats even after his accident.

Knowing Toñejo invalidates any excuse you could ever give yourself for why you can't do something and reminds you of the power of the human spirit.

No Dickheads:
Extending Mindset
(From One to Many)

It's not what you preach, it's what you tolerate.

Jocko Willink
(Navy SEAL)

WHAT'S THE BIG DEAL?

Over the last chapters, we've delved deep into the key variables in the *Mindset* block of *The Optimal Performance Formula*, and hopefully you have a good understanding of how huge of an impact they can have on your performance. If all has gone well up to this point, you're all fired up to start implementing these yourself. Now the question arises:

If you're part of a team or organization, how do we ensure these skills and tools are implemented by everyone?

This is where we start to differentiate great individual performers from leaders, who not only perform at elite levels, but have the magic ability to elevate the performance of others around them.

It's no small task to ensure that all members of a team share the elements we've seen in a way that creates synergies, allowing the group to generate more value than the sum of its parts. Specifically, leaders must ensure:

I.   A powerful and common group identity, in which each individual's unique fit and contribution are clearly mapped

II. A growth mindset and unspoken commitment to continued improvement both individually and as a team

III. A shared, unwavering belief in the team's ability to achieve their most ambitious mission and firm expectations of maximal success

IV. A common commitment to uphold the same daily standards across the board, despite how they may feel on any given day

V.   The foundational skills to drive empowering *meanings*

VI. A non-negotiable commitment to operating in *CAGE-mode*

The glue to hold all that together is a carefully curated culture driven by real values that are personified everyday, especially by leadership. Sounds logical, right? It is, and most leaders in business and sports will get it at a theoretical level and agree. The problem is that when it comes time to measure, design, and implement a culture, the same people will draw a blank.

My good friend Lorraine Steele, who is a world class executive coach, jokes that culture is the *"c- word,"* as if it were some forbidden, foul term. Lorraine's joke highlights the elephant in the room in most corporations and competitive sports organizations: leaders still feel very uncomfortable and uneasy when talking about culture. It has almost become taboo. Sure, many CEOs and head coaches *say* they need to address culture, but they are just doing lip service to it if it's not burnt into the DNA of the organization and personified by every member of the team.

I'd like to take you deeper into understanding why culture is such a powerful performance driver—or a performance killer, if you allow a toxic culture to take hold. Before we dive in, let me just note that culture is such a broad and important topic that we won't be able to properly cover it in one chapter. However, I do want to highlight some critical aspects that you can start working with right away.

If you can't see or touch it, how are you supposed to believe in it?

The first question to look at is: *why is culture such a complex subject for leaders to get right?* The problem starts with being able to define what it is. Albert Einstein once said:

> "The definition of genius is taking the complex and making it simple."

That's precisely where so many struggle right out of the gate. Culture is complex for many reasons. I'll share some of the most common challenges I've seen clients struggle with, and I'm sure you'll feel at least a couple of them resonate with your organization.

First, culture is about how humans interact, and humans are always complex. We're not taught in school—or in any other venue—how to understand each other at a fundamental level and align paradigms, expectations, and values. As anyone who has ever had a child can tell you, humans don't come with instruction manuals. And, if you're talking about an organization's culture, you need to integrate tens, hundreds, or even thousands of individual humans and align them.

That's complex, but not impossible! It is much easier if you understand the drivers of human behavior and have methodology and tools like the ones in *The Optimal Performance Formula*. Leading people on a transformational journey requires uncovering limiting paradigms, prioritizing effective communication, and helping people overcome the fear and uncertainty linked to change. Understanding the humans who have to make the journey is essential to overcome resistance—or as I like to call it, *antibodies to change*.

Another reason culture is so difficult is because most organizations don't know how to measure it, let alone how to drive it. Companies are good at measuring the tangible stuff related to *tactical performance*, like productivity, profit, revenue, etc. But how do you measure culture? This impacts what's called *adaptive performance*, which is the ability to adapt to the unknown variables along the way and innovate. While *tactical performance* techniques, such as headcount reduction, are well-known and easy to execute, *adaptive performance* skills, such as creating a culture of trust and safety where people can test and risk in order to stimulate innovation, is more of a black box for most CEOs and head coaches.

One challenge that makes culture difficult for organizations is that people confuse their *personality* with *culture*. I recently read an interview with ex-NFL and MLB star Deion Sanders, who is now the head coach for the University of Colorado Buffaloes football team. In the interview he said,

> "Culture, culture, culture, culture, culture ... What the heck does that mean? ... I don't care about culture... I don't care if they like each other. I want to win. I've been on some teams where the quarterback didn't like the receiver, but they darn sure made harmony when the ball was snapped."

Judging from that quote, he seems to think culture is just about team members liking each other. So even though Sanders is, in fact, creating a culture in Colorado, as we'll see in a moment, he seems unaware of the variables linked to establishing a solid and sustainable culture. By the way, that's one of the key differentiators of organizations with high performance cultures—they shape their culture deliberately instead of letting a *default* culture emerge from the mix of personalities and behaviors that occur spontaneously.

Now, *Prime Time,* as Sanders is known, is a unique animal. He's extremely talented. He played both pro football and baseball at the *same time,* and was very successful in both. He was even selected as an All Pro in both sports. That's an amazing feat and there's no questioning his talent and work ethic. He was an elite performer. However, what's fascinating is that, when people are that skilled, there is a lot they do right, but they do many of those things *innately.* That's the case with *Prime.* If you hear him speak about his personal mindset when he trained, it's fantastic. He doesn't call it mindset but that's what he's talking about.

What he doesn't seem to realize is that everything he is discussing, including how he coaches, has already been invented and modeled. He says it's just *"me"* [him], and he has projected his personality on the team. He seems to think culture is just about team members copying him.

So the really interesting part is this. Yes, he does embody many of the traits he wants to implement in the *culture* (the term he doesn't want to use), but he didn't invent them. As a result, he thinks culture and method are BS. He seems to believe that it's just a matter of *Do what I say. Be a mini-me and good things will happen.* Leaders like this are limited for several reasons. First of all, if you want to populate your organization with copies of yourself, forget about leveraging the value of diversity, in any of its facets, be that cognitive diversity, unique experiences that could add value, or unique skills the organization does not currently have. Secondly, leaders that don't build the culture from the bottom up leave a house of cards that falls as soon as the coach or CEO leaves, or even loses power and influence.

By contrast, legendary coaches like Bill Walsh, who led the San Francisco 49ers to five Super Bowl championships or Bill Belichick of the New England Patriots dynasty that won six championships, built organizations with such ingrained cultures that they were able to win despite changes in key people in the organization, and have often achieved great results without a team of all star divos.

On the other end of the spectrum, leaders who don't have that hard-wired set of skills often try to model winning cultures but stay at a very superficial level and don't usually walk the talk, so it never sinks into the organization.

Culture, like character, creates trust and respect

I believe culture comes down to whether you are really committed to living your values. I've seen many clients talk about values in the boardroom, then contradict those values with their behaviors in their day-to-day interactions. A classic example most people can relate to is promoting the typical top performer who is a toxic team member. This person does more harm than good, but leaders who are not really committed to culture allow them to remain—and often reward them—because they provide tactical performance (i.e. sales, profit). However, the damage they are doing to the organization—and the performance of the rest of the team members—is far greater. If you say you want team members who trust each other and support each other, yet you allow toxic team members to thrive just because of tactical performance in the short term, you're selling your organization's soul for short-term gain.

Pep Guardiola, when he coached FC Barcelona, was a great example of betting on culture and reaping huge rewards in terms of performance.

He held tight to his principles and often removed extremely talented, big name players from the roster who just didn't fit with what he wanted to create. The final product was an FC Barca that won an unprecedented number of titles with a minimal number of high profile superstars. Even the greats on the team, like Leo Messi, played in a way that was very team-oriented and aligned with the culture. He was happy to play a specific role when he was asked to, even if he was not the guy scoring or getting the attention. That's the power of culture.

So let's get back to defining culture. Basically, culture is a set of norms that define how an organization *does* things. As humans, the vast majority of our daily decisions are formed in our subconscious mind, so we can say that an organization's culture is made up of the unconscious behaviors of its members. If you want to start understanding the culture of your organization, ask yourself sincerely the following questions:

What is the default response, standard, or action when there is a challenge?

Do team members always support the greater mission irrespective of their individual roles and protagonism?

Are politics always present in promotions and other key decisions?

Does the whole organization understand they are empowered to do whatever they deem best to drive client satisfaction, or is it frowned upon to stray from the standard rules and guidelines?

All that, and much more, is defined by culture. One way to prompt a response from people as to what the culture is like, is to ask:

What does it feel like to be a part of this organization?

In organizations with strong, high-performance cultures, you will find answers revolve around having high standards and strong relationships. The more connected people feel to the group, the better the culture is, and when those relationships serve to establish, support, and enforce standards, team members will buy into how the standards are an essential part of the identity of the organization. As a result, norms are consistent, well-entrenched, and a good reflection of the values. In other words:

A strong culture is one in which behavior is consistent from one person to the next and predictable over time.

Here is where the rubber meets the road for leaders. Leaders need to recognize that, by displaying a behavior—or even just tolerating a certain behavior from others—they are endorsing that behavior. It's that simple.

The quote at the beginning of this chapter by Jocko Willink, Former Navy SEAL, illustrated that in the most no-nonsense way possible.

"It's not what you preach; it's what you tolerate."

Organizations such as the SEALs and other special operations units that cannot permit uncertainty about how their members will behave have zero tolerance for any behaviors outside the culture and values.

The value of being strict in curating your culture has been confirmed in other circles too. Stanford University professor, Robert I. Sutton, is known for what he calls the "no a-hole rule." Negative people are like viruses, and their attitudes spread and seep into every aspect of an organization. Sutton wrote the following about the potential negative impact of tolerating toxic team members:

"They [assholes] are the Fellowship of the Miserable. . . and they are the killers of the dream . . . The damage that assholes do to their organizations is seen in the costs of increased turnover, absenteeism, decreased commitment to work, and the distraction and impaired individual performance documented in studies of psychological abuse, bullying, and mobbing."

It's no coincidence that legendary sporting organizations, such as the New Zealand All Blacks, have similar rules. The All Blacks version of Sutton's rule is summed up very simply with the phrase *No Dickheads*, which served as the inspiration for the title of this chapter.

When a team lacks any shared cultural values or history, money becomes the core value holding the firm together, and history has shown that economic incentives are a weak glue. So *carrots* (bonuses or raises) and *sticks* (loss of bonuses or termination of employment) puts teams into survival mode, and drives them away from their maximum potential. Moreover, team members operate as missionaries, maximizing personal gain in the short term and with little or no concern for the wellbeing of the group.

High-performance cultures are based on intrinsic motivators

An important part of the formula to keep in mind if you want a high-performing culture is to thoughtfully design the motivators for team members. The best way to motivate people and drive optimal performance is not through extrinsic motivators such as economic rewards or threats, but by inspiring people through the main intrinsic motivators of *play, freedom, purpose,* and *potential* in their craft. Let's quickly explore these powerful drivers in greater detail.

117

PLAY

Play is about what Dr. Mihaly Csikszentmihalyi called *autotelectic* experiences. *Autotelectic* means something you do for the mere love of doing it, not the external reward that may result. When you love what you do and are allowed to put your own personal, authentic touch on how you execute it—in other words, when you see it as *play* and can experiment—the result is performance that goes through the roof. When you love the process of doing the hard work—and enjoy testing and improving every little piece of your job or role because it is your personal masterpiece—you have found what psychologists call *play* in your craft. Additionally, *play* generates a feeling of control over one's life since it allows you to shape how your work is done. That sense of being an architect of your life, and not a victim of your circumstances, according to *Self Determination Theory*, drastically improves your self-esteem and happiness.

FREEDOM

The *play* driver is closely linked to the second intrinsic motivator—*freedom*. Research has shown that top performers feel more fulfilled and satisfied if they have the freedom to choose what they work on, how they work on it, whom they work with, and when they work. According to author Daniel Pink, in his book *Drive*, freedom or autonomy motivates us to think creatively without needing to conform to strict rules. By rethinking traditional ideas of control, organizations can increase team member autonomy, build trust, and improve innovation and creativity, as well as stimulate top performers to experiment and aim higher.

PURPOSE

Purpose occurs when the team is driven by a shared mission. Many organizations have trouble articulating the mission except for some outdated poster in the halls with a generic message such as *we create shareholder value through high valued services for our clients*, but in no way does that mission engage and energize people or identify what makes the organization unique. Apple has done a legendary job attracting people aligned with their purpose and empowering them to stretch the limits of what's considered possible.

POTENTIAL

The fourth driver of performance is *potential*, and I sum it up as follows. The most valuable thing you will ever gain from what you do are not the trophies, titles, or money you may win, but rather *who* you become in the process. That's basically the power of potential. When people see that doing a specific role or being part of a specific organization will transform them and grow skills that will make them better and more valuable, you have created an almost unstoppable force of motivation. Consider the allure of *potential* in an organization like the Navy SEALs and other elite organizations. Likewise, being part of a legendary team like Manchester United or the All Blacks gives the player an opportunity to leave a mark on history.

When I chose to study for my graduate degree at an Ivy League university, a part of the rationale for the high investment was the *potential* it provided graduates by just being an alumni of such a prestigious institution. Once you achieve these things, no one can take them from you, and you feel you have gained in the process. That is a strong motivator.

The power of intrinsic motivators was brilliantly illustrated by Alan Stein, Jr., a performance coach who worked with NBA stars Kevin Durant, Stephen Curry, and Kobe Bryant when he recounted a lesson from working with Christian High School basketball coach Stu Vetter:

> "Stu Vetter always used to talk about the difference in mindset between renting and owning. When you rent something . . . you view it as temporary . . . When you buy, it's an extension of you. Those who look at a job as just a step on the ladder or a paycheck are a drag on that place's culture. They're renting their job. . . . [by contrast, when] everyone sees the company as an extension of themselves. . . . they will walk through fire for the company because it's a part of who they are. That's the power of culture."

Great leaders don't measure success exclusively by wins and losses or the P&L, but also the culture and experience they create for every team member and client.

Soccer coach Dave Brandt of Messiah College expressed a similar view of culture when he said the following, which I love:

> "For me, winning isn't enough. I had a very idealistic vision. I wanted to coach the team I wanted to play on. I essentially wanted Camelot in a soccer program."

Coaching Case File: Leveraging culture to empower bottom line impact

I was asked to come in to help turn around a poorly-performing business unit of a large logistics provider. The first thing that struck me was how disjointed and separate each area or function appeared. The company provided end-to-end service from range planning, sourcing, procurement, transport, warehousing, handling, and delivery to final customer.

After I interviewed a few people, I started to understand why everything felt so poorly integrated. The unit was the result of the acquisition of three businesses that were thrown together in one business unit with the idea of giving clients an end-to-end service. To make the situation worse, they had a few key suppliers who were external companies but operated as strategic parts of the service, and they were run completely independently. The fundamental problem that jumped out to me was that they did not have one company, just several small groups, all with very different cultures and understanding of what success looked like.

Although top management had severe doubts about the approach, I started the turn-around by bringing in the different groups and working on what culture they wanted to have. No one had ever actually *asked* them how they wanted to work or even how they could improve their productivity, and they gladly jumped on the opportunity to shape their new company and their own roles. Remember that *freedom* and *play* are key factors in driving intrinsic motivation, and that proved to be the case here.

Teams began by defining what their joint mission was, and then how each of the integrated companies could contribute. We agreed that one trait of culture was *radical transparency*, and they engaged in sharing their frustrations and feedback in a constructive way with other areas. The magic was evident as they were all invested in defining and making the new model a success.

Another trait we defined for the business unit's culture was *simplicity*. They all agreed that legacy ways of working and corporate policies made things much more complicated than they needed to be, and had a negative impact on the strategy of providing the highest quality services at the most competitive price. This common understanding and agreement gave them the *freedom* to challenge the existing paradigms about how things needed to be done. They asked themselves if certain steps were really necessary—or if they just added bureaucracy to the process—and were empowered to implement the changes they agreed to as a group.

The teams worked across functions for several months and, within a year, the unit had turned around from seven-figure losses to break-even, all driven by a change in culture that unleashed the potential of each part of the value chain.

BLOCK 2:
MAPS

*If you don't know where you are going,
you'll end up someplace else.*

Yogi Berra
(Major League Baseball Hall of Fame Catcher)

Think in Decades

The way we spend our time
defines who we are.

Jonathan Estrin
(Film Producer)

WHAT'S THE BIG DEAL?

As we've seen, having a burning passion to achieve your dream or mission is essential. It can help you find strength and energy to work the long hours and do *the unrequired*. However, there is a big gap when people begin chasing their dreams that you can cover by learning and implementing this element of *The Optimal Performance Formula*.

Being prepared to work hard is great, but designing a plan to decide where and how you will invest that time and energy is even more important. Chasing mastery requires more than just will; it requires knowledge and meticulous planning. Although it may look like top performers have just been blessed with natural talent, if you look closer, you'll see that their success is built upon the foundations of a structured plan that has been meticulously executed over a significant period of time.

This last point is key. If you aspire to achieve anything exceptional, you need to *think in decades*. Moreover, you need to *plan* those decades. I always suggest building a 10-year *Mastery Map* that details the path of what optimal performance looks like for you and a structured, phased program to get you there.

I know that in our hack-driven, short-term focussed world, talking about decades seems like the ravings of a lunatic, but I assure you every single elite performer has a long-term view. There is a quote I often share that captures the essence of this principle very well. I first heard it from Tony Robbins, but it has also been attributed to Bill Gates. Either way, these two legends in their respective industries coincide on the same advice:

> "Most people greatly overestimate what they can do in a year and underestimate what they can do in 10 years."

I implore you to write this on a piece of paper and put it somewhere you can see it daily—or copy it directly on your phone or desktop. I guarantee, if you meditate on it consistently, you will find over time that it is more powerful than you might believe, and can set you apart from the rest of the pack. Although elite performers all follow this advice, for the rest of humanity it is a glaring weak spot.

Why is this such a game changer? Remember that mastery requires thousands of hours of *focussed practice*. If you're serious about driving your performance to your maximum potential, you need to play the long game. You need not just a clear picture of who you need to be to achieve what you want to in the future but also a structured, detailed roadmap to guide your decisions and actions along the way. Since it's a long journey, it's not reasonable to think you can just keep two or three vague ideas in your head and trust that will keep you on track.

Your *Mastery Map* is essential because, like a road map when you take a long trip, it helps you keep perspective on how each leg of the journey contributes to the final goal. Without that, you won't be as motivated to incessantly drill the boring, but essential, basics of your craft over and over, because you haven't linked them to your final vision. Remember, in the *Mindset* block, we explored how *CAGE-mode* is essential for top performers to keep going through good days and bad—when they feel like it and when they don't—to consistently advance along their mastery journey. Well, a *Mastery Map* is one of the most powerful tools to help you keep that focus on your long-term goals and consistently work with the focus and intensity necessary to compound skills over time.

Maps help reduce frustration and injury

One of the biggest advantages of a normal map, when you're traveling, is benefiting from the experiences of others who have gone on that path before and can tell you which roads will lead you where you want to go. This is easy to understand when you use Google maps or a similar alternative while you're driving or walking. You benefit from knowing that 2 km ahead, you need to turn right, so you can prepare and position yourself in the exit lane. Likewise, your map may indicate that there are no gas stations for the next 100 km between two points, so you know you need to ensure a certain amount of fuel before you start on that stretch. The same value can be garnered from your *Mastery Map*, which is why it's so valuable to leverage mentors, teachers, and other resources that help you understand what will be necessary each step of the way. Just as importantly, your *Mastery Map* can help you identify the proper sequence in which you need to develop skills and foundations to optimize your results. You can learn through testing on your own—and there are some things you will need to customize—but why would you want to forfeit the head start you can gain by standing on the shoulders of those giants who came before you?

If you're an athlete, you need to understand which components of skill, strength, coordination, and other physical traits are necessary before you can try to master the next one. For example, if you don't have the necessary strength, speed, or stamina, there are certain techniques that will be impossible for you to master. Imagine a ballet dancer trying to execute a turnout without having the required strength and flexibility in their hips to properly execute the movement. The result would be sloppy, far from ideal, and most likely would lead to injuries over time due to overcompensating with the knee and/or ankle. Similarly, gymnasts need strength and flexibility before they can execute floor routines.

For this reason, your *Mastery Map* can benefit from being developed with the help of experienced coaches and mentors who really understand what it takes to be world class. With these insights, your *Mastery Map* needs to plot out each component over time and have a plan for then integrating them together. A prime example of how elite performers implement this concept was given by Kobe Bryant in a 2019 interview. Kobe describes his zero-point summer playing basketball as a 12-year-old and how he developed a plan, similar to a *Mastery Map*, to excel past his peers from then onwards.

> "That [the summer league experience] is when understanding a long-term view became important. I wasn't going to catch these kids in a week, I wasn't going to catch them in a year... What do I want to work on first?. . .
>
> For 6 months I did nothing but shoot. After that, [you work on] creating your own shot. Jump shot from 15 [feet], my 3 point shot, not miss open shots, be able to shoot it with speed... I started creating a menu of things, and then next summer I came back and I was little better... What I had to do was work on the basics and the fundamentals, while they relied on their athleticism and their natural abilities.. . .
>
> It's a simple thing of math, if you want to be a great player. If you play every single day for 2-3 hours, over a course of the

year... how much better are you getting? Most people will play, maybe, an hour and half, two days a week. Do the math on that. That's not going to get it done! If you're obsessively training 2-3 hours every single day, over a year, over two years—you make quantum leaps."

The exact same principle applies in business. I often encounter companies where team members are suffering from "change fatigue" resulting from being asked to work on multiple initiatives, without seeing how each one contributes to achieving the mission. However, you can change that dynamic if the team can see the same list of initiatives as part of an integrated plan and understand how each one contributes. If you place them on a coherent map, over a reasonable period of time —usually several years if the goal is lofty enough—then each day of *struggling* with new initiatives and feeling uncomfortable becomes a step on the path to mastery and achieving the overall mission. My experience is that people don't need to be motivated; they are already motivated. What leadership has to do is to stop demotivating them with what appear to be disjointed and conflicting initiatives and lack of a clear path forward.

Pre-work required

When I start working with a client, we delve into the key elements they need to step up their performance, and then structure each one in a phased plan. It creates a global view of where we want to go and what steps we need, and the map provides a reminder that each new skill is a step along a path to developing the most complete version of that performer.

To start the process, I try to establish with my clients where they are starting from. To do this, we need to take into account some essential variables of their situation through a multi-step process I've designed.

STEP 1: At what point are they in their journey?

If I'm working with an ATP player, is he new to the tour? Is he an established veteran? Is he evolving upwards in the ranking or struggling and falling? What factors are affecting his current trajectory?

If we're talking about a business, the same idea applies. Is the company growing or stagnating? What's the view and overall temperature of team members? What challenges or gaps do they see?

STEP 2: What motivates the client to reach out

Unfortunately, most people don't reach out unless they feel stuck. Here I need to understand where they are mentally. This means not just whether they are optimistic or depressed, but how deeply open they are to really getting help and doing whatever is necessary to improve their performance.

Often, you need to break through barriers to get clients to open up. Leaders or professional athletes feel they're visible, under scrutiny, and thus fear that sharing their concerns and fears will be seen as a weakness that will be used against them

Essentially, I want to gauge if they are ready to rethink every part of their performance and what they've done traditionally, or are they looking for a quick fix?.

STEP 3: Mapping out a self-diagnostic

The next area I will focus on is to try to get a picture of how they see themselves. If we don't have an accurate view of what we've got to work with, it's highly unlikely that we'll have success. This is much more difficult than it sounds, because more people than you might expect suffer from a *Dunning-Kruger-like effect*. The *Dunning–Kruger effect* is a cognitive bias in which people overestimate their abilities in a particular domain. Although the original *Dunning-Kruger effect* is based on people with low skill levels who overestimate their abilities, a similar pattern occurs in high performers who feel pressure to *not* recognize any weaknesses in their skills due to social or cultural pressures.

As a quick example that's easy to understand, imagine you are working with an athlete who needs to improve a physical skill, say jumping, but the player is unwilling to recognize that they have a weak link in the kinetic chain (e.g. weak calf muscles), then it's going to be difficult to get them to put in the work necessary to improve that skill. Similarly, players are often not honest with themselves about how they prepare and manage pressure, or even the technical parts of their game they feel insecure about. When working with executives, it is very hard for them to identify and admit areas where they need to improve, be it technical knowledge, or leadership skills that generally are never properly measured yet can impact tremendously on an organization's performance.

This reluctance to admit improvement opportunities makes it harder to design a map to drive performance, because there's a psychological resistance to even looking at the problem, which is a necessary building block for improving.

So what I'll do here is often ask them to self-rank themselves on different parts of their game, with regards to specific techniques (e.g., in tennis, that could be things like second serve, backhand, etc.) or in relation to their ability to respond in critical moments of a match. I will then map out on a sort of "spider web map" I use, where you can clearly see strengths and improvement areas.

This provides me a tool with which to start objectifying what needs to be improved. So, if a player ranks himself as a 9 or 10 in every part of the game, the question that tends to upset them is: why are you not in the top five of the ranking? There's no shame in identifying the need to get better. As a matter of fact, the greatest athletes obsess about getting better. It's only when we identify an area we need to get better in that we can start to work on it.

STEP 4: Prioritize and program improvement areas across the *Mastery Map*

With the picture of where we are, we then move to identify what ambition we want to set for what needs to improve. It's vitally important to correctly gauge *ambition*. Although there are no right answers to what is the correct level of ambition, there are implications. If a player wants to be the best in the world, or top 5%, the dedication and training requirements will be different than if they just want to enjoy and ensure longevity in their career. Both are perfectly acceptable goals, but the *Maps* to get there are quite different, and even the specific priorities we will focus on first in the roadmap will change. So, once we know what we want to achieve, it's about defining the elements or *ingredients* needed to get that done.

I'll usually build with my clients a plan that schedules and prioritizes those areas we will work on. Thus, over a period of time, they have a well-structured program to develop more fully. It's impossible to get where you need to be in a day or a week or a month, but if we prioritize, find synergies, and program properly, we can build a *Map* that not only works, but helps players remember where they're going and how far they've advanced.

How do you know what better looks like?

When looking at improving specific dimensions, the measure of progress can be defined in several different ways.

Firstly, you can reference against someone else who clearly has a strength in that specific trait. Examples could be: *I want a serve as fast as this player's* or *I want to speak in public as well and clearly as co-worker X.*

Another way to set improvement targets is based on outputs. A tennis player can set a goal of converting 35% of break point advantages, or a sales professional can define a higher target conversion rate. When using output measures, it's important to remember that they serve as data on whether you're advancing, but to get the results, you need to focus on the inputs, processes, or skills that impact those metrics. The numbers are just the confirmation of whether you are improving or not.

Another very powerful target is to set process goals, such as training an extra hour on free throws or watching two hours of game film a day. They can even have a slightly subjective flavor, such as an athlete aiming to make *every training session full intensity.* The great thing about process targets is they are 100% within the performer's control to execute and improve, so if you don't hit your targets, there is no one to blame and no acceptable excuse.

Whatever the measure, the most important step is to identify the individual components that drive performance in that dimension and draw out a development plan for each one, drawing support, guidance, and experience from specialist mentors and coaches.

To help you structure the process, here are some suggestions on how to identify the areas you should include in your *Mastery Map*, how to order them, and how to define what targets you should define.

I. Study top performers and content experts in your space and try to draw up a complete inventory of the fundamentals for your craft. What do the best of the best say you must be great at to unleash your potential in your specific calling?

II. Benchmark values for what great looks like. If your vertical leap is key in your sport, see what the best performers can do. If you are a business striving to give the best customer service, benchmark how long competitors take to resolve issues and how satisfied customers are. Compare where you are with the best benchmark you've found, and that's the gap you need to cover. Do this for each fundamental, then prioritize them based on the impact they can have on *your* performance given your current level. In other words, if you're really weak on one point, prioritize it.

III. The next step is to find all the resources possible to understand how to develop the foundations you are missing. This may be working with a coach or mentor who has deep knowledge or finding training material in book or video format or any other means to get a deeper understanding of what will move the needle. It also involves testing and discovering on your own in order to adapt, and adopt where necessary, what works best for you and what creates the greatest impact.

IV. Build a *Map* that gets you to a specific target of improvement in each of the key areas over a defined period of time.

For example, you may have identified three fundamentals you really need to prioritize, and you decide this year will be focused on number one during the first four months, then you will add in work on the other two, or whatever makes sense in your individual case. When you are prioritizing, make sure to keep top of mind the dependencies between areas. In other words, if you work in a multinational where English is the working language, and you are not a native English speaker, you may need to improve fluency and vocabulary before working on your public speaking skills.

V. Make sure you define how you will measure progress and set up a system to track those variables. Based on the progress you make, review what you're doing, problem shoot, consult coaches, and fine tune, then launch another micro cycle.

It is probably obvious from the process above, but in order to gain the most, you need to leave your ego on the coat rack and embrace the journey.

This is a never-ending process. The more you learn, the more you will want to take it up to the next level that you previously couldn't even have imagined. So embracing a growth mindset and getting comfortable with being uncomfortable will bring you great returns.

Train movements, not muscles

One final principle to keep in mind when building your *Maps* is what I have labeled *Train Movements, Not Muscles*. The logic behind this is simple. World-class performance is complex, and it is rarely the result of one simple variable. As a result, you need to design detailed plans within your *Mastery Map* that identify all the related and synergistic parts that contribute to the performance outcomes you want to achieve.

Although this concept is modeled from the evolving science of performance in the world of sports, I've found it is an exceptionally impactful tool when applied in complex business organizations. In fact, the larger and more complex the organization, the greater the impact. However, let's first introduce the concept in the context of athletic performance.

The genesis of the concept *Train Movements, Not Muscles* is the shift in the physical training space from focusing only on strength and range of motion of specific muscles, to designing exercises that are structured around function and movement. What athletes and physical trainers have discovered is that, although strength, flexibility and endurance are important, the greatest impact on performance comes from proper movement mechanics. This requires a holistic view of how all the muscles, joints, and connective tissue in a given chain work together and—no less important—the neuromuscular training necessary to ensure they function in harmony.

Gone are the days of just working a single muscle, say biceps. Instead, the question is what movement do you need the help of that bicep to perform, and what other pieces of the chain need to work flawlessly with the bicep? Then, and only then, can you design a coherent program to optimize your performance.

For example, if you want to enhance your tennis stroke, working only on your biceps will net you very modest gains, even though they do play a role in the swing. What's more important, though, is practicing movements that engage and strengthen the entire kinetic chain involved in generating speed and power in your stroke, including legs, hips, back, core, and arms. Only by working on the holistic movement can you aspire to optimize your performance.

The same can be seen in martial arts training, where the focus isn't solely on the prominent muscle groups like quads and hamstrings. To maximize speed, power, and technique, it's essential to develop the deep hip muscles: rotators, extensors, abductors, and more.

The equivalent paradigm shift that needs to become the norm in the corporate world is swapping the outdated view of optimizing siloed functional departments for the new vision of optimizing the entire process that cuts across the different areas.

Improper movement mechanics and unbalanced segments of the kinetic chain result in reduction in performance capacity—and often injuries. For example, athletes that tend to run, jump, and land with more femoral rotation (i.e. *thighs turned in*) and genu valgum (i.e. *knock-kneed*) suffer more stress on the ACL and more ruptures. Likewise, lack of proper range of motion in a specific part to the chain, for example lack of proper pelvic rotation, can result in other muscles, such as hamstrings, that overstretch to make up for the restricted part of the chain, causing restricted ability to generate power, greater wear and tear, and eventual injuries.

Translating this to the corporate world, again, all too often, organizations have areas that don't function as well as others, and more importantly, don't communicate and collaborate fluidly between departments. To make matters worse, often the objectives and performance metrics are focussed just on the small part of the process that a given department does, resulting in no overall view and optimization of the end-to-end process. All too often, clients of companies suffer the result of this. If you've ever called customer service of a company and been transferred from department to department without anyone solving your issue, you have experienced the problems of processes that are designed by training muscles instead of movements.

In team sports or businesses, you not only optimize individual movements, but also team dynamics, which would be the equivalent of *team movement*. All too often we see superstars who don't know how to work together. These teams never reach their maximum potential, because there is a synergy in each part of the chain functioning optimally and in an integrated, holistic manner with the other parts. Masterful leaders and coaches like Bill Belichick in the NFL, Phil Jackson in the NBA, or Pep Guardiola, especially in his tenure with FC Barcelona, built teams that achieved multiple championships because they built and trained *whole teams*, not collections of disjointed superstars.

Coaching Case File: Building a *Mastery Map* for an ATP player resulted in a significant rise in his ranking

When I began working with this particular player, he'd fallen out of the top 50 in the ATP ranking. We both believed he had the talent and potential to do much more, but over the previous 18 months, he'd been hopping from one coach to the next without getting traction. It was clear to me that the first thing we needed was a *Mastery Map*.

I asked him to rate himself on the following, from one to ten:

1. Technical skills
   - √ Forehand
   - √ Backhand
   - √ First serve

√ Second serve

√ Volley

2. Tactical and Mental skills

√ What was his identity and what was his *power mode* of play?

√ How good was he at dictating the tempo and style of the match?

√ How good was he at holding a lead?

√ How good was he at recovering when he was behind?

√ How meticulous was his planning before matches in each of the following: strategy, film review, nutrition, physical warm up, mental warm up, hydration?

√ How did he handle mistakes?

√ How well did he manage his emotions?

√ How did he manage pressure?

√ What were his process drivers?

3. Physical skills

√ How good was his stamina?

√ How flexible was he and how much strength did he have in end ranges?

√ How fast was he in both phases: identification and execution?

Those first sessions were interesting because they also allowed me to not only see how he viewed himself, but also see how comfortable or uncomfortable he was admitting and exploring areas where he felt, deep down, that he was not extremely strong.

After we mapped everything out and broke down the ego barriers, we identified a series of areas to improve and prioritize based on what would impact his game most. From the list, we chose three to start with:

√ Flexibility/mobility
√ Managing pressure
√ Strategy and preparation

We then sought out expert support in each one. He wanted someone who had worked with other known players, but we agreed to find the best in class in each area. In the strategy and preparation phase, we teamed with a well-known coach on the tour who is tactically excellent and has worked with several top ten players for the strategy and preparation. With him, we set up a process for every step of the pre-match process, from scheduled sessions to review rival game tape, to strategy and contingency planning, all the way to what time the player would wake up (relative to match time), his eating and hydration protocol, physical warm-up and mental warm-up protocols.

I led the mental skills training on managing pressure and also coached him on more advanced mobility and end range strength work derived from my experience in the martial arts and working with dancers.

The sum of the marginal improvements of each of the pieces ended up producing some significant results, and within a year the player was in the top 20 and had managed several victories against top 10 players, which gave him great confidence that he would progress even more. The player made more finals and semifinals than in the previous two years combined, and won two new titles.

The most important benefit was that he finished the first cycle of the plan and was excited to start another round of improvement. Most notably, he was proud that he was working on improving, instead of ashamed that he had things to improve, as had been the case when we started.

Coaching Case File: How a high growth multinational used a *Mastery Map* to drive efficiency and bottom line value

Let's see what this looks like when we apply it to the world of business. My client was a large multinational that had grown to a dozen countries via twice as many acquisitions over five years. The time had come for the client to integrate all the operations and begin realizing synergies. Specifically, the first order of business was to reduce costs across the business. This is a common ask from clients, especially in moments of economic downturn or rising inflation.

The common approach—in other words, the *training muscles* approach—would be taking one department or function, usually procurement or finance, and telling them to *slash costs*. This is where our client had started. Finance had first launched emergency restrictive measures to control internal costs. These are often marginal in impact, given that they focus on reducing travel costs or free coffee but don't really address the big buckets.

The second action was by procurement, calling suppliers in to slap them around, telling them they needed to provide a tangible percentage cut in cost. This led to all kinds of problems, because suppliers are usually not set up as non-profit entities, and squeezing them too much generates survival behaviors such as drops in service levels, hidden costs that appear later in the service and—the most damaging in my opinion—the loss of a partnership relationship with those suppliers.

But, wait, it got worse. The big problem was that they were only looking at part of the puzzle, i.e. a *muscle* approach. To sustainably optimize costs, we set up a *movement* model that involved the following missing links in the chain:

ONE

We mobilized and worked jointly with key players in the supply chain, both internal and external. I firmly believe that important suppliers of critical services should be considered part of your team, regardless of whether they are employees or suppliers. These actors are essential to deeply understand what levers drive costs. More often than not, you will see savings can be had only by improving information flow, reducing double work, and improving and coordinating scheduling. In this case, that was exactly the case, and suppliers formed part of the solution. Instead of imposing arbitrary targets, the joint team identified process and technology improvement that would allow third party suppliers to reduce their cost to serve, sharing those savings with the client.

TWO

Operations teams needed to be involved to work on things like improving their planning, in order to enable third parties to plan resources in a more cost-efficient way, so they could pass on cost savings of optimized scheduling. Operations teams also brought insights on measures like segmenting delivery based on service (and value), initiatives to accelerate processing, more efficient assignment of works and related admin, just to name a few.

THREE

Technology teams participated to drive technological solutions to integrate faster with clients and suppliers and provide one source for information and documentation, saving time spent chasing and aligning parallel systems and document repertories.

FOUR

Commercial teams also added value by re-working terms and conditions with end customers that allowed laxer delivery times and thus reduced delivery costs.

Each of the above tended to be siloed departments in the company, with lack of clarity on who has ownership over the end-to-end process. Without coordinating across the different areas, or *muscles,* the overall improvement would have been marginal.

The solution was to break down the process, identify how each block works, optimize it, then figure out how to streamline the entire process, stitching it all together for an improved, end-to-end process. One of the most important parts of the process was identifying what to *stop* doing. Often legacy ways of working or culture lead to doing things that do not bring value and yet drive costs way up, both in terms of time and money.

As you can see, it's much more complicated than it first appears. The most important point is that true improvement in performance requires that you understand each link in the chain. In the same way that you can't spot-reduce fat, you can't drive down cost or improve service if you just look at one piece of the puzzle, which is what most companies do.

The biggest challenge is re-educating teams to look at issues with a *movement* mindset, instead of a *muscle* view. This goes against everything they have been taught in their careers. Even incentive models are often structured to drive department thinking vs process thinking, and the truth is that you get the behavior you measure.

How Humans Learn:
Programming The Skills Roadmap

I want to keep pushing the
limits to see what's possible.

Lindsey Vonn
(World Champion Alpine Ski Racer Olympic Gold Medalist)

WHAT'S THE BIG DEAL?

In order to properly fill in your *Mastery Map*, it is essential that you understand the fundamentals of how humans acquire skills and improve to the level of mastery. Understanding how we are wired to learn is something everyone aspiring to master their craft should study in depth, although the sad truth is that very few people ever do. Meta-learning, i.e. understanding the science of how we learn, should be a mandatory skill for any performer aspiring to reach their maximum potential. After all, knowing the principles and strategies of effective learning will maximize the time and energy you put into any phase of your training.

Let's start by setting a few principles you need to understand if you want to properly structure your process to optimize your training and performances. If you haven't read it, I highly recommend Dr. Carol Dweck's excellent book *Mindset*. In the book, she explains in great detail the difference between a growth mindset and a fixed mindset. For our purposes, let me summarize the key findings and implications of fixed vs. growth mindsets.

In a nutshell, people with a fixed mindset feel that their skills are determined by genetics and are set at birth. This is similar to your height, which you can't influence. Likewise, the majority of people believe that all abilities, including intelligence, are fixed or genetically predetermined. Science has shown, however, that this is not true, because of the concept of *neuroplasticity*. When it comes to learning skills, whether that be learning to play the violin, improving your math skills, or working on your martial arts techniques, our brains change as we learn by recruiting more neurons and building complex neural networks to make you better at that particular skill. The more you work that specific neural pathway, the deeper it gets and the more automatically you can access it, and most importantly, the faster and more efficiently it works. That speed results largely from increased layers of *myelin* as we practice. *Myelin* works as an insulator around neural pathways and increases speed of exchange between neurons. The more we use those pathways, the more layers of *myelin* we build, turning those pathways into super speedways.

Okay, so back to the concept of fixed vs. growth mindsets. People with a growth mindset understand the concept of *neuroplasticity* and that radically changes the way they approach learning and challenges. Dr. Dweck explains how people with a fixed mindset see all challenges as tests that they either pass or fail. Just as when you go to an amusement park and they measure your height for certain rides, you are either tall enough or you aren't. In the same fashion, people who have a fixed mindset feel that talent or genetic predisposition sets their skill, and so they become discouraged and are much less resilient in the face of challenges during skill acquisition.

People with a growth mindset, on the other hand, understand that skills can be developed through the right training methodology. This chapter lays the foundations so you can understand how we, as humans, learn skills and what the major steps, phases, and tools used in skill development are, so you can then factor that into the phasing and interdependencies of your *Mastery Map*.

There are broadly six phases for acquiring and mastering a skill. Let's take a quick look at each one, then we'll delve into greater depth to understand how they work and how you can leverage them in your journey.

PHASE I: IDENTIFY

In this phase, you'll need to explore *what to do* to develop your craft. This is the period during which you gather guidelines and discover the essentials of the craft or skill you want to learn. The goal here is to identify the most important aspects of your craft and a rough idea of how to work on them over time. For example, if you're learning tennis, you would identify a series of strokes and skills you need to play tennis and you'd start to construct an idea of how they piece together.

PHASE II: LEARN

At this point, you'll be gathering instructions and moving on to learning *how to do* things. This is about learning the basics and fundamentals of your craft. This is where you learn the technique or parts of the techniques and try to become proficient at them. So, in our tennis example, you'd learn how to grip the racket depending on what shot you want and what spin you want, and you'd learn about racket path, weight transfer, etc.

PHASE III: PRACTICE

Once you have an idea of the basics, you enter the phase of practice. Here is where you work on deepening the neural pathways of the skill so you can put the pieces together and automate them so you no longer have to think about how to execute technique. This leaves you free to focus on other dimensions of performance later on like strategy, tactic, environment, and what your opponent does, that you need to take into account. In our tennis example, this phase would include things like drilling basic strokes with buckets of balls, working with a coach to get a consistent number of balls over the net, etc. Until you have the most fundamental basics under control, you can't advance to the next phase. In any case, even when you do start to explore more complex learning scenarios, you will always come back to *practice*, because the best of the best never stop working the basics.

PHASE IV: BRIDGING

As practice advances, you enter the phase of *bridging* or integrating all the elements so you will be able to use them when you perform. Bridging is an intermediate phase between practice and performance that simulates real execution, but in a more controlled environment. In our example, this would be the equivalent of playing practice sets or points with limiting guidelines like *hit two forehands crosscourt, then change to backhand, then play the rest of the point,*

PHASE V: PERFORM

The fifth phase is to begin to actually perform or compete. This phase, despite what most people believe, is *not* the end of the process. In certain ways, it's the beginning. It's where you start to apply your craft in the final setting you envisioned and begin learning and adapting based on real experience. Our tennis player example would begin to go to tournaments—first basic, then more advanced—facing rivals in a real environment and having to win matches to advance in the draw.

PHASE VI: REFINE AND IMPROVE

Finally, you enter the never-ending refine and improve phase. Here is where you use data and feedback during practice and performances and start to fine tune your performance. In this stage, you enter into deeper and deeper levels of understanding of the basics and begin achieving levels of performance you previously could not imagine. Examples here for our tennis player would include things such as using match results and coaching feedback to identify improvement areas, tracking ranking points, developing resilience during pressure points, etc.

In reality, the whole process is one of reiterative cycles of the six phases that are like concentric circles, with each one bringing you closer to optimal performance. You will run cycles of identifying, learning, practicing, and so on, each time working on more advanced skills and more refined execution of the basics. Those are the fundamental steps for learning and mastering any skill. It's simple, but definitely not easy, of course.

Deeper understanding of each phase

Now that we have an overview of the different phases, let's delve into—and get a better understanding of—the characteristics of each stage so you can better program them in your *Mastery Map*. In this section, I've included two examples in each phase—one of an athlete and one of a businessperson—to help you understand the kinds of goals and learning objectives that occur in each phase, so you can later leverage this more easily in mapping your own journey.

PHASE I: IDENTIFY

At this stage, your practice is based on cognitive learning. As you advance, the skills will be so ingrained that you won't have to think about how to execute them, and they will pass to the subconscious part of the brain, like walking or any other skill you now do automatically.

When you're in identification phase, what you're essentially doing are two basic steps:

1. **Exploring:** This consists of different types of research to break down your craft into the main components and understanding what's necessary to develop ability in each part. This phase provides information on how accomplished performers currently structure their practice and how all the pieces fit into the overall craft.
2. **Understanding:** Once you've gathered information, you then move on to identify the relevant implications of all that information. Here, you can leverage observation of more skilled practitioners, written or other training material, and video resources to identify best practices or parts of the craft that you can't do now, but that are essential to being a top performer. You use this time to get a deeper understanding of what experienced practitioners do, how they do it, and how they train to develop those skills.

Let's illustrate this phase with examples of what it might look like for an athlete and for someone in the business world.

Athlete example

For illustrative purposes, imagine you've decided to take up the martial arts. In this phase, you're identifying the different styles and the technique included in each style, trying to identify what progression looks like in each discipline, and starting to lean towards some specific areas you feel drawn to, such as the grappling arts or arts with high and dynamic kicking.

Business example

To facilitate an example, let's assume you've decided to study business to further your career or as your university major. At this stage you'd be discovering the different branches of business education, such as finance, marketing, sales, manufacturing, etc. You will then delve deeper into the areas that attract you, to better target what you ultimately want to do and what skills you will need. Say you decide you want to do finance. You may go down the rabbit hole of corporate finance vs. financial services. Within corporate finance, you'll need to understand treasury, accounting, auditing, among other related functions, whereas in financial services you'll discover a wide range from commercial banking to investment banking and more. From here you'll be able to identify what area you are most attracted to, and then can start an inventory of the key fundamentals of that area that you need to learn.

PHASE II: LEARN

In this phase, you pass from trying to understand what your craft entails, to focussing on learning how to execute all the pieces and components you've observed in your first phase. Your learning will mostly come from two different paths:

▶ **Explanation**: As you'll see in a later chapter, having an expert coach or mentor to break down the subject is priceless and allows you to stand on the shoulders of giants, leveraging all they've learnt working with other similar performers like yourself before.

▶ **Test & Adjust**: No matter how good the coaching you get, you will ultimately need to work on the elements you've seen and try to figure things out on our own. You will do this more as your skill level advances, but beware of starting before you have a basic understanding and proficiency in the fundamentals, as it can lead to frustration and consolidation of bad habits and flawed mechanics that are later difficult to fix.

One of the most important points I'd like to highlight is that we understand and memorize information better when we are engaged and we pay attention to what we consider meaningful, interesting, and relevant. This is why, if you have a powerful passion for your goal, mission, or objective, you will focus on small details others miss, because you care deeply and will pay attention to everything related to your craft.

Let's see what this would mean in our two examples:

Athlete example

In this phase, if we continue with the martial arts example, you'd start taking classes in the disciplines you think fit best for you. You may complement your training with books or videos from recognized teachers. As you begin to learn and execute the basic techniques, you will start playing with different variables such as your balance, the position of your feet and hands, and you may start discovering through stretching what limitations you have in your basic flexibility that are hindering your progress. At this stage you're no expert, but you start to get a feeling for what your craft entails.

Business example

In the example of someone looking to study finance, at this point they will start taking classes in specific areas, such as capital markets if they're interested in working on Wall Street or accounting if they want to work in auditing or corporate finance functions. During that process, they'll begin identifying more specific and advanced skills. The person interested in capital markets might identify the need to understand valuation finance and study about different debt and equity vehicles. Just as occurs with the athlete above, at this stage, you're far from being an expert, but you start to feel what each discipline is about and evaluate if it excites you and fits with your personality type.

PHASE III: PRACTICE

At this point, we move from the theoretical side of knowledge to learning how to apply it in practice. You will notice that here there is an important change in the weight of each type of activity you prioritize to improve. We highlighted that cognitive knowledge can be transferred through books, videos, or coaches' explanations. However, when it comes to being able to execute the skills ourselves, we have to develop it through consistent practice over time. As such, here you start to *do* much more than *study*. Although you will clearly be receiving coaching from more experienced practitioners, the focus will be on specific technical aspects, and you will take the guidance and feedback and immediately try to integrate it into your performances by practicing and drilling the cues you receive.

When practicing, it's important to separate practice into two main objectives. The first is hardwiring the skills you already have, and the second is increasing and expanding your skill level in your craft. Both types of practice are useful—but at different moments and in different areas—and you need to understand where each one fits in order to properly structure and phase your *Mastery Map*.

PRACTICE GOAL NUMBER ONE:
Solidifying existing skill levels and abilities

When the goal is making a skill more automatic, we need to focus on *repetition*. Remember, this helps us hardwire the abilities and techniques we currently have, but it doesn't help us expand our skills. Although there is definitely huge value in focussed repetition, this can also lead to the common trap we have seen where people get *good enough* or *competent* and stop improving.

A very important point I want to reiterate here is that the main role of repetition is reinforcement. However, it does not discriminate between desired behaviors and techniques vs. undesired ones. So, if we repeat bad habits or keep making the same mistakes, that's what we'll reinforce and automate, making it harder to correct later on.

Athlete example

The martial arts student would use repetition to hardwire the basic skills into their nervous system such that they achieve the ability to execute techniques without having to use the cognitive part of the brain. A beginner might have to think of the process cues for each part of a kick. For example, in doing a spinning back roundhouse kick, they would consciously remind themselves of the following points: *bend knees, begin rotation from the hips, spin on the balls of the foot, look at the target, lift the knee high, etc.* Through repetition, the practitioner will integrate those cues and movements into their subconscious, where skills reside, so they can execute the kick as a single move, automatically piecing all the components together into one fluid movement.

Business example

In our business example, the student of finance may focus on doing a multitude of practice problems where they write accounting entries for different concepts. At the beginning, the performer will need to think about each entry, and possibly consult reference sources. For example, they will be given a problem of a cash outflow, and will need to figure out if that is an operating expense or an amortization cost, to what account it should be posted, and then what posts have to align the accrual vs cash perspective. With repetition, however, the performer achieves the ability to do these actions automatically and learns to see several steps ahead in the process, understanding the impact on the different accounts and financial statements.

PRACTICE GOAL NUMBER TWO:
Expanding current skills/learning new skills

As we said above, repetition is good for consolidating what we know how to do and making it more automatic, but top performers are usually always seeking to improve their repertoire of skills and abilities. For that, the best model I've discovered—which is confirmed by science as being the most effective method for improving skills—is *Deliberate Practice.*

In order to grow, you need to plan on your *Mastery Map* progressions that meet the following criteria:

1. Your training must push you outside your actual skill level, requiring you to work just beyond your current abilities. Mihaly Csikszentmihalyi, the father of Flow, called it the

right ratio of the difficulty of the task over our ability to perform or the challenge/skill ratio, and he believed that it only requires stretching our current capabilities by about 4%. For another estimation of what *just outside your current skill level* means, Dr. Ericsson suggests the level should be where you can get things right between 50 percent and 80 percent of the time.

2. As a result of the above, you need to be working at a level that demands maximal effort, so you can't just mail it in or go through the motions. You need laser-like focus on what you're doing, so multitasking won't cut it.

3. Your practice can not merely have some vague objective such as *overall improvement*, but rather it must be structured around well-defined, specific goals and often focuses on improving component parts of your performance. The idea is to include in your *Mastery Map* a plan for making a series of small changes that will add up to the desired larger end goal. To be more precise, you need to build upon previously acquired skills by focusing on particular aspects of those skills and working to improve them. Over time, this step-by-step improvement will eventually lead to expert performance. It's all about deconstructing skill into the component parts, optimizing each one, then stitching back them together seamlessly.

4. Your practice requires feedback and modification in technique in response to that feedback. Top performers crave and seek out feedback (we have an entire chapter on feedback later on).

5. Another thing you should keep in mind, if you aspire to reach mastery, is that you must get comfortable with solo practice. World-class performers—even those in activities that require teammates, such as basketball or football—spend long hours practicing alone. Michael Jordan and Kobe Bryant were both known for spending thousands of

additional hours, beyond team workouts, refining their craft. Likewise, Martial Arts masters worship the long, solitary workouts where they are able to focus on chasing perfection in the hope of achieving excellence. It's essential that you learn to get comfortable being uncomfortable, or as is commonly said, *embracing the suck* of consistent, hard work done alone. As Pablo Picasso said,

"Nothing can be accomplished without solitude."

Athlete example

In practice to expand skills, our martial arts student would work on advanced versions of the base technique they worked during the repetition phase. Examples might include advancing from the basic spinning back roundhouse kick to the same kick but jumping in air. Other progressions could include more complex combinations that string together pieces of the basics such as kicking combined with footwork or combinations of techniques executed one after the other. Note that, once the performer is able to execute these new techniques, they will revert to repetition to consolidate and perfect their level of execution.

Business example

Our finance learner may begin working on more difficult and complex problems, such as consolidating accounts across subsidiaries in multiple countries with different regulatory requirements. The goal of this type of practice is to have the student make mistakes. The more the better, because that indicates that their performance is being stretched and skill is being increased.

PHASE IV: BRIDGE

As an extension of practice, we'll then move on to what's called *bridging*, which consists mainly of simulations or rehearsals. This step is meant to transfer the skills we developed in the context of practice to performance situations, thus the name of *bridging*.

Think of *bridging* as an interim step towards full-out performance. *Bridging* is still practice, but it's made to simulate the look and feel of real performances, including the environment, the pressure, and the plethora of exogenous variables you'll need to deal with. The justification for *bridging* is that, in many crafts, the jump from practice to performance is too extreme to be done all at once. Consider the example of boxers or full-contact martial artists. The challenge of going from isolated practice to the pressure and complexity of a real bout is too big of a jump. Fighters need a way to progress while remaining in a controlled environment. They bridge the gap between practice and performance by simulating fighting scenarios with their coaches and sparring with fellow practitioners.

Bridging practice and performance is crucial for all professions where stakes are high, including the Navy SEALs. Leif Babin explains about SEAL training,

> "I don't think people realize the amount of rehearsals and walkthroughs we conduct before every operation."

When introducing bridging, there are two fundamental types of exercises: *simulations* and *rehearsals*.

Simulations

Designing *simulations* requires scenarios where our practice is structured to simulate the conditions of a real performance. Anything we do to make our practice more realistic is a form of simulation. *Simulations* are usually the first step from practice to performance and are first structured around simple, specific parts of our performances, and can then evolve into more complex, multi-part exercises.

One way to generate simulations is to modify the normal rules or constraints you'll find in your craft to make practice harder than performance, thus preparing you better. Great performers often do this in one form or another to drive themselves harder. For example, swimmer Michael Phelps would sometimes swim in his sneakers or wearing a scuba vest or with water in his goggles. Likewise, *The Great One*, Wayne Gretzky would do drills with tennis balls instead of hockey pucks because they are harder to control.

Athlete example

Our martial arts student might partake in *simulations* to learn to fight against different styles of fighters. The athlete's coach can find sparring partners to roleplay different types of fighters, such as strikers, grapplers, or southpaws. These are situations that the martial artist may not have encountered but needs to prepare for, as they can easily occur in a performance situation. The simulations allow the performer to struggle through unknown situations in a controlled environment, better equipping them should they encounter this in a real-life situation.

Business example

In our finance example, the person may be given roleplay situations where they have to simulate being an entrepreneur and presenting a pitch to a make-believe venture capital fund. In these kinds of *simulations*, the leaner may make many mistakes and be humiliated, but since it is in a learning environment, it serves as a powerful experience and valuable training exercise because the instructors can stop the *simulation*, give guidance, and then ask the student to try it again, using a different technique or approach.

Rehearsals

Although similar to *simulations*, rehearsals vary in one significant way. While in *simulations* we are practicing individual parts of our skill, in *rehearsals* we are putting everything together the way we would in a real performance. In *rehearsals*, we are not stopping and starting to examine lessons and consolidate learning. *Rehearsals* are trial performances, and they are the closest you can get to real-life situations before stepping out on your particular stage, whether that be a football pitch, a tennis court, or a board room.

Athlete example

For our martial artist, *rehearsals* would include full-length sparring matches where the conditions are the same as a real contest. For example, rounds would be the same length as in a real bout, protective equipment could be removed, and if the performer begins to struggle, the match would continue until they won or lost or the time limit was up. This type of *simulation* allows the performer to get a much better idea of what the entire match experience will feel like and will provide inputs on coping mechanisms and tools that will be necessary to develop in order to properly manage the ebbs and flows of the encounter.

Business example

In our finance example, an aspiring broker might be given a make-believe portfolio based on real stocks and a time to optimize that portfolio, setting a significant reward or punishment based on the result of their decisions and the value they create. An extreme would be a two- or four-week trial at a real firm, where the outcome of the *rehearsal* will decide if the person gets hired or not.

PHASE V: PERFORM

Performing your craft in the situation you have ultimately trained for is the final step. For team sports it's competing in games vs. other teams. In tennis it's playing tournaments. In acting it's getting on stage or in front of a camera in a real show or movie.

When we *perform*, we are not actively trying to learn. Instead, we want our training to flow so we can access our skill, which is in the subconscious part of the brain at this stage, and that allows us to focus on the variables in the environment, what opponents do, and what strategies and tactics we want to apply.

Performing is not practice, but it does provide important learning opportunities by reinforcing our knowledge, building our experience, and providing valuable insight into what needs additional practice. Experience in competition or real-life situations over time becomes extremely valuable for performers.

Firstly, *performing* allows for the development of a larger and larger data set of situations we have to deal with, and eventually can be integrated into any given performance. In a later chapter, we will look in detail at *mental representations*, but for the moment, just understand that as performers gather more and more data points through both physical and cognitive filters, they are able to hone their skills and choose more quickly and more accurately from a larger array of potential options to any given situation, giving them another distinct advantage over less-experienced practitioners.

Also, although *simulations* and *rehearsals* help performers manage stress, real *performances* represent a whole other level of psychological pressure. Experienced performers benefit from both *systematic desensitization*, which is the psychological method by which people are progressively exposed to situations or stimuli that may generate fear and activate the fight, flight, or freeze response. As a result of that phased exposure, the situations lose power over the performers, and they are able to access all of their talent even in the most tense situations. Experienced veterans in any field, from basketball to the military, are able to better perform and lead their teams during the most critical moments, largely because they have lived similar situations before and do not freeze up as easily as performers who are less experienced in those situations.

Athlete example

Returning to our martial arts example, *performance* would be any contest where you put your skills to the test in real world conditions. That may include different types of tournaments, sparring in other schools where you are not in a controlled, protected environment, or if you work in a field that requires you to use these skills, such as law enforcement, use of your techniques on the street. Of course, street fighting would also be an example of *performing*, although I strongly suggest you refrain from doing so unless it is unavoidable and a matter of self-defense.

Business example

In our finance example, if our hypothetical student had chosen to work in mergers and acquisitions, *performing* would include actually working on deals in whatever area they are specialized in, be that valuation, deal structure, negotiation, due diligence, or post merger integration.

PHASE VI: REFINE AND IMPROVE

The final step is to continue the cycle of training and competing, each time shifting our focus more from learning to improving. In this stage it's essential to use feedback—be that data, mentors, coaches, video, or whatever—to fine-tune our abilities and training

It's important to dig deep into feedback and data. It's not enough to say *I lost. I need to improve.* Rather, we should strive to understand *why* it didn't go well. Some questions you can use to drive you to deeper insights are:

What did I execute well?

What was not up to par?

Am I progressing?

What area, if I can improve it, would bring the most impact?

Is there something I need to do more of?

Is there something I need to do less of?

How can I get objective feedback and improvement instructions?

Masters take this process to the extreme. They practice their craft to the point where they can execute technique at world class level without thinking consciously about how to do it.

Athlete example

A martial artist might live this phase as follows. They compete in tournaments, perhaps win a few rounds, then lose. They should take away the film (if available) and feedback from their coach as to what worked and what did not. Perhaps they got stopped by a competitor with a very different style of fighting, or the other competitor simply had better stamina and wore out the performer. This would trigger a cycle of training those weak areas, including programming *simulations* to allow the practitioner to learn and implement improvements in the areas needed. In the case of insufficient stamina, the simulations might include higher intensity rounds with shorter rests to drive the needed improvements. In the next tournament, the team will have to evaluate if the performance in that area has improved or continues to be an area to focus on as a priority.

Business example

A business person doing the mergers and acquisition role may receive feedback from a client that an acquisition had not been successfully integrated because the leadership teams of both companies had terrible chemistry. The learning would drive the aspiring expert to seek out training and support in the areas of evaluation of executive teams, personality profiling, and design of post-merger operating structures to be able to include these in their next assignment, improving the outcome and client satisfaction.

Summary

The above detailed breakdown should provide you with the understanding and insights to ensure you plan each phase properly and in the corresponding order on your journey.

Identify, learn, practice, bridge, perform, refine, and improve. That's the process for developing skill in anything and the phases you should keep in mind when programming your *Mastery Map*.

Note: Due to the extensive nature of the methodology in this chapter, I have opted for including examples in each step for easier understanding of how each one applies. As such, this chapter does not contain Coaching Case Files, as it would be redundant and a key premise of this book is to be useful and easy, not clunky and overly dense.

Fundamentals:
The Pillars Of Your Map

Winning ... starts with complete command
of the fundamentals. Then it takes desire,
determination, discipline, and self-sacrifice.

Jesse Owens
(4x Track & Field Olympic Gold Medalist)

WHAT'S THE BIG DEAL?

As you start to design your *Mastery Map*, it's essential to keep front
and center a list of the fundamentals of your craft. The fundamentals
or basics of your craft are the cornerstones upon which everything
else is built. Sounds obvious, right? Well, the shocking truth is that
only a small minority of people place the fundamentals at the forefront of their training, no matter how experienced they are. That
small minority are almost always the elite performers in any field.

I like to think of the fundamentals as the metaphorical middle of the
body. In physical disciplines, the kinetic chain transfers energy from
the middle of your body out. If you only work on the extremities,
you will never be able to generate the speed and power necessary for
masterful execution of technique. A ballet dancer initiates a turnout
from the hip sockets, not the feet or the knees. A boxer or martial
artist generates power from what the Japanese call the *hara (tanden* in
Chinese), which is the center of gravity and energy, located halfway
between the navel and the pelvis, out to the extremities. If you are

just working on your arms or legs you're probably not transferring power and won't be able to achieve world class performance.

It's tempting to think that anyone who has advanced in their discipline must have the fundamentals down pat, but that's not the case. If you investigate, you will see many experts who share the same opinion. For example, former NBA player Oscar Robertson is quoted as saying,

"There's so many young people who start to play basketball and never learn the fundamentals."

Likewise, PGA legend Jack Nicklaus warned,

"Learn the fundamentals of the game and stick to them. Band-Aid remedies never last."

While working on the ATP tour, I witnessed several experienced coaches echo the sentiment expressed by one coach as follows,

"Very few players in this era understand tennis. They just hit the ball really hard and chase it, but they are missing so many of the fundamentals that the more experienced players can poke holes in their game."

There is a gross misperception that fundamentals are just for beginners. They are *essential* for beginners—otherwise they wouldn't have the base with which to progress to even a medium level of proficiency—but they are also the key to unlocking elite performance.

As we saw in the *Mindset* block, most people get to a level of *acceptable* execution, then stop improving. It seems that when people get to *decent* or *good enough*, they feel that working the fundamentals is beneath them. Most people apply this to almost every part of their lives. Even most professional athletes get good enough to make the pros, then flatline.

Elite performers, however, have a different way of operating. In stark contrast to what the average performer does, the greats like Michael Jordan, Tom Brady, and Rafael Nadal, to name a few, work their entire careers on chasing mastery. Although they know it's impossible to achieve perfection, they double down on improving the *fundamentals* because they know this can give them the millimeters of separation over their competition that define the legends for the rest. NBA Hall of Famer Julius Erving, aka Dr J, said exactly this,

> "I had to spend countless hours, above and beyond the basic time, to try and perfect the fundamentals."

The road to mastery passes necessarily through a continuous and obsessive analysis and focus on improving the fundamentals. And the reason it is such a game changer is that it separates you from the masses that get to *good enough* and stop even thinking about the basics. By logic, the fundamentals are called such because they are the necessary cornerstones upon which everything else is built. Like all things, it's only through long-term, focussed practice that you can ever aspire to deeply understand them and execute them at world class level.

Even if it feels like regressing at times, the passion and commitment of elite performers to becoming the best they can become is much stronger than the desire of their egos to feel good about themselves. The top performers *embrace the suck*. They are willing to feel less than competent and struggle with something outside their current skill level because they know it's the only way to break through to the next level.

Let me share what I've seen in the world of professional sports and business, so you can see how this traps so many people in sub-optimal levels of performance. When you don't have a clear view of what moves the needle in terms of fundamentals of your craft, you will likely stay focussed on the things you either already do well, or the ones you like most. Either way, once you've achieved a certain level of proficiency, your current habits will only give you marginal benefits. One well known ATP pro, whom I did not have the pleasure of working with—but did cross paths with over the years while on the tour—had a physical trainer who was very knowledgeable and respected on tour. This trainer confided in me his frustration that the player didn't want to follow the guidance of the trainer to work on his explosiveness and other fundamentals. He wanted to work biceps, which made him feel better because of the aesthetics it gave his body. That's a clear example of missing a ton of improvement because you don't focus on the fundamentals that will drive performance.

In companies I often see a similar problem. Whenever I hear clients saying how overwhelmed they are with the volume of work they have, I dig into *what* work they spend their time doing. I teach them to frame priorities with a concept I call *AOI*, or *Area of Impact*. Basically, we want to know what the activities are that allow each person to bring the maximum value to the company. Each person has a few areas where they have a disproportionately positive impact. Then the question is, how much time do you dedicate to those activities vs. the hundreds of other things which come across your desk daily. The average is that people spend 5% to 20% at most on their *AOI*.

This to me is about understanding the fundamental levers of the business and what unique contribution each person can bring to drive value. We then work to re-engineer the team's tasks, eliminating or handing off certain lower value items to allow each person to focus more time on their *AOI*. The results are stunning as performance skyrockets, and not coincidentally, people are happier because their *AOI* tends to be linked to what they most enjoy doing also. So they get to do more of what they love while bringing greater value. Seems like a no brainer, right? Well, you'd be surprised how few organizations ever do the work to fine tune this.

Realizing you don't know is a superpower

Another big problem is that many people don't work the fundamentals because they don't understand what they are or how impactful they can be. I've heard firsthand how pro athletes dismiss the importance of proper rest, nutrition, sleep, flexibility, and even technical skills like footwork and balance. They just don't get it. That's where having a mentor or coach makes such a huge difference.

There are tons of examples across sports where well-known athletes have been able to improve their performance by receiving coaching from experts in specific areas of the fundamentals such as footwork, balance, proper body mechanics/use of the kinetic chain, or mindset/ mental skills.

Tom Brady is a great example. As he advanced in his career and began accumulating Super Bowl rings, he sought out experts to improve his footwork and flexibility, to not only become better, but also bulletproof his health, allowing him to be a top quarterback well into his forties and retire while still being at the top of his game.

Another example I love is Roger Federer. Most people think Federer had so much natural talent that he didn't need to work hard. Although he is undoubtedly one of the most talented tennis players ever, he worked very hard, especially on the fundamentals. In an interview with well-known coach Darren Cahill, who has coached a plethora of superstars including Lleyton Hewitt, Andre Agassi, Andy Murray, Jannik Sinner, Ana Ivanovic, and Simona Halep, Cahill recounts his shock at Federer's work ethic when he first worked with him,

> "I had a week with Roger Federer in Dubai... and was stunned how hard he worked on the practice court. Four or five hour blocks! And I never knew about this Roger, because if you go and watch Roger on the practice courts warming up for a match, it looks like he's going out to play with the country club boys... so everything is done away from the public's eyes."

The reason Federer's play seemed so effortless was because he obsessively worked the fundamentals. I've always been especially fascinated by his footwork, that I'd say was the best I've ever seen. And he worked it hard and intentionally, because he understood the fundamentals of performance of his craft.

Many players think just hitting hard is enough or having a big serve, but footwork is one of the key essentials in tennis because, to hit properly, you need to reach the ball and position yourself at the exact distance to be able to unleash your maximum power in the most effortless way. While Federer's contemporaries such as Rafa Nadal or Novak Djokovic are exceptional fighters and could often be seen lunging to reach almost impossible balls, Federer seemed to always be in position, and that's because his footwork was so superior that he avoided having to arrive late and lunge. This is also how he protected his body and had very few injuries until he was almost 40.

In martial arts, I see so many people suffer long-term damage because they don't work the fundamentals in terms of proper hip mobility and strength. As I've said here several times, if you have weak points in the chain, the rest of the system compensates. So when a martial artist lacks proper range of motion in the deep hip structures, then the hamstrings, knees, or other parts of the chain compensate to achieve the end result, and over time, this can cause serious damage.

If, on the other hand, you have a proper *Map*, built with someone who deeply understands all the key components of performance in your craft, you will focus on the basics and their component parts. This will change the way you train, as you will work on the basics until you have mastered them, and only when you have a solid foundation will you work on the more advanced parts of the technique.

Having worked with coaches and trainers across many disciplines, the one common thing they all see is that people want to jump ahead to the flashy stuff before consolidating the basics. Sometimes they don't work the basics because they haven't been taught properly, but the end result is the same. This is why so many athletes have significant hip, knee and shoulder injuries, because they lack the proper deep mobility and strengthening work necessary to enable the body to perform those high-impact techniques without taking an unbearable toll on the overworked and compensating structures.

The problem of not knowing what you don't know does not just plague athletes. Here's another example of not understanding the fundamentals, but this time from business. All too often I see organizations wanting to run transformation programs in 6 to 12 months. Now, the mere name, *transformation*, indicates that we're talking about very significant change, not just a slight adjustment in how the company works. That type of change requires learning new skills and often working on the culture and values. As we know from the work of Dr Anders Ericsson, gaining mastery in any domain takes thousands of hours of focussed practice. This is a foundational truth. If you understand how people learn and teams grow, you then understand that you need to program and structure time and safe spaces for people to practice and embed the necessary changes to drive the transformation you have designed, and that is not a 6-month endeavor. You can advance along the path, but you can't expect to be there in such a short time.

Lack of clear understanding about the fundamentals of change, skill acquisition, transformation, and performance are at the root of these well intentioned but poorly executed programs, and the result is a failure rate above 80% of all transformation initiatives, and all too often, change fatigue in the team members.

Fundamentals of training vs. match play

One of the most often ignored fundamentals I see when people build their *Mastery Maps* is ignoring the fundamental difference between training and match play. Programming both properly is essential, but you need to approach them in fundamentally different ways. To be clear, by *training,* I mean any work you do on improving yourself and fine-tuning your performance potential. With that definition, I hope it's clear how this also applies directly to companies and corporate team members.

In the corporate world, the overwhelming viewpoint is it's a trade off between *training* and doing *real work.* In fact, most companies normally don't program space and time for team members to learn and practice new skills in a safe environment. It's normally a half-day training at best and then back to your desk. As you've seen in the previous chapter, the process of skill acquisition requires a *bridging* phase to transition from a controlled, practice setting to the much less predictable environment of real world application, which is why Baseball Legend Yogi Berra brilliantly pointed out,

"In theory, there is no difference between theory and practice. In practice there is."

One of the biggest realizations that helps my athletes change the way they see their craft is the fact that, in any sport, the vast majority of your time is spent training, not competing. Take the example of NFL players. They play one game per week. The other six days are training days. And that only occurs over a period of time, so if you count the regular season 17-week schedule and add in 4 pre-season games and (being generous) another 4 post-season games, that's a total of about 25 days over the course of a year. Even if you allow for the off season, that's about 25 out of 300 working days that are spent in actual competition, or about 8%.

That proportion is true across most sports, give or take, and is even more extreme in Olympic athletes who train for four years for a few minutes of competition.

Businesses actually face similar situations. Take the example of a sales representative. No matter how active and hungry that rep is, the actual time sitting with a client is usually less than half of their total working hours. The rest gets used up in research, preparation, administrative tasks, travel time, etc.

The big *so what* is this: *how you train severely impacts how you will perform.* Although there are some principles you need to apply in both training and competition, such as extreme passion for your goal and your craft, there are some fundamental differences in how you approach each one and, if you don't have this clear, it is very unlikely you'll reach your full performance potential.

Let's look at some of the apparently contradictory approaches between when you train vs. when you compete. I think one of the best definitions of this basic distinction comes from Brian Levenson in his book, *Shift Your Mind*. He writes,

> "Preparation involves learning, growing, and improving, whereas performance is pure execution, carrying out an action or pattern of behavior designed to achieve a goal."

Think about that for a moment. During training or practice is when we learn, grow, and hard wire the skills, techniques, and flawless execution into our nervous system. Achieving that requires thousands of hours of *Deliberate Practice*, which by definition leads to mistakes, errors, and putting ourselves in situations where we are not yet proficient.

Performance, on the other hand, requires you to be able to execute as well as possible, so it ideally means you are operating within the skill level you dominate perfectly. When you realize how little time you spend performing, you realize that you need to structure your practice time to address both becoming better, and also consolidating your ability to perform in competition. A classic problem I've seen with many athletes is that they prepare to be good at practicing, but do not work on carrying that over to the performance or competition phase. This leads to what is often called in tennis the *king of the practice court*, which is used to refer to players who seem world class when training, but then are not able to access that level of talent in match play.

So it seems the challenge would be, as former New York Giants head coach Tom Coughlin said, that you need to be,

> "...humble enough to prepare, confident enough to perform."

Let's take a look at some of the differences in approach and mindset between training and practice, starting with my favorite which is focus on perfection in practice vs. focus on flow in competition.

For me, this gets to the heart of one of the most *fundamental* differences between practice and competition. In practice, you're working to expand and perfect your skills. To do that and chase mastery, you need to log thousands of hours of focussed practice. We will delve deep into the details of *Deliberate Practice* in the *Mojo* Block, but for this discussion, let's have a quick look at a few dimensions that, by design, are different in practice than what you need to do when performing or competing.

When you structure your training to expand your skill level, you need to ensure the following:

FIRST: You need to break technique and overall performance into component pieces, practice each one, then stitch them back together.

SECOND: Consistent progression requires you to push just beyond your current level of ability, so you're always training at something you're not already great at.

THIRD: You need to ensure you get feedback, as immediately as possible. That means you stop, analyze, make adjustments, then try again or redo the technique. The more you focus on excellence, the more you work the fundamentals and stop the flow in the middle to correct tiny micro-movements in order to attain exceptional technique.

As a result of these three points, you approach training with a perfectionist mentality. You look to nail every tiny detail and you not only accept, but value and crave feedback that identifies what you are not doing well to help you improve every millimeter you can. Great performers will redo and drill the same thing over and over until it's hardwired into their nervous system. By doing this, you make great technique automatic, and this an essential first step to later transition it to competition/performance.

Now let's look at those three principles again, but from the lens of competition. When you perform, you need to change the focus of the above points as follows.

FIRST: As we mentioned above, in practice you break technique into component pieces, practice each one, then stitch them back together. When competing, you want the opposite. You want to be able to effortlessly execute techniques and seamlessly deliver full performances. Instead of looking at all the pieces, you want the resulting final skill, and you want it to be automatic, so you can focus on the exogenous variables that could impact during your performance, such as what your opponent decides to do, the wind, uneven terrain, etc. It's only by doing the training with a focus on the basics and obsessing over the minor details that you can later flow when performing.

SECOND: We mentioned in practice you want to work on new skill levels, just beyond your current level of ability. When performing, you want to ideally be operating with skills you fully dominate and can execute with near perfection. So again, in practice you want to feel clunky and out of your depth, to stimulate growth, however when performing you want to feel that your skill flows almost effortlessly.

THIRD: We mentioned how, in practice, you need immediate feedback and you use it to stop, fix, and redo technique as you try to get it perfect. When you perform, on the contrary, you need to be able to ignore small errors in execution and keep going. If you don't, you'll lose the flow and be unable to perform at your maximum level. Competitors who are perfectionists often freeze in competition when any small variable doesn't go as planned, so your mindset in competition needs to be very different.

Let me pause here and take you through the distinctions between practice and competition/performances that we've just seen, this time applied to business.

FIRST: In business, you want to create safe spaces for teams to analyze and optimize each part of a process or function and to practice new skills. They need to be able to stop the process, experiment with new options, and implement improvements. This can't work if you're *performing* with a client. For example, if you're working on customer service, you need to do the practice and innovation off-line, then have those improvements implemented and be able to execute them perfectly to deliver exceptional service when you are engaged with a client. You can't stop the interaction and start thinking about the parts of the process. You need to have that work done before.

SECOND: We mentioned working on new skill levels, just beyond your current level of ability. The poisonous word in business is *competent*. You want people to be good at what they do, but that means they can never experiment to get better. After all, no one picks up a violin and plays perfectly the first day or picks up a tennis racket and is pro level in a day. However, in business, companies tend to give teams a short training on something, then expect people to be able to execute at that level. You need to embed planned and structured times and spaces to practice new skills in the *non-performing times* (i.e. non-client-facing or non-critical process times).

THIRD: Finally, when a sales rep is in front of a client, things may go wrong, but you can't freeze because of that. Ideally, they should prepare for that interaction, trying to identify the possible challenges from the client and take time to develop responses or solutions before meeting the client. In the worst case, they can do the analysis later, where they can go back and replay the interaction, stopping at the parts that need to improve. On this point, approaching practice with a focus on perfection sets the foundations for exceptional performance. New England Patriots head coach Bill Belichick is famous for saying: "Do your job." But he meant: "Do it to the exacting standards established through training." Likewise, legendary San Francisco 49ers head coach Bill Walsh had a similar concept he called *Standard of Excellence*, that he later taught at Stanford Business School. No wonder they both became iconic leaders and two of the most successful coaches ever.

Another nuance in mindsets between performance and training is having the humility to improve in practice, while later holding unwavering belief when performing. When training, it is essential to have a beginner's mindset and be immensely open and humble to feedback in order to consistently improve. The greatest athletes have always remained open to any feedback in training that could help them improve, no matter how famous or successful they have become.

By contrast, when it comes time to perform, you need to have an unwavering, even exaggerated, belief that you are able to outperform anyone else. When the lights are on, if you don't believe in yourself, absolutely nobody else will.

The interesting part is that the confidence to trust your skills with insane belief when performing comes from the humility of training to challenge everything and working to improve. Knowing you trained harder than anyone could expect, makes you feel prepared and gives you greater confidence when you later perform. As the ancient Greek poet Archilochus said around 600 B.C.,

"We don't rise to the level of our expectations; we fall to the level of our training."

This is why the best of the best prepare with a feverish work ethic, so that their level of focus and effort in training frees them up in performance. Remember, by practicing outside your comfort zone, you need to train while feeling uncomfortable and not fully competent at times. Yet this hard work allows you to compete at a level where you feel you have full mastery over your skill, and thus it can become an *autotelectic* experience, where you enjoy merely *doing* the activity, with no concern for the outcome.

Remember, *autotelectic* experiences are one of the key elements to induce *FLOW*, that divine-like state defined by Mihaly Csikszentmihalyi that unleashes optimal levels of performance.

When performers face competition or key moments with stress and tension, this hinders output. When the performer is enjoying and allowing their talent to *flow*, that's where the magic happens.

Imagine what work in most corporations would look like if you *prepared* as if it's *work*, yet *performed* as if it's *play*. This is a learning we teach clients, and the impact on performance is huge.

As author Mark Twain warned us,

"Prepare for the future because that is where you are going to spend the rest of your life."

Despite Twain's always amusing sense of humor, the core message is extremely powerful. Investing in optimal preparation pays dividends in the future. Muhammad Ali held this concept in the forefront of his mind, admitting the following,

> "I hated every minute of training, but I said, 'Don't quit. Suffer now and live the rest of your life as a champion.'"

NBA coach Kevin Eastman, who formed part of the coaching staff of the legendary Doc Rivers, also confirms that the best of the best put preparation at the top of their list because it provides huge benefits that separate elite performers and teams from the rest in terms of counteracting pressure and fueling confidence.

Size matters: Focus on the small things

As you progress in skill level along your mastery journey, you should become obsessive about perfecting the *small things*. I know the word obsessive is frowned upon nowadays, but when I say it, I mean it in the most positive sense. I mean to give high priority and focus to something and to feel such passion for upping your performance that you work at each tiny detail until your execution is flawless.

When I reference *small things*, I mean the fine details that most people don't even see, but that can make all the difference. Those fine details can set you apart, whether you are searching for innovative solutions to complex, important problems, or working to dominate your sport.

In terms of skill, think of the small things as the next level you need to understand and master once you start getting good at the basics. It's like *turbo basics,* and only the best of the best even know they exist, let alone how to work them. As my friend Donna Flagg, ex-professional dancer and respected faculty member at several prestigious dance academies says, it's the micro moves within the move and within the body which make all the difference. And they do!

Let me use Donna as a first example. I've been training and teaching martial arts since I was a teenager, so I've worked on my flexibility a lot. When I began working with Donna, I was trying to recover from an operation to fix an inguinal hernia, which messed up my fascia and misaligned my hips, causing all types of compensations in my kicking that I have had to undo and rebuild. The point is that I was already well above the average in terms of flexibility, yet Donna taught me the small things that took my flexibility—and my understanding of my own body and what it is designed to do—to another level all together.

At first, she put my body through drills to help me learn to articulate each joint independently. This may sound obvious, and easy, but it's quite the opposite, especially when you look at complex structures like the hips. I'd venture to say that 99% of adults, including professional athletes who are not dancers or gymnasts, are not able to control and move the individual components of their hip joints. Most people aren't even aware that there are different pieces, and they just move them like one chunk. Here's where you see the importance of small things or fine details. You need to have a deep understanding of what each component should be doing in order to identify which part of the chain is compensating for weaknesses in other parts.

Not putting in the time and effort to master the small things is very common, especially amongst ambitious, type A personalities. Competitors in all fields are after the *outcome*, whether that be the ability to do a high kick, run fast, move from side to side, or whatever your specific activity requires. In the case of business, these outcomes are all types of operational indicators such as getting a project finished, meeting production deadlines, or meeting sales targets. Very often, these competitive types hit their targets by any means necessary, but the long-term cost of achieving these goals can be significant.

As long as the outcome is occurring, you ignore the underlying weaknesses and risks, over-stressing and eventually breaking some essential components of the chain, and then you have a real problem. In sports, that looks like a muscle such as the hamstring, or a joint like the knee or hip, suffering a serious injury because of the weakness of the underlying structures in the chain. This can end your season, and sometimes your career. In the case of a company, the dynamic is similar. Key people in the chain burn out and you are unable to get your product out, or the quality decreases and it threatens the very essence of your competitive advantage in the market.

My experience with the best of the best is that, once you can do the basics reasonably well, you need to invest in cycles of understanding the small details and working on your weaknesses. Although you will inevitably feel like you're going backwards, trust that eventually it will strengthen your overall ability to perform and take you up a level. However, here's an important caveat. This is only for those who are committed to becoming the best they can be, because working the small details is hard, frustrating, not sexy, and takes time. You'll only stick with it if you have a bigger *why* that drives you. You need to be comfortable being uncomfortable. I'd say you even have to learn to enjoy it, because it means you're doing *the unrequired*.

Small stories of big impacts

Andre Agassi is considered one of the greatest tennis players ever. His career, though, was split into two parts. During the first phase, he was a rising star and child prodigy, and although he had undeniable talent, he was deeply unfulfilled and unhappy. At one point, he broke down and wanted to leave tennis. He dropped in the rankings to about number 200. He was ready to quit until, as legend has it, an unexpected event changed his perspective. The daughter of someone on his team suffered an accident, and Agassi observed how hard she worked on rehab. He thought to himself that if he had worked half as hard on being a better tennis player as that girl worked on being able to walk again, he could be so much better. He realized he was wasting away his potential, and that sparked the second part of his career, where he became known as the *Zen Master of Tennis* and rose back up to number one.

That second phase of Agassi's career is where he began discovering the fine details of his craft. For example, his then coach Brad Gilbert asked Agassi how he decided on his strategy of where to place each serve. Agassi looked blankly at him and explained that he decided while he was tossing the ball in the air to serve. Gilbert, who was a master strategist, wasted no time teaching Agassi that studying serve placement and developing a strategy adapted to each rival could bring huge dividends.

Agassi then leveraged experts like Gil Reyes to get his body in prime condition, focussing on things he had paid no attention to before, such as ensuring he had a proper hydration programming for the 24 hours before a match.

Working each little detail was uncomfortable at first, but as he started to master the small details, it made Agassi better and better. And he began to love what he was doing, as opposed to the hate and anxiety he felt earlier in his career.

One very significant example of how skilled Agassi became at leveraging the small things to gain advantage is recounted by Agassi himself in an interview. By focusing on the small details most players don't see, Agassi realized that one of his main rivals, Boris Becker, had a very slight twitch that gave away where he would place his serve. Based on where Becker placed his tongue, Agassi could move to the spot where the serve would go, out wide or down the T. Agassi years later told Becker the secret over a beer. Becker admitted he had felt very frustrated and helpless because it was as if Agassi was reading his mind and knew what he was going to do before he did it. All that just by focussing on the small details.

Here's another example, this one from the world of medicine. Years ago, my wife and I were trying to have a child and we had suffered several miscarriages. We went to several specialists and no one seemed to have an answer. One day, by a stroke of luck, my wife went to visit the doctor who had been her family physician when she was a child. This doctor has a special eye for detail and, after observing a few things and asking some questions, he zoomed in on some symptoms and linked it to a family history with diabetes, and that allowed him to identify my wife's problem. With some simple medication, he rectified it. She became pregnant with our son, and we are now the parents of a wonderful, perfectly healthy young ball of infinite energy.

This doctor's ability to care for the small details proved life-changing for us. That's what great performers do—they identify the small important details. The other specialists had not even noticed these details. That's the difference between an elite performer who studies the fundamentals of their craft and the rest of the field. This is a good place to note that the key is not being a perfectionist or obsessing about every detail, but understanding which ones are important and performance drivers. That comes from obsessively studying the *micro-basics* of your craft.

Identifying the *micro-basics* also allows you to generate more value from the work you put in, because you are operating at a higher level. This sentiment was echoed by none other than the great Michael Jordan:

> "You can practice shooting eight hours a day, but if your technique is wrong, then all you become is very good at shooting the wrong way. Get the fundamentals down and the level of everything you do will rise."

So when building your *Mastery Map*, make sure to think about what small details make all the difference in your craft. Ask mentors who have more experience in your field and then figure out a plan to work on those *micro-basics* obsessively. If you do, you'll discover your performance will rise to a whole other level.

I often say that driving performance is much simpler than it might seem. Note, I said *simple*, not *easy*. It's really hard, which is why the vast majority of people—be it well intentioned individuals committing to New Year's Resolutions or ambitious competitors aiming for world class—never get close to reaching their full potential. The truth is it's hard because people don't have a deep understanding of what drives performance, and because of that, they lack the commitment to work on the fundamentals obsessively and over their entire careers.

Coaching Case File:
How a hospitality business leveraged
the fundamentals to drive performance

Before I begin sharing a client case that illustrates the impact of successfully working the *fundamentals*, let's quickly talk about management vs. leadership, which to me is the starting point of this discussion. A key thing to keep in mind is that management and leadership are two different things. They are both useful, but you'd be wise to not confuse them.

Management is about ensuring repeatable, predictable outcomes. In other words, you want to make sure all the widgets of your factory come out the same, at the same time, and at the same cost. It's about doing your best to install processes and systems so things don't change day to day. This is good, except when something needs to be improved. At that point, you need leadership, which is about finding new and better ways to do things—and new areas to grow.

Again, both leadership and management are necessary, but they are different, and they require different skills. Management is about well-defined processes that are strictly followed, and the outcome is then all but guaranteed. Leadership is about navigating less-defined waters and examining the *fundamentals* of your craft and your industry and figuring out how to gain an advantage by challenging the paradigms that have been limiting you.

Just as in sports, when what you're doing is killing the opponent, then keep doing it (management), but if it's not working for you, you need to shake it up (innovation) and rethink how to structure your game plan and what new skills you need to develop. In business, these same concepts apply. Now on to my client. . .

A few years ago I worked with a hospitality business in the US. They had an assortment of higher end restaurants, nightclubs, and bars. The owner was obsessed with driving performance and wanted to optimize all the *small things* to create unique experiences in each establishment. One of the challenges was that the part of the US where they did most of their business was a real melting pot of cultures, thus it wasn't feasible to define a vanilla service process and think that would satisfy everyone.

We began a series of waves with the team at all levels, and also ran a program of mystery shopper experiences to see how a client would view the interaction and compare with what the staff thought was happening. The program spanned from servers to the executive team, and over two years, the change was really impactful and touched a broad range of points. I'd like to share some of the *small things* they implemented that marked a really significant change.

One of the first things we worked on with the staff was asking, at a fundamental level, what do clients look for and value when they come to your establishments? This seemingly stupid question is actually amazingly powerful, because if you don't ask what your clients most value, you run the risk of not paying attention to what it is that will keep them raving about you and coming back for more.

So we structured a series of experiments to get data from different perspectives. First, we did a couple of mystery shoppers, who went to the different restaurants several times and documented what they saw, how they felt, and how they were treated. We specifically wanted to know what made them feel great and made the place stand out, and what detracted from the experience.

In addition, we took servers out to other similar establishments run by the competition and examined how they felt about different parts of the service. What made *them* feel valued or like a commodity when they were clients?

Finally, we reviewed all the findings in workshops with the team and challenged what they believed was important and what they thought had no impact. Here are some of the findings that most shocked and surprised the client.

Eye contact and being acknowledged during waiting times was one of the most impactful variables that determined how happy or frustrated the client was. This is something servers rarely think about, but it's one of the *fundamentals* of great service. Have you ever been in a restaurant waiting to be served and, as the waiters swoosh by, they look away to avoid making eye contact? This is probably the most frustrating thing a server or manager can do for several reasons.

First, if someone pretends to not see you, it dehumanizes the experience. You don't want your patrons to feel like a number; rather, you want them to feel special. Just making eye contact, stopping for literally five seconds, and acknowledging that you know the person is trying to get your attention and you will be there as soon as possible, allows the customer to know that they *are* important and you are monitoring to try and take care of them, even despite the shortage of resources to attend to everyone immediately.

Secondly, your patience and mood will be different if you feel ignored vs. if the person acknowledges you, listens to you, then tells you they'll be right back. You may wait the exact same time in both scenarios, but it will seem much shorter and less frustrating if the server has acknowledged your presence and desire to get their attention.

Overall, it's about saying, *you are my client and I care about you.* They may still have to wait a few minutes, which almost anyone can understand without being bothered, but they will never feel ignored and not informed. Setting expectations goes a long way

Here's another small thing that can make a huge difference. Always remember people's names. Our own name is one of the things that we value most, even at a subconscious level, so when someone can't be bothered to learn our names correctly and pronounce and spell them, it feels like this person does not value us. Servers objected that no one in the restaurant business learns the names of the guests, except those who are regulars. That's the management view. It's not *efficient*, but that's exactly the opportunity! No one does it, so how impactful is it if you ask and take people's names and put them next to the orders, so when you bring the food, you can name each person and match it to their order. *"The chicken was for Bob, right? And for you, Mary, the pasta?"* That's innovation. It's challenging the existing paradigms to bring greater value with a simple step that hardly consumes any time.

Another thing that came out of the studies was the fact that time spent waiting between courses of your meal is very important. Once you start, you don't want to wait a lot between courses. In fact, many customers say it ruins the experience and they stop being hungry, so the actual food tastes less exciting and impressive. So we defined the maximum waiting time between courses and timed it on all the tables. This also had an additional advantage in that it sped up the time customers were using the tables and allowed greater utilization per night. And, on this subject, one fatal flaw was bringing partial orders. By this I mean, serving some customers at a table while not bringing out the food of one or more of the others at that same table. People go to eat together, and if they can't eat at the same time, together, it detracts massively from the experience.

Other things that came up—and were considered premium by customers if the establishments did them—included remembering a frequent customer's birthday or anniversary. When the date would arrive, the establishments would program an alarm and reach out and wish them a happy birthday or anniversary, even if they did not have a reservation to return. You'd be amazed how people appreciate it. It sends a message that you care enough to make the effort, and that sets off a positive dynamic that really can't be underestimated.

Perhaps the most impactful innovation came from solving the problem they had in the bar areas. Many restaurants had adjacent bar areas, where customers could go after dinner, especially on weekends, and spend a few hours drinking and dancing. Management was very concerned and annoyed that the staff in the bar areas were careless with slippage and free giveaways, resulting in terrible profit margins. Here's where challenging paradigms around the *fundamentals* proved to be such a powerful tool. I got the team together and posed the challenge,

> "Even if you think it's impossible to achieve, tell me which of the fundamentals, if we somehow changed and improved something, would completely transform this area and make it work at world class level."

The key was inviting them to identify things that they thought were impossible to change, but would have an impact. The question got kicked around for a while and, as people warmed up and started to think out of the box, they began shouting out what they thought were insane or even sarcastic and funny ideas. One person jokingly said,

> "We should get the bar staff to pay us, instead of paying them, and they might take it more seriously."

The room broke out in laughter, but I saw an opportunity and we decided to discuss it so I said,

"Here's a good chance to challenge our paradigms. Why do they have to be employees?"

There were a series or mumbles and exasperated comments in the room, until someone spoke what the rest were thinking,

"What do you mean? What a stupid comment. How are we going to run a business without employees?"

That's where we were able to break the paradigm, so I launched the following challenge,

"What if, instead of having employees, you rented out space at the bar to entrepreneurs, and they managed their own little bartending business in their corner of the location. You provide traffic and, in exchange, they pay you a rent plus the cost of whatever they consume, whether they give it away, sell it, or spill it on the bar. They become responsible for their own profit and you have a solid, projectable revenue stream without the stress of managing the service."

After a half hour of discussion, the team started to embrace that this might actually be a viable idea. We worked through the mechanics and the numbers and they agreed to test it in one site. The model worked so well, they quickly rolled it out to all locations and the profit of that part of the business rose exponentially, while reducing stress and frustration around the performance. Sales also rose because the entrepreneurs renting bar space now had a direct incentive to maximize profit, since it was their profit, not the owners'.

Here's one final example from this client that illustrates the importance of challenging your paradigms. The owner decided to hire an external consultant who was a designer, to visit all the locations periodically and spot defects that needed to be cleaned up. His theory was that the walls would be stained or the bathrooms would have a faucet break and if it didn't get fixed right away, the team would get used to seeing the stain or the broken faucet and after a while, would not notice it. Only by bringing in fresh eyes from someone trained in the fine details of decoration and design would they be able to keep the locations in top shape year around.

Coaching Case File: Fixing the fundamentals to unlock an ATP player's performance

Remember that, when we refer to *fundamentals*, we're talking about any element that forms the base for everything else and is essential for mastering the skill. That's a broad definition, but essential if you want to optimize each millimeter to drive your performance. That's why one player I worked with on the tour was shocked when I told him he needed to improve in four seemingly unrelated areas to improve his confidence while on serve: *form, flexibility, breathing, and solo training.*

This player struggled at times to hold serve comfortably against rivals with a strong return game. As a result, he'd push his first serve harder, lowering the percentage of first serves he got in, and found himself having to struggle with his second serve, which he felt insecure about. We ran through what we thought caused this situation and what it would take to make him approach these situations with a much higher level of confidence. The answer to the question *what would improve your win rate with second serves?* yielded the following answer from my client:

> "More speed and kick on the ball on second serves, making it a weapon instead of a liability."

That answer gave us four areas to work on, all of which, to me, are *fundamentals* for a professional tennis player.

First and foremost, I asked the player to put his ego aside for a minute and tell me if he could admit that perhaps his technique on second serve could be better. He admitted reluctantly that maybe he could improve a small percentage if a super expert on serve helped him. Good enough! I told him I'd take it, even if it's a 3% improvement. We found a serve coach, and I knew that the expert coach could also help him improve his choice of serve placement and accuracy, which players like Roger Federer have used to make their serve effective, even at lower speeds than other pros.

I then suggested that he could generate more power, and thus speed and spin, if he improved his flexibility and could load and generate more elastic energy to explode into the ball. This one perplexed him, but I explained that he lacked significant flexibility in certain areas of his body—specifically in his lats, back, and hip complex—and that restricted how far he could flex his back to get under the toss, limiting the speed he could generate and the power potential he could get on his serve. I convinced him to work on a mobility program to target these specific areas.

Also, his speed and range of motion were limited by the tension he carried at all times, so we worked on breathing techniques to relax his body before a serve. After he loosened up the muscles of the kinetic chain, and began breathing to relax his muscle tension, he discovered his serve shot out much faster and with less effort. He was amazed that relaxing could augment his power output.

Finally I told him he needed to work on one of the least spoken about fundamentals: solo practice. Solo practice is one of the best things we can do for our progress. No one can limit how much extra time we invest in our craft, and doing so tells your subconscious that you're serious about all your goals. He agreed to do an extra 90 minutes daily on his serve that compounded over the weeks and resulted in a noticeable improvement. You may lose in a given competition, but you should never be outworked in your preparation.

My client was already a top player, but this took him to another level, and his results improved on court as his confidence on serve also increased. All that because we worked on some fundamentals like flexibility, relaxing inhibitive muscle tension, and deep breathing.

Obsessively Seek Feedback: Data and Experts

Performance is meant to be an expression of who we are, not a definition of who we are.

Dr. Micheal Gervais

(High Performance Psychologist)

WHAT'S THE BIG DEAL?

Over the last few chapters we've explored the importance of a detailed *Mastery Map* that sets out a complete and integrated picture of all the pieces you need to work on to turbo charge your journey. The next piece all elite performers put in place is a system to track both outputs and inputs so you can fine tune how you are working and identify what needs to be improved. If you're serious about realizing your full potential, it is absolutely indispensable that you seek out and embrace data and expert feedback.

This seems so simple that you're likely to skim over it and not be diligent. My advice is *DON'T!* I know this sounds like common sense, but I bet you're not doing it now—at least not as precisely and consistently as you need to be. This is an area that I repeatedly find my clients can benefit greatly from implementing. If you remember in an earlier chapter, I shared the research of Annie Duke, from her book, *Thinking in Bets*. Duke's research showed that, on average, people tend to overestimate their merit when things work out well, and underestimate their responsibility when things don't work out. Well, that dynamic is human nature, and one of the side effects is that we tend to believe we have done more than we actually have, and you can be giving yourself a free pass if you don't contrast it with cold, hard data.

I promise you that, if you track how consistently you do the work, with what level of intensity and technical precision, you'll usually be shocked. We tend to warp how consistent we are in our minds, especially when the path is difficult. This is one of the reasons that people fail with really ambitious goals. If you don't track and review systematically, you'll let yourself off the hook for minor deviations from your plan, thinking *it's just one day, one set, or one meal*, whatever the area may be where you deviated.

I'll be the first one to put myself out there and admit that I teach and coach people on this stuff, yet I still catch myself deviating without noticing. I love training, and I consider myself as a test laboratory for *The Optimal Performance Formula* variables that I've developed. Despite all that, when I track myself, I realize that I'm often not as rigorous in following my plan as I think I'm being.

Now, the gaps between how diligent I think I've been, or what my programmed schedule dictates I should have done, and what I really do, may not be huge, but accumulated over time, they can make a real difference. For example, I'll find that if I have six or seven training sessions programmed in a week, when I track I may have shortened one, or skipped it due to client commitments, or I may know that I did not bring the focus and intensity I should have and am capable of.

I don't do this to beat myself up. Shit happens and that's okay, but by tracking, I can quickly connect to my mission and passion, commit to holding myself to a higher standard, and correct course. Everyone will veer off course at some point, but the greatest get back on track quickly. The point isn't to reproach any tiny deviation, but rather to avoid the compounding effect of small deviations. Remember that you are always consolidating habits, whether they be good or bad, so catching yourself when you start to slip brings much more value in the long run than you might imagine.

For an easy-to-understand and illustrative example of how this plays out, just observe how most people try to lose weight. The theory is pretty straight forward: eat healthier foods, manage portion sizes, drink more water, and exercise more, resulting in caloric deficit. If you do that, you'll probably get some positive results. Why do so many people struggle then? One main reason is they don't really track their diet or their exercise plan. Let me share a personal anecdote that I often tell to get a laugh, but is actually very illustrative of the importance of feedback. This story is a bit of a caricature, but that's what makes it such a great learning tool. My wife decided once that we were going to clean up our eating habits and reduce body fat for the summer beach season. Well, to be more precise, *she* decided this was a good idea and she also mandated I would take up the challenge with her. I agreed, as I'm always into anything health and fitness, but I set some guidelines in exchange for my participation. The basic one was no radical, extreme caloric deficit diets, mainly because they're unhealthy and never sustainable, but also I didn't feel like being so low on energy that I couldn't perform in the areas that are important for me.

She agreed and we looked for a good app to help us track our calories and macros, which we had never done properly. We found a really simple and user-friendly app which allowed us to tailor the plans to our lifestyle and goals. It was a small investment, but I didn't expect it would make much of a difference. Boy, was I wrong!

The app has a cartoon vegetable that serves as your conscience, and allows you to scan or manually enter whatever you're thinking of eating, and it tells you how aligned it is with your personal macros and caloric targets. Sounds cool, but not game-changing, right? Well, my mission is helping people improve performance, and I know the theory. Yet, this reminded me how easy it is to let yourself off the hook if you don't have any objective way of tracking what you're actually doing.

I quickly realized that, every time we were going to add something to our meals that we fundamentally knew we shouldn't, the cartoon vegetable from Hell showed up on our screen with a frowning face and said something like, *Well, it's up to you, if you want to throw all your progress in the garbage, but I wouldn't if I were you.*

This sounds too simple to be relevant, but we found the impact to be really significant. By tracking, we could see how certain small deviations were sabotaging our progress. It's so easy to convince yourself that it doesn't matter that much, until the data stares you in the face. Things that we usually thought *well, it's only a little bread/a cookie/[fill in the blank]* ended up throwing us off track and resulting in zero progress in our fat loss journey. When you see the data, it's shocking the impact it can have. You think they are just little deviations, but the compound effect is very relevant.

Expert mentors and coaches: the "other" key source of feedback

The first part of the learning about the value and importance of feedback coincides with one of the key variables of any practice on the path to mastery:

For your training/work to bring the best results, it has to, among other things, be coupled with accurate feedback, received as immediately as possible, that allows you to correct the fundamentals and make micro-improvements that, over time, drive you closer to mastery.

That feedback, as we saw above, can come from data, but there is another source that provides you with extremely valuable information on aspects that are harder to evaluate. No matter how experienced you are or how accomplished, there is no substitute for guidance from the fresh eyes of an expert mentor or coach, who can help you identify tiny details in foundational elements that are holding you back.

Let's take a quick look at some of the most valuable insights you can gain from the fresh eyes of an experienced mentor or coach.

Awareness

Experts provide you with a whole new level of awareness on how you perform. You don't see yourself when performing or practicing. Even if you could see yourself with a mirror, you would only have a fraction of your attention available because you need to concentrate on executing your craft while you try to view and evaluate yourself. Moreover, you haven't seen, studied, and helped many others in your field improve, whereas a coach or mentor has a wealth of knowledge from working with others and identifying what works better and how different approaches impact different styles of performers. Taking all of this into account, it's highly unlikely you can have the same awareness and ability to identify technical details in your execution as an expert coach or mentor who is observing you.

I've lived this phenomena with athletes when we discuss how their body language or style of play changes depending on what's occurring in a match. At first, they are not even aware of what they are conveying in a match, and often need to see film of themselves to believe it. Once they see it, they then need help in making the connection to how this is influencing the dynamic of the game. Often you can see rivals visibly get a second wind because a player's body language reveals they were insecure, tired, or frustrated. Finally, once they understand the whole scene and the impact, we can finally work on strategies and tools that will allow them to make a conscious decision about how to use their body language to convey what benefits them most when performing.

Performance-enhancing techniques you are were not even aware of

The second big advantage of working with an expert is that you can discover, and learn how to implement, techniques or dimensions that you don't currently even know exist, but can drive performance improvements.

Often, the problem isn't just improving the technical skill; it's developing other skills you've never even thought about that will drive your execution. Here are some areas I've helped clients explore that have netted them very positive returns.

For athletes, learning and incorporating any of the following from specialists in each area can be game changers:

- Mental skills training
- Advanced flexibility and strength work in end ranges
- Strategy and tactics
- Hydration and nutrition
- Proper sleep patterns and programming

- Different types of physical training to be more explosive, faster, etc.

Novak Djokovic, Cristiano Ronaldo, and a long list of Who's Who of professional athletes have leveraged some or all of these categories.

For corporate performers, the list will often include topics like:

- Great communication skills
- Creating spaces of psychological safety
- Understanding (*really* understanding) culture and personifying the values
- Learning how to eliminate things and say *No* to projects, tasks, and requests

A common theme in both business and sports is the surprise that performers experience when seeing how much of a lift they get from working on one of the above categories, and the corresponding realization of how much potential performance improvement they have been forsaking.

Skill development tools and training

Often, performers actually have identified areas that they need to improve, but they don't know how to develop these skills or increase their current skill level. Here, a coach or mentor can provide deep knowledge of how things work and a broad universe of experiences to draw from to help them customize the strategies to break through a performance plateau.

An important point to keep in mind here is that you're best off trying to find a mentor who has been through the learning process. What

I mean is someone, no matter how good their pedigree is, who has worked on improving themselves and/or others. I've often seen this mistake in professional sports, thinking that a former player is the best coach, without evaluating that person's experience and skill set in elevating performance in others. If a player had a lot of talent, but no structure, and did not fulfill their full potential, then you're not looking at a mentor. You've found someone who, at best, can share what worked for them, but that's not what you want. You want someone who can help you craft what will work *for you*.

I've seen former players who achieved high ranking during their playing careers, but who are pretty average coaches. Likewise, I've met players who never rose high in the rankings but are spectacular mentors and coaches that help their players develop. There are also those who come from outside the industry and can bring value, like Clive Woodward, a former teacher, who led England Rugby to international glory as a coach because of his methods and the value he could add to training and competitive strategies.

Some varied examples of the value of mentors and coaches

If you want a fantastic firsthand account of how impactful expert mentors and coaches can be, I encourage you to google *"Atul Gawande surgeon coaching"*. You'll find a wonderful TED Talk by Gawande, who is an accomplished surgeon, telling the story of how he felt he had stopped getting better, so he went to visit one of his former teachers from Med school, Bob Osteen, and asked him to observe him in the Operating Room.

Gawande explains how, after that first intervention where his new mentor was present, Gawande had felt it had gone perfectly, but when he asked his former teacher, now coach, what his thoughts were, he was shocked to see a page dense with notes. Seeing his former pupil's surprise, Osteen explained,

> "Just little things. . . Did you notice that the light had swung out of the wound during the case? Another thing I noticed, your elbow goes up in the air every once in a while. That means you're not in full control."

Gawande declares in his talk that Osteen's coaching provided him with

> "...a whole other level or awareness."

Despite it being difficult for his ego, over time, applying the insights from fresh eyes, Gawande's performance improved significantly in terms of all key indicators such as reduced number of operations with complications.

Over the years, leveraging experts is something I've come to understand and use more and more myself. I will now seek out anyone who can teach me something new, even if that's just a nuance that can improve a skill I already have by 1%. I'm an avid reader and consider my time well-invested if a book gives me one new and useful idea. I have also found it's well worth the investment in a coach if I get one performance tip (usually I get a lot more). The more micro you go with the concept of *expert*, the more you gain potential to drive your performance to greater levels.

Some of my greatest leaps in performance have come from working with experts in very specific fields, including, but not limited to, the following:

EXPERT: Donna Flagg

Stretching guru Donna Flagg is a former professional dancer and dance teacher. I often joke Donna has forgotten more about flexibility than most performers ever learn. She has challenged my belief in what my body is able to do, showing me that my limitations were based more on lack of knowledge and proper training than on physical limits. It's so tempting for us to accept that something is *not humanly possible*—or only possible for genetic freaks—but the truth is that the vast majority of goals you will ever set are limited more by your lack of technical knowledge and insufficient/improper training. As Michelangelo, the legendary sculptor and painter (not the Ninja Turtle), stated,

> "If people knew how hard I worked to get my mastery, it wouldn't seem so wonderful at all."

EXPERT: Sensei John Stevens

During my time studying martial arts in Japan, I had the great fortune of meeting and training with the legendary John Stevens. Stevens Sensei is a high ranking Aikido master under the lineage of Rinjiro Shirata Sensei, a direct student of Ōsensei, the founder of Aikido. John generously shared all the secrets he had learned from decades in Japan with anyone who had pure intention and love in their heart. It was during this time that I learnt one of the most valuable lessons on performance that has stayed with me for over 30 years, that I call *"learn and forget, learn and forget."* Essentially, through changing the structure of the class each day, over months, I learnt that the key was to consolidate the fundamentals, then free that talent to be applied as each situation unfolded. Sensei's advice was to learn what we did in class, then forget the specific application and retain the underlying principle, leaving us free to adapt as necessary in every situation.

EXPERT: David Kingsberry

David is a highly-respected fitness coach, sought out by Hollywood stars when they need to transform their bodies. I've had the luck of working with David, and his depth of knowledge and experience have allowed me to pinpoint where I needed to strengthen weak links to eliminate pain from overtraining and improve my strength and explosiveness.

As you can see from the above stories, developing mastery requires working outside of your current skill level in very niche aspects of performance, allowing you to consolidate new knowledge and abilities. Since you'll be executing in an imperfect way during most of the journey, getting immediate feedback with detailed instructions on how to improve is a key part of driving performance improvements. Performers who are open to feedback will eventually find a path to improve their skill. Those whose ego won't allow for it will plateau, or even lose skill over time.

Let me add one last consideration. Often, the feedback you receive at a given point in time doesn't give you the whole answer, but it gives you clues about another piece of excellent execution. You need to take it, work on it, integrate it into your current technique, then work on other pieces and add them in also. Then continue this cycle repeatedly as you hone your craft like a Japanese blacksmith produces a masterful *katana* sword. In case you don't know the process, the *katana* is heated, then pounded into shape, then heated and folded again and again until after thousands of times, the blade is incredibly strong and flexible. This is how elite performers are forged. There is no shortcut.

Essential parameters of feedback

To maximize the effectiveness and value of feedback, you should ensure it meets the following key principles.

Firstly, feedback needs to be as immediate as possible. Ideally, feedback should be available in the moment, so you can redo and correct whatever needs to be improved, consolidating the improvement by feeling what it's like to do it differently. If you do something wrong, then get feedback 24 hours later, you may not be able to relate to it as well. Imagine a dancer executing a technique and their teacher makes a technical correction, such as lifting the knee higher before extending the leg. This is a very subtle difference, and will take the practitioner time to integrate it as a natural part of great technique, so stopping in the moment to get the feedback, then re-doing the move with the process improvement, is the best way for the dancer to feel the difference.

Of course timely feedback applies not just to physical skills. If you have a disagreement with someone, trying to give them feedback on how you felt after a month may be less efficient because you both will have less clarity about the details of the conversation.

The biggest argument for making feedback immediate in my opinion is the principle that you're always practicing and consolidating technique, whether that be right or wrong technique, so having a way to increase your awareness of when you commit the error, and being able to fix it, accelerates the consolidation of proper execution, be it physical technique or behaviors.

Another key attribute of effective feedback is that it should be as concrete as possible. You will never find a master teacher giving feedback such as *it's not sharp*. Whether you're critiquing a presentation or a pirouette, feedback has to be actionable, and *not sharp* tells us nothing about what needs to change for it to become *sharp*. Great teachers will give you specific instructions such as *initiate the movement from the hip* or *your presentation needs to have the following structure and storyline—use graphs here, not tables*. Specific, concrete feedback allows you to implement it immediately, gaining all the benefits mentioned above.

A final piece of guidance on feedback is that it should be structured and given at the appropriate moment. An avalanche of concepts and improvement points can overwhelm a performer and lose impact. Great mentors and coaches choose a few pieces, the most important ones, and work on those first. They know that, if they coach too many concepts at once, it may scatter the focus of the performer and take away the concentration needed for proper practice.

Feedback and your *Mastery Map* phases

As we've seen, most ambitious goals require a realistic timeline, measured in years, not days. It's important to trust the process, because you probably won't see the results in the short term, even though all the work you're doing is, in fact, setting up the foundations for improved performance in the future. A clear and illustrative example of this is when you start going to the gym. You can have the most well-suited and designed program in the world, but the first week all you will feel is tired and sore. You won't see more muscle or less body fat. That doesn't mean it's not happening, but you need to distinguish what your final goal looks like from the smaller progress indicators along the way.

The same is true for any skill, be it physical or cognitive. When you start working on your forehand or practicing giving feedback, at the beginning, you won't notice any performance lifts. However, over time, if you are consistent, you will see a performance improvement. The key is to have a realistic *Map*, as we've been discussing, that will allow you to gauge progress in the context of where you should be at this point, as opposed to measuring progress vs. the end state you imagine.

The impact of measuring vs. the right benchmark can serve to motivate you or deflate you. If you have been playing violin for three months and compare yourself to a professional violinist, you will feel terrible. However, if you have a clear *Map*, with well-thought-out milestones, you might see that, three months in, you should be able to play a simple piece of music or some scales, and you may be doing well vs. that target. Far too many people compare their day one to the skill of an elite performer who has been working on their craft for 20 years. Seeing the enormous gap, they conclude that they are just not gifted enough and quit, whereas if they had continued over several more years, they would probably have a much more optimistic view of how good they can get.

Let's link this concept of the importance of linking skill and mastery milestones to time periods on a coherent map, to a real case. Joao Fonseca is a young player who I predict will be a top seed in the ATP in a few years. He's a 17-year-old Brazilian who just stormed onto the ATP scene with a wildcard in the Rio ATP 500 tournament. Fonseca played two or three fantastic matches and then lost in the quarterfinals. Here's what I saw and what I think is most important for him in order to keep growing.

First, I saw some fantastic talent. He reminds me of a young Jannick Sinner, because he's tall and has a complete game, but with the power of Carlitos Alcaraz. So, he clearly has great potential, but potential is not enough. He's also very young and still needs to gain physical strength and endurance, improve his game strategy—especially when his trademark power doesn't work to overpower opponents—and work on his mental performance skills. None of these is worrying; in fact, it's more than normal at this point in his career.

Now here's where the story can go one way or another. I believe he needs to take the data from his games against top players, identify what worked, and be relentless about improving what he still needs to develop. If he does that, and sets a realistic and well-structured map to continue developing—without expecting to be world number one by age 18—I believe that within three to five years, he has the potential to be a top five, and maybe even number one level player.

History is always useful, and Fonseca would be wise to take note of the evolution of Carlos Alcaraz, who is another incredible talent, but his meteoric rise placed so much pressure on him that he appears to expect to win all the time, and that has greatly hurt his progress. I know it's hard when the world starts drooling over you, but Fonseca really has to not listen to the hype and adopt a *CAGE-mode* mentality where he commits to improving consistently and agrees with himself that he can be so much better. If he feels he needs to be unbeatable now, he'll just get frustrated because people will figure out his game, like they have with Alcaraz, and if he's not prepared and willing to keep evolving, each loss will feel like a harsh test that he has failed. That's the importance of evaluating data and progress in the context of a *Mastery Map*. It can mean the difference between feeling that you've improved—but still have a lot of room to keep growing—or feeling like you are a failure because you're not there yet, even if that is objectively unrealistic.

THE OPTIMAL PERFORMANCE FORMULA

Taking the feedback of what he learned, and what his opponent did to beat him in the quarter finals—together with a realistic plan to keep developing over the next few years—Fonseca has insane potential. To fulfill that potential, he should also seek out the best experts in the areas he needs to improve, so they can help him unlock the details he isn't even aware of yet. If he doesn't give himself the time and room necessary to walk the road to mastery, and expects himself to be a *finished product* at 17 or 18, he will become his own worst enemy.

Coaching Case File: Using data to change culture in a large corporate client

One of the most valuable benefits of feedback is it increases your awareness of how you perform in reality. Often, it is a bucket of cold water to realize that you are performing worse and differently than how you think or believe you are.

One corporate client called me to embrace a culture change and revitalize the high level of disengagement of the team. The senior leadership team could not understand the problem, because they were convinced that they had the best place to work and some really solid values that were displayed in beautiful posters on the walls of each floor of the building. After carrying out a series of interviews with team members at different levels in the organization, I was convinced the problem started with the gap between what the leadership team believed and what they really did.

I'm known for giving clients radically transparent feedback, because I consider that the greatest gift I can give them is to start improving performance. Sometimes, however, people don't want to hear. They think they want to be mentored, but will then refute everything you point out. This was the case with several members of the leadership team of this client, so I decided they needed to see data and objective feedback in order to come to the conclusions themselves.

We set up a two-day session and ran through the values. They all sounded great, but I challenged them vs. the data I'd picked up. Here's an extract of the discussion that marked a turning point in the meeting.

Me: *So trust is one of your values. Define what you mean by trust. Whom do you trust? Everyone? To what extent?*

Leadership team member 1: *It means two things. First, clients trust us because we always deliver. Secondly, we trust our team and stand behind them.*

Me: *You trust your team? Define what that means for you. How much do you trust them?*

Leadership team member 1: *It means we stand behind them. They are part of our corporate family.*

Me: *Sorry, I'm not sure I know what that means. Does that mean you trust them like you'd trust your family? Your closest family or a more extended family like crazy uncle Bill who you know is a good guy but you wouldn't bring him to the office? Pardon the joke, but I really want to understand how much you trust your team.*

CEO: *Fully! We trust them completely.*

Me: *Ok, great! So, do you track vacation days? How about travel expenses?*

CEO: *Why yes, of course. That's pretty standard.*

Me: *Why? I mean, if you trust them fully, just tell them to be responsible and then know that they will only take the days they need and consider fair in terms of vacations. Likewise, they'll manage* *travel expenses as if it were their own money. Why waste time and incur costs by tracking and controlling this? I don't feel the need to track my wife's expenses. Isn't that the level of trust you mean?*

An uncomfortable silence fell over the room. After about 30 seconds (that seemed like 10 minutes for the participants of the session), someone spoke out.

Leadership team member 2: *What if someone takes more vacation days than they have allotted or spends more than our travel guidelines allow? We need to control these things.*

Me: *If you need to control them, then you don't fully trust them. I'm not judging, just giving you data that does not support those posters on the wall with your values. Let me ask you another question. You've got 'Be a team player' on your list of values. Is that a value that is mandatory or a nice-to-have?*

Leadership team member 3: *Mandatory of course. All the values are mandatory.*

Me: *Okay, so here's another interesting piece of data I picked up in the interviews. Several people commented about recent promotions at second and third level of the organization of people who are considered toxic by their co-workers, but produce operational results. One example was person X, a sales rep who exceeds his numbers, but is generally considered a lone wolf and a terrible team player. How should the team interpret that if the values are mandatory?*

Leadership team member 3: *People need to understand that a business needs to hit its targets.*

Me: *At any cost? What you're essentially telling people is that team players are nice to have, but you can be an asshole if you sell a lot or produce a lot. In that case, the company is willing to flex its values.*

Another uncomfortable silence fell over the room...

Me: *Look, my only objective is to hold up a mirror and give you accurate feedback. You wonder why people are disengaged? Simply because what you say and what you do don't align, so they don't believe you. Leadership is hard because it requires hard choices sometimes, but people follow you because you stand for something. They won't follow you just because you use the right buzzwords, then do the opposite.*

We stopped for a coffee break, and when we came back, the CEO stood up and said that he had to admit that they were not being diligent enough as a leadership team and wanted to spend the next day and a half of the workshop identifying where they had been incoherent, and designing ways to fix it. Most of all, he said, he'd learned that they needed clear and timely feedback mechanisms to see if they were living the values. That last realization was the biggest breakthrough of all.

Coaching Case File: How niche experts helped drive performance for a professional athlete

One tennis player I worked with wanted to improve, but had an extremely narrow view of where he could seek help. His basic approach was to cycle through tennis coaches who had been former players to see if they could help him break through to the next level. For this player, a tennis coach was the base of his own personal hierarchy of mentors.

If you imagine a pyramid, similar to the one depicted in Maslow's hierarchy of needs, this player placed all his attention on the lower rungs and didn't understand that there were almost an infinity of progressions within a given level. Let me take you through the process we worked through, using the pyramid as a mental structure, so it is easier to visualize. The first time we did the analysis together, I kept it to just three macro areas, but I have taken this down to a dozen key areas with other clients. The three levels of coaching hierarchy my client had identified were: technical coaching, physical trainers, and mental skills coaching.

First, I'll run through his starting view of the hierarchy, which is a pretty common example of what I've seen with average players. Then I'll break down how we identified that he could drive performance by digging deeper into each part of the hierarchy and finding niche experts.

Level 1: Player's original starting point

As I mentioned, this player thought that the one fundamental area he needed to have covered was to have a tennis coach. What he was looking for here was a former player to teach him the missing pieces of technique, tactics, and some strategy. If that sounds general and ambiguous, it is, but that's as far as he'd thought about it. He wasn't able to articulate further what he needed, so it was no surprise he hadn't found it up to this point. One of the key values of a *Mastery Map* is to ensure you have a complete view of all the component pieces necessary for mastery in your craft, so that you can seek them out and fill in gaps in your knowledge and skill set. Without one, you run the risk of having a high level idea of what you need, but not detailing that enough to know how to go about it and what support you need to get there. That was the starting point for this client.

Level 2: Player's original starting point

On the next level, this player thought he needed to find a good physical therapist and trainer to improve his overall strength and endurance. As in the previous level of the pyramid, he didn't have a clear inventory of all the component parts he needed to work and find expertise on, such as explosiveness, endurance, flexibility, or speed. He simply believed he needed a trainer, but wasn't able to define what outcomes he expected the trainer to provide.

Level 3: Player's original starting point

As a recent revelation, the player had started to think he might benefit from mental skills coaching, although again, he could not articulate what kind of support he needed and what outcomes he hoped to gain from working with a mental skills expert. As a corollary, he had no real grasp of the magnitude of the effort he would need to put in to benefit from this coaching. He just thought getting an expert would bring some benefit and allow him to compete better.

Now let's see how we ran through the same three levels of the pyramid, but with a focus on specialization, identifying significant potential performance improvements to be gained by leveraging deep expertise in each area.

Level 1: Expanded view

It's rare that your coach is an expert on all things, so we thought about which specialists could help clean up the weaker aspects of my client's game. Note that I'm talking about a player who had consistently ranked in the top 50, so the fixes may seem minor when seen in isolation, but put together, they can have a significant impact on a player's success.

We sought out a recognized expert on serve mechanics. This was a super specialist whose career had centered around helping professional players up their serve in terms of speed, power, spin, and placement.

The result was that my player improved average serve speed (on first and second serve) and learnt about placement details that gave him more variables to tweak so as to make his serves more efficient.

We then found a well-known coach who has coached several top ten players and is one of the smartest thinkers in terms of strategy and tactics. My client had worked with some fantastic coaches, so this is no knock on his previous coaches, but that's the whole idea behind an expert: it's someone who's thought about, studied and understood a smaller but very specific area more deeply than almost anyone else, and thus can bring you insights and fresh eyes on the basics of that niche like no one else. In this case, the coach helped him understand smarter and lower-risk strategies in certain situations that resulted in the player giving away less free points to rivals. When you're competing at that level, scratching out a dozen points you would not have previously won is a big deal.

Level 2: Expanded view

On the next level, we looked at physical therapists and trainers. Although many are excellent, I've found common gaps. For example, many athletes are negligent of the performance and injury prevention potential of proper flexibility and end range mobility strength training. One player who figured this out was Novak Djokovic, and it not only improved his performance, but has allowed him at age 37 to continue to be competitive. This client had very limited movement when lunging for shots, so we brought in a flexibility expert and, again, the level of play improved while reducing soreness, wear-and-tear on hips and knees, and injuries. Just to give you a feel for how significant a performance lift this can represent, take a look at what Rafa Nadal had to say in a recent interview. When asked if he would have won more Grand Slams than Djokovic if he had suffered less injuries, Nadal, in his typical no-nonsense fashion, said,

"Novak has had a better body than me.. and that counts."

In other words, the sum of all the small niche area improvements Djokovic implemented with the help of specialists has raised his performance over his entire career significantly.

An interesting data point is that this expert was not a former tennis player or even specialist trainer for tennis players. This expert had worked with gymnasts and dancers who needed extreme flexibility and was able to adapt that knowledge to the needs of this particular client.

Other micro-niches that can have a huge impact in this section are expert nutritionists (again Djokovic leveraged this too with great results) or sleep coaches (Federer and Cristiano Ronaldo, among others, hired sleep coaches). It's rare that your PT has world class knowledge across the domains of flexibility, nutrition, and sleep. They may know the basics, but the insights of an expert can prove to be a game-changer.

Level 3: Expanded view

The third area I explored with my client was the area of mental skills. Although he had engaged me to work on his mental game, I thought it was worth it to help him understand that different needs required different specializations. Grossly simplifying, a clinical psychologist is the one to help you with deeper emotional issues or traumas (or a psychiatrist, if medication is recommendable), whereas a sports psychologist will focus more on helping you cope with the pressures of your sport. A performance coach may provide an even broader view including how you plan, structure, and develop your training and transfer it to match play. The point is that the areas of specialization within *mental skills* are vast and, if you find the right support, it can take you up to the next level.

In the case of my client, he had a series of issues around stress, tension, and freezing up. We worked techniques and wove them into the other areas of preparation such as physical training and technical tennis training, such that he could develop tools and techniques to manage pressure in the context of his sport, raising the probability of successfully bridging those skills to real-time match play.

Draft, Develop, and Relentlessly Fine Tune Your Roster (From One to Many)

The intangibles are a euphemism for we have no idea what we're looking for but we know it when we see it.

Brian Billick
(Super Bowl winning NFL Head Coach)

WHAT'S THE BIG DEAL?

One of the greatest challenges when constructing a *Mastery Map* for a company or sports team is finding the right mix of talent for each particular organization and integrating the key performers together. We've talked about the importance of culture and values, but the great mystery remains how to efficiently and effectively find and recruit the right people to drive the mission in line with your culture and values.

Empirical data has shown that scouts in professional sports, and recruiters in businesses, are notoriously bad at choosing the future superstars of their organizations. Not only do they spend very significant amounts of money, time, and effort to recruit team members who later perform way below the average, but they also pass over players that later become legendary performers. This happens across the board in all sports and in most corporations. Here are just a few of the many data points that prove the point.

The NFL is ripe with terrible draft decisions. QB JaMarcus Russell was chosen by the Raiders with the first overall pick in the 2007 draft. In three years with the team, Russell would start 25 games and go 7-18, costing the Raiders nearly $40 million. Likewise, Ryan Leaf was chosen second overall in 1988 by the San Diego Chargers. Leaf's NFL career was over after four seasons that cost $31.25 million. More recently the New York Jets drafted Zach Wilson in the first round in 2021 and gave him a $35 million contract, only to trade him away for a sixth-round pick in 2024.

On the other end of the spectrum, legendary quarterbacks Joe Montana and Tom Brady were selected 82nd and 199th overall in their respective draft years, yet went on to lead the dynasty years of their teams, the San Francisco 49ers and the New England Patriots. Clearly, the NFL talent identification process needs work, but it's no better or worse than other professional sports leagues. In the NBA, Sam Bowie was selected second overall in 1984, ahead of the best NBA player of all time, Michael Jordan, yet his career was ultimately deemed a flop. Michael Olowokandi was taken number one overall by the Los Angeles Clippers in 1998, ahead of three Hall of Famers that they passed on: Vince Carter, Dirk Nowitzki, and Paul Pierce. Olowokandi only scored more than 10 points per game twice in his career and was deemed *talented but uncoachable* by former NBA player Kareem Abdul-Jabbar, a Clippers assistant in 2000.

In the NHL, the New York Islanders used their first-overall pick in the 2000 draft on Rick DiPietro and signed him to a massive 15-year contract worth $67.5 million. After several disappointing years, the Islanders used a compliance buyout in 2013 on the final eight years of DiPietro's contract, paying him $1.5 million each year until 2029.

The world of business has not historically done much better. Kevin Kelly, former CEO of Executive Search Firm, Heidrick & Struggles, shared the conclusion from an internal study of 20,000 searches,

> "40 percent of executives hired at the senior level are pushed out, fail, or quit within 18 months. It's expensive in terms of lost revenue. It's expensive in terms of the individual's hiring. It's damaging to morale."

It would seem that the value of talent identification skills and methodologies in leading organizations is similar to that of Wall Street traders, as highlighted in 1973 by Princeton University Professor Burton Malkiel. In his best-selling book, *A Random Walk Down Wall Street*, Malkiel claimed that,

> "...a blindfolded monkey throwing darts at a newspaper's financial pages could select a portfolio that would do just as well as one carefully selected by experts."

Empirical tests later confirmed that his estimation was about right.

So what's going on and how do leaders in pro sports and business blind themselves? This is a topic I've worked on a lot with organizations and there are several root causes worth noting here and looking at.

The past may not be the best indicator of the future

The first problem with existing talent scouting is that we've been taught to look at past performance as a trustworthy indicator of future performance. That may work if all the relevant variables stay constant, but unfortunately, the way organizations and their talent scouts use the information of past performance is faulty, as they don't take into account different environments, different requirements, and varying degrees of uncertainty that can impact performance.

A very simple example to illustrate this is something you see very often in companies. When choosing a new sales director, the criteria is often which sales rep is hitting the highest number. They then name that person as the new sales director. Now that's fine, except that being a sales *director* requires a series of skills that you don't necessarily need to be a successful sales *rep*. Among others, the ability to communicate, give coaching, carry out strategic analysis, and create high-trust, high-performing environments are essential. A rep may be great at selling a given product to a segment they know, but making strategic adjustments and decisions to enter new markets or sell other types of products are not necessary to hit their sales targets, so these may be skills they have never learnt.

Here's another example. College athletes often have success at the NCAA level, but when they get to the professional leagues, they find the game goes much faster and they often struggle. History has shown that physical talent is not enough, and things like grit, a growth mindset, being coachable, and having the will and ability to study film and playbooks all make a huge difference in the level of success an athlete may have when entering the next level of competition.

In both examples above, we don't have concrete historical data on how people have performed in their new environments. In other words, we've never seen the promoted sales rep act as a director or the rookie athlete play at the speed of the professional leagues. So what can you do? Well, I believe personality attributes can provide valuable insights to identify the type of person who will thrive in new roles and environments where we don't have historical data to evaluate. Often the mistake in these cases is to mistake *attitude* with *aptitude*. Performance psychologist Jonah Oliver illustrated this distinction perfectly,

> "One of the biggest errors we have made . . . is we use the word confident when we actually mean competent. I can't sing. I am not competent at singing. Put six beers in me in a karaoke bar and now I'm confident ... but I am still terrible at singing."

So how can we know if someone has the potential to get good at something, even if they haven't developed that skill so far? Essentially, how can we evaluate potential for specific abilities that are new, or at least new to the performer we're trying to evaluate?

This is where attributes and other types of personality profiling indicators can be very helpful. There are no guarantees, but a solid attributes evaluation will give you clues as to what things come more naturally to a given person, as well as providing insights to the values the person holds closest, how coachable they are, the learning style of that particular individual, and even the motivators that drive that person. These insights can allow leadership teams, whether in business or sports, to have greater understanding of development areas, how to coach the person for best results, and even ensure a fit with the organizational culture.

Most importantly attributes allow for a reasonable estimation of performance in a particular role when the person does not have direct experience in that role and environment to use as valuation data. With time and sufficient data, organizations can identify the core attributes that correlate strongly in a given role with output performance measures for that role. This discovery is fascinating and is changing the way organizations look at talent and potential. The historically flawed love affair with perceived *natural talent* is quickly fading. Talent is how fast skills improve, but achievement is the outcome or result when those skills are used. Attributes like grit have been proven to be better indicators of potential achievement. The reason is because focused, consistent effort impacts more than talent. Wharton Professor Angela Duckworth established the following formula to explain it clearly in her landmark book *"Grit"*:

TALENT x EFFORT = SKILL
SKILL x EFFORT = ACHIEVEMENT

So effort impacts twice as much as talent! Thus, identifying team members most likely to apply effort consistently over the long run is key to predicting potential top performers.

Even if you find potential, you need to nurture and develop it

Research into talent identification in sports has concluded that elite athletes require both intrinsic values (talent, grit, etc.) and extrinsic factors (coaching, structured trainings etc.). In other words, even if you manage to identify and recruit talent, performance will be limited without well-designed training programs through each phase of skill acquisition and fresh expert eyes to help guide the evolution.

This conclusion is just as valid in the corporate world, even more so because the second factor—well-structured training programs with adequate time allotment— is rare. The dominant model in most companies today is some sort of classroom training, usually a half-day or a day, and then teams are sent back to their day jobs and expected to implement the new skills. This is as naive as receiving a three-hour class on how to do a spinning back roundhouse kick and then expecting the student to be able to execute it effectively without any follow-up training.

As we saw in the phases of learning, practice is essential to master a skill, be it physical or cognitive, and—if you remember—one of the reasons is that repetition increases the amount of myelin around a neural pathway. This fact is essential to leverage in redesigning skill acquisition in the workplace. To really integrate skills or behaviors into the culture of an organization requires myelin power. To do that, in addition to class room training, corporations need to design programs that provide the following variables.

Frequency

To get sufficient practice time to develop new skills, organizations need to conceive job-imbedded development routines. The existing paradigm that employees are either learning or working needs to be replaced by the sports model that sees athletes either training or competing, but both are considered core functions. Looking at it this way helps to view the time dedicated to developing and consolidating skills as a profitable investment in performance, as opposed to a cost that needs to be managed.

Focus

The development routines need to have specific learning objectives structured around the fundamentals for each role. To do this, it is extremely valuable to have experienced team members or external experts come in and provide awareness around how the team members are developing and make corrective suggestions that keep the focus on the basics.

CAGE-mode

To ensure skills initiatives don't become the flavor of the month and fizzle out, you need to ensure teams stay in *CAGE-mode*, i.e. ensuring they work consistently, over extended periods of time, focussed on developing world class execution, despite challenges and setbacks. In order to feed this drive, it is very important that organizations ensure all team members are driven by a common passion for a compelling mission. Situational enthusiasm is common, but enduring passion is rare.

Invisible Obstacles

After reading the guidelines to drive sustainable skills development and performance optimization in organizations, you're probably thinking *duh, no brainer.* Well, conceptually, yes, but why then do so few organizations manage to do it? There's a key difference between the *change* you want to make, and the *transition* to get there. *Change* is the end state or result you're after, while *transition* is the human journey people go through to achieve that *change*. What you need to keep front of mind is that changes in the environment require you to evolve, yet the subconscious instinct is to resist change. We are wired to seek homeostasis, which is a state of balance among all the body systems needed for the organism to survive and function correctly. If your body temperature goes up or down too many degrees, your very survival is put at risk. Likewise, the mind resists cognitive changes that take us out of our comfort zone. *Transition* is often ignored when trying to optimize performance, but it's the source of some of the most significant barriers to change. Here are some of the most common invisible obstacles I've seen clients crash against over the years.

System Justification Bias

Individuals who have been most successful in a certain system or model are the ones most likely to qualify it as fair or just. This is a natural bias hardwired into humans because the implication of not believing that the system is based on merit would be to question if you deserve the success you have had within that system.

The paradox is that, in an organization, these are the senior leaders who must drive change. As a result, people higher up in an organization will be the least likely to see the need to change the system because it has worked well for them, and they have convinced themselves that it is a fair measure of value contribution. In addition, there is fear of straying away from what has worked in the past. This is especially visible in athletes and C-suite executives who have reached a certain level but then plateau because they need new skills to continue to grow.

Blinded by Success Syndrome

The ego mistakes *you've had some success* for *your success is the result of you having reached your maximum potential.* This causes two problematic and faulty conclusions. Firstly, optimal performance is a continuous endeavor, not a unique milestone. Even if you have performed well in the past, it does not mean you have reached your maximum potential. However, stepping out of that comfort zone to embrace a beginner's mindset and learn new skills is scary and difficult, which is why most people don't do it. The second false conclusion is linked to Annie Duke's finding that people tend to overestimate their merit when things work out well. In other words, just because you've had success does not mean you have maximized your potential.

Here again, the value of expert coaching or mentoring is a game changer. Having independent experts act as objective eyes and ears to help you identify improvement opportunities is the best strategy to break through plateaus and realize that your past success should be a stepping stone upon which to build, not an indicator that you have no more upside potential.

Progressive Change vs. Big Bang

A clear vision of the outcome is important, but it is naive to think that will be enough for any improvement in performance. No real change, be it physical, cognitive, or cultural is immediate. Believing you will lose 20 pounds of fat in a week (and keep it off) is self-deception. Likewise, thinking you can change your team's culture in a week shows a lack of understanding of what drives performance. Doing the hard, disciplined work *is* the performance hack.

Skewed systems that produce biased outcomes

Perhaps the most harmful obstacle is one that is invisible to most people because they have accepted it as universally true and correct. The biggest problem with organizations over the last century is the obsession with standardization. On the surface, standardization sounds great, be it in a factory or a sports organization. The theory says that standardization serves to maximize the efficiency of a system by eliminating individual variations, allowing leaders to boast that outputs are consistent. It is essentially about getting your athletes or managers to perform the same way, ignoring their individual strength and unique abilities. In other words, the standardization model views uniqueness as a problem. Are you starting to see why talent identification is so flawed and biased? Stay with me; it gets even more interesting.

Most organizations in our society are designed to shape, mold, or conduct people down a certain standard path. This pattern starts with our educational system, that is based on standardized course material, standardized textbooks, and standard grades developed from standardized tests that allow you to earn a standardized degree.

Schooling is designed to prepare you for the corporate world, but still focussed on the industrial model, designed to meet the needs of a factory. As an interesting tidbit, have you ever thought how schools are designed to emulate older factories, even including school bells announcing changes in activities, just as factories did to announce shift changes?

From an early age, we are taught to strive for standardized environments and strongly coerced to follow rules that are the opposite of what drives optimal performance. For example, schools teach you the following gems of wisdom:

Work alone (collaborating with others is cheating)
There is only one right answer (so much for innovation)
Memorize and repeat (don't challenge or question the lessons)
Failing is bad (if you do it too many times, you get punished with expulsion)

So, from the age of schooling, the message is *if you want to be successful, do what everyone else does, and try to be the best at it... but don't do other things or things any other way.* Is it any wonder that talent identification in businesses and sports organizations is as myopic as it is? Actually, the way talent is currently scouted is a reflection of the tenets that underlie standardization (and they are performance detractors instead of performance drivers).

The system is designed for a very specific, narrow definition of *talent*. There are tons of examples of people who struggled in school and later shone in their own particular way, starting with Einstein who was called *retarded* by one of his teachers. Despite all the talk about diversity, it's the ultimate irony that cognitive diversity and unique skills or attributes are still frowned upon and excluded.

The implication is that *unconventional talent* that might drive innovation or new points of view, under the standardization model, is not rare due to a smaller universe of people with these profiles, but rather by institutional decree. Elite organizations like Ivy League universities, professional sports teams or symphony orchestras, to name a few, have a fixed quota of candidates they accept from a large pool of aspiring applicants. As such, recruiters search for those that have already exhibited some talent that they feel is a good proxy for success in that specific environment. The implication is that they're not recruiting to drive optimal performance, but rather selecting talent that seems familiar and fits in, because the goal is to keep the system working as it is, and not to try to improve it. That explains why so many people in leadership positions hire or promote people based on the rudimentary criteria: *They remind me of myself [or in best case, of someone else in the organization].*

Relentlessly fine-tune your roster

Once you manage to implement a talent identification system that works and complement that with skill development processes and culture, you need to constantly be analyzing and optimizing the composition of your team. Balancing strategic long-term relationships with the need for new skills and insights is a delicate balance, but is the trademark of leading organizations in both business and sports. I call this *relentlessly fine-tuning* your roster.

Even when great sports organizations win a championship, they examine each role and each player, questioning how they can develop the existing players and what new players with new skills are currently missing in the team that would improve overall performance. Bill Belichick, former head coach of the New England Patriots, was famous for his consistent focus on the roster and asking how they could strengthen it. This approach allowed him to take the Patriots to nine Super Bowls, winning six times, often with very few superstar players, but rather brilliantly constructed and coached role players who fit together in a solid roster.

Companies should be asking themselves the same thing. Markets are evolving so fast, and new skills are needed to continue to lead in your industry. However, companies tend to resist bringing in new talent to the leadership team. Bringing in new skills does not mean the team is bad; it means you identify new needs and want to make the team even stronger. Again, leave the ego on the coat rack and focus on creating value.

What Artificial Intelligence (AI), and the Internet before that, have done is change the landscape because they give everyone access to a wealth of knowledge they didn't have access to before. This happened in consulting 30 years ago when I was just beginning my career. Back then, international firms could sell the added value of having benchmark data from other companies in the same sector from around the world. With the arrival of Google, access to that knowledge was *democratized*, resulting in a need for the firms that wished to survive and thrive to find new ways to add value. When we think about schools and education, what technology has done is similar—it has raised the bar for teachers to bring value. Instead of just sharing previously hard-to-access knowledge, they now need to really teach kids skills on how to use that information to innovate, think critically, and combine it with their own unique skills and abilities.

Here is where the model is broken. As British mathematician and philosopher, Bertrand Russell, pointed out over half a decade ago,

> "I think men in control of vast organizations have tended to be too abstract in their outlook, to forget what actual human beings are like, and to try to fit men to systems rather than systems to men."

The current corporate model was designed for a different economic world model. It is based on the fundamentals of an *industrial economy* where capital was in the hands of a select few able to own land and factories that produced profit, and where employees were just cogs in a bigger wheel. If you want to see this reflected graphically, just study the structure of a corporate balance sheet. Assets are the *good* things, and they are all linked to capital: land, factories, cash, and short-term assets like receivables. Notice that people are nowhere to be seen there. In fact, they come into the equation through the income statement as a *cost*, i.e. a necessary evil that reduces profit but that is required in order to operate.

Sadly, most companies still operate in this fashion, and the only skills you need to keep that running from a human standpoint are people to carry out *algorithmic* tasks, where you follow a set process to achieve a certain result, such as tightening screws on an assembly line. However, the reality of markets has changed, and now capital is available to anyone with a good idea, and those *algorithmic* production skills are commodities that can easily be reproduced and have all fled to low-cost markets.

So now, the value that can differentiate a company in its niche comes from team members who carry out *heuristic* tasks, where you need creativity and problem-solving to reach a desired outcome. This requires companies to review their *rosters* and find new team members versed in these new skills, or to develop those skills in people currently in the company. Likewise, sports organizations need to change how they choose talent from just historical physical performance to evaluating other skills like leadership potential and coach-ability.

One of the big challenges in updating your roster is that these new performers, be it athletes or corporate workers, are motivated by different factors than the industrial era factory workers. Sticks and carrots such as bonuses or threats of loss of employment, or in the case of athletes, getting cut off the team, do not allow you to bring in the required talent. So you need to modify your measurement and rewards model to provide the three variables that people who excel at heuristic tasks most value:

1. **Autonomy/freedom** that allows these top performers to have input into how to best do their work, with whom they want to work, and how they organize their own time
2. **Mission**: Being part of a compelling mission or contributing to something bigger than self is a strong driver for top performers
3. **Growth**: Opportunities to learn and become better from the experience/role/job

The bottom line is that you will need to keep revisiting the *Mastery Map* for your organization with an open mind and identifying the skill gaps and missing profiles you need to keep leading your competition in a quickly-changing world.

Think of relationships in a long-term context

Just as the first chapter of this block advised the importance of designing your *Mastery Map* with the mindset of optimizing performance over a decade, likewise it is extremely important to build, curate, invest in, and care for long-term strategic relationships if you truly want to compete at the highest level in your craft. I've observed the tremendous impact this can generate both in the world of sports and in business.

Whether you're a company or an athlete, you need to really focus on the key relationships with all the partners, coaches, mentors, suppliers, sponsors, and other individuals or companies that may not strictly be a part of your organization, but in many cases, represent a significant advantage if you are striving to become world class and achieve ambitious goals.

Let's explore how this plays out in sports, and then we'll explore how this is such a powerful lever for driving performance in the world of business.

Sports relationships

When working with athletes, I've observed that the first relationship that brings stability and tends to result in positive performance lifts is that of coaches and staff. Let me differentiate here between individual and team sports, because the dynamic is slightly different, although the principles are the same.

Let's use the ATP tour as our individual sport example, where I have a wide range of data and examples from my time working on the Tour. A growing number of players, especially young players, are very fickle and tend to cycle through different coaches with surprising frequency. When speaking of coaches, I'm referring to the whole team, including tennis coach, physical therapists/doctors, physical trainers, and mental skills coaches. Here's the thing though:, when you look at players who have generally had success over the long term, you will find a strong correlation between their outputs and stability of relationship with the coaching team.

Rafa Nadal spent his entire career coached by his uncle, until they started the academy and Toni stepped away to run it, and since then, he's had only one main coach in Carlos Moyà, longtime friend, mentor of Rafa and former world number one. He's also had the same physical trainer for years. I believe this stability is one of the key factors in Nadal's tremendous career.

Nadal is not by any means the only example, however. David Ferrer had a multi-year stint in the top five, which can actually be considered being almost number one because above him he had prime era Rafa, Novak Djokovic, Federer and Andy Murray, so being world number five and four is actually an amazing feat. During this time he had a long-term relationship with coach Javier Piles, who was critical in shaping him as a player and helping take him to the top.

Djokovic himself had the two greatest periods of his career with longtime coach Marion Vaira, and later during the long term-and stable relationship with former Wimbledon champion Goran Ivanisevic who served as his coach.

Likewise, Feliciano López's greatest run came later in his career during his stable relationship with Jose Manuel "Pepo" Clavet that lasted about a decade.

Even just one area, like mental skills training, can make a huge impact. When I have had long-term relationships with players in the ATP, they achieved their career high ranking and secured a majority of key titles during the time we worked together.

Now the interesting part is not the length of those relationships per se, but the dynamic that made them last, and as a result, the ability to impact on performance by coaches above and beyond what can be achieved in a shorter, more transactional relationship.

The longer term relationships result when both parties see each other as a critical part of the equation. If tennis players can hire and fire trainers at will, as I've seen in many less successful players, it becomes much more difficult to help them develop outside of their comfort zone. Since the player has all the power, coaches may be hesitant to say,

> You need to start changing the intensity in your training and structuring your pre-game preparation much more.

If the player is made to feel too uncomfortable, then they can just decide to move on to a new coach. There's no leverage to help the player enter into the space of focussed practice, where they're outside their comfort zone. Given that many pro athletes have fragile egos, they short-sightedly refuse to even look at their own performance and why they are not getting the results they want, which makes it impossible to help them improve.

If you look at the above examples, such as the one of Rafa Nadal with his uncle, you see a trend. Toni Nadal has two brothers, one of which is Rafa's father. The three had an agreement that Toni would train the boy and the other two would run the family businesses, and they all shared in the profits. So when young Rafa might not have wanted to follow Toni's guidance, he had no choice. The family did not let him fire his coach at 12 years of age, as I've seen other players do. The benefit was that Toni was able to teach Rafa not just technique, but foundational skills such as consistency, emotional regulation, humility, etc. By the time Rafa was old enough to decide, he realized that having been *stuck* with the same coach was an incredible blessing.

The other advantage over time is that a long-term relationship allows coaches to understand players much better—what their drivers are and how to better help them. In the case of Nadal, Toni was his uncle and so he deeply knew his player, but the same applies for, say, the David Ferrer relationship. Urban legend amongst pro players here in Spain has it that Ferrer had quite a temper as a younger player. Piles used to lock him in the equipment shed until he got over his tantrums, and when Ferrer stated at 18 that Piles wanted him to work too hard, David's father told Ferrer that he was taking a season off and would work with him on construction jobs. After starting at 6 am all winter and spending 12-hour days laying bricks, David Ferrer decided that touring on the ATP tour wasn't that tough after all. The ability of Piles to influence the education and foundational values of his player is one of the factors that turned David Ferrer into—as Roger Federer said at Ferrer's retirement ceremony—*the most professional, disciplined player on tour*. He never deviated from his meal plan; he was incredibly consistent doing his cardio; and he became a formidable returner and one of the most consistent base-liners in the history of the game.

For a long-term relationship to work, the player and coach have to constantly find a balance of give and take. The player, over a long-term period, trusts that the coach knows what he's doing. When the coach pushes the player more than he likes or gives him harsh feedback, the player knows in the long term it will benefit him. This allows the coach to push his players to higher levels and make them more teachable. On the other hand, coaches need to balance the pressure with reward and giving players proper phasing to make the long road bearable.

In a long-term relationship, the coach's influence increases and players get the benefit of discovering and integrating new dimensions beyond what they've experienced previously. I worked with one top player over several periods of his career. At times, I pushed him out of his comfort zone and he felt like he didn't want to listen. But he always came back and, during the last stint of his career, he confided,

> "I now understand how impactful performance training has been in my career and I actually wish I'd realized earlier."

The theme here—that you'll see applies also when we talk about this in the realm of business—is that, if you don't view coaches, mentors, specialized experts, and other strategic partners as long-term components of your team, you handcuff yourself and greatly limit your performance potential.

Let's take a look at how this plays out in team sports. The principles are the same, but the dynamic includes ownership and coaching staff. Coaches in team sports are hired by team owners, so players have much less freedom to not listen to, or fire, coaches. However, team owners need to have a long-term view together with the right coach in order to build a winning culture. This means both sides have to give and take. Coaches need to have autonomy and control over certain decisions, and ownership has to have a long-term commitment, allowing coaching staffs to have rebuilding years which don't give immediate results but set the base for future success. If you look at the most successful teams, ownership and coaches had a mutual commitment to working together long-term. A best-in-class example is the Rooneys, the family that owns the Pittsburgh Steelers. All their coaches have been with the team over long periods of time and the results have been winning records every year over decades, as well as six Super Bowl titles. Bill Belichick and Robert Kraft of the Patriots, or Sir Alex Ferguson with Manchester United, are other examples to study.

Now let's switch our focus to the world of business. My team and I find ourselves having this conversation over and over with big multinationals, and I find it amazing that we should have to discuss it, but here's the truth. The world has evolved and companies are specializing more and more in their unique *Area Of Impact* and outsourcing other parts of the value chain. The clear example is the automobile industry, where car manufacturers used to own everything from the steel mills to the dealerships and every part in between. Now, they've discovered that they need to focus on their core skills, like engineering, design, and efficient production lines, and have specialized suppliers who bring specific value in each part of the value chain. There are companies specialized in making specific components, like the electric window openers, and they are able to create higher quality products at more competitive prices.

The implication is that strategic partners have become the equivalent of coaches, mentors, experts, and coaching staff. They do not belong to the company, but if you want to dominate your industry, you had better establish productive, long-term relationships based on mutual trust and mutual benefit.

This is where many big multinationals totally go off the rails. Mediocre management teams view and treat these suppliers as an outside entity that needs to be squeezed for the lowest price. They mistakenly believe those suppliers have to make up for the internal inefficiencies of the company. That's a big mistake. First off, suppliers are in business just the same as their larger multinational clients are. They need to make sustainable profit over the long term; otherwise, they cease to be viable enterprises. For some unfathomable reason, companies feel they need to limit their suppliers' profit. This is the same limited thinking that leads to capping sales commissions. You should want your suppliers (and sales teams) to make very healthy profits, in exchange for creating extreme value for you.

To do this, when companies need to drive costs down, instead of following the remedial procurement director's playbook of shutting suppliers in a room and threatening them to bring down prices or they will be substituted, companies need to work with their strategic suppliers to see how, *together,* they can restructure how both parties work so suppliers can provide better quality at lower costs.

When you're talking about strategic suppliers—just as when we spoke of the dynamic between athletes and coaches—a long-term relationship allows the supplier to know your organization much better and propose innovative improvements that will drive enterprise value. For that, they need to be seen as strategic, and their ideas and guidance need to be sought out and valued.

The next time you want to negotiate with a supplier, sit down with them to understand what your company does that drives up their costs to serve or slows down their service, and work together to make the changes that will jointly produce better results. Sometimes that means improving your internal systems so suppliers can be integrated and get faster, more accurate information that avoids mistakes and rework. Other times it may mean modifying your commercial terms to your end clients that change how you consume services from your suppliers. Perhaps you need to change things so you can plan demand much further in advance, and more accurately, which allows your suppliers to manage their resources and give you better quality and better response times at a lower cost. These are some of the levers my team has used in many companies to drive incredible performance improvements and positive economic impacts.

Like so many aspects of performance, it starts with mindset. Whenever I hear company execs talk about suppliers as a *necessary evil* that needs to be closely controlled and squeezed, I know they will never optimize their performance. You really need to see strategic suppliers as your long-term partners that are basically an extension of your company. They represent critical functions that you need in order to be competitive in your industry. The only difference with your internal departments is that they belong to another owner and get fees instead of salaries. So what? You need to get away from those industrial-aged paradigms and start to understand how true value is created.

I often use the metaphor of a marriage. A marriage is never world class because the two people are tied in by a complex contract and are afraid to step away or they get penalized. It only works when both parties want the best for each other—and for the family unit as a whole—and thus they realize two important truths that must never be forgotten:

1. Sometimes one party will give more than the other. That shows you care. However, over time, there has to be a balance where both parties are helping the other be better.
2. Both parties need to feel and realize that their contributions are *equivalent*, although they will rarely be *identical*. In

business, people often mistake the contribution of the *payer,* or the one contracting, to be greater than the supplier. That's actually very low-level thinking, and as many clients have discovered, the cost of losing a really good, strategic partner is often orders of magnitude greater than what you paid them. So this is important. Suppliers want to work with you and get paid—that's the reason they have a business. But if you treat them like second-class citizens, threaten to substitute them if they don't give away margin *just because,* and fail to create an environment where you are open to benefitting from their specialized knowledge about your business, then you will eventually find you have a weak link in your business that will cost you much more in the long term.

Just ask yourself how your employees would react if you treated them like you do your suppliers. Most of them would seek another job. And, just like great employees, if your suppliers are top tier at what they do, they may value your business, but they don't need you to survive.

Whether you're an athlete or a business, I invite you to think long and hard about investing in long-term, strategic relationships with experts in all capacities. It could be the missing key to unlocking amazing performance gains for you.

If you're an athlete, consider your coaches, mentors, staff, and expert advisors as strategic members of your team, and make sure they are invested in your long-term success. Likewise, you need to think of how to make them want to stay with you and bet on you long term. The magic happens when all parties are working toward an ambitious objective and they realize the best probability of achieving it is together.

As a business, be smart and leverage external talent and specialization to make your core business more efficient and capable of providing greater value. Remember that, just because they are different companies than yours, that doesn't mean they are less valuable to your business. Often it's the opposite. Being external allows them to specialize in a specific part of the value chain and become much better than you ever could in that function. That's the whole idea behind specialization.

Apply this concept in the design of your *Mastery Maps,* keeping in mind that the skills and abilities you need on your team may be internal to your organization or may be provided by third party strategic partners. Identify where you will find experts to help drive your performance and how you will integrate them into your journey.

Coaching Case File: How a large multinational leveraged attributes to select talent for a new function

A large multinational I worked with for a while was in the process of transforming the way they provided support services from a controlling model to a partnership model. At one point, they decided they wanted to create a new role that would lead strategic transformation in support functions across different countries. The challenge they had was choosing the internal candidate to lead the role, because they had never done anything like this, so their traditional model of using historical performance in a similar role was rendered useless.

This was when I introduced them to the concept of *attributes*—character or personality traits of each person that, when used properly, are powerful predictors of performance in certain functions. I always note that no attribute is good nor bad in absolute terms, but rather is just more or less aligned with the skills and behaviors a certain role requires. As such, certain people will find it easier to perform in new functions than others, depending on the requirements and their attributes. For example, someone who is risk averse and a very meticulous decision-maker may find a role in finance more aligned with the things they are naturally good at than a role in innovation. Again, this is neither good nor bad, but it is helpful to try to assign team members to roles more aligned with their attributes, even if they have never performed that role before.

In the case of my client, since the role was so new, we needed to define what capabilities would be necessary to perform well. I worked with the client to define a series of competencies in each of the following four domains:

Business Domain: Including attributes such as openness to new ideas, creativity, willingness to learn, interest in advancing one's own success agenda, among others

Leadership Domain: Including such variables as competitiveness, self-confidence, willingness to take measured risks, desire to drive and be in charge, interest in the financial success of the company, etc.

Interpersonal Domain: Comprised of traits such as approachability, willingness to take a stand, charisma, willingness to help others, and team approach

Intrapersonal Domain: Including balanced emotional demeanor, organized *can do* approach, appropriate interaction with hierarchy and structure, integrity, and willingness to have fun in the workplace and take prudent risks

I then worked with the client to identify in each domain which traits were essential for the new role, which ones were nice to have, and which ones were irrelevant. The *essential* traits were weighted with a value of 1, *nice to have* with 0,5; and *not relevant* got a 0.

We then tested four internal candidates and were able to rank them based on attributes that would facilitate or hinder performance in the role, giving us a clear picture of the level of fit per candidate on each of the four key domains.

This experience provided a paradigm shift for my client and they began integrating attribute analysis not just into internal promotion, but also in recruiting to ensure new hires matched traits needed for success and also gained insight into alignment of the candidates' values with the corporate culture.

Coaching Case File: Using personality profiling to help drive a player's performance

I was asked to help a promising WTA player who was struggling with managing pressure and expectations. My experience is that many times people won't tell you what's wrong because they don't understand what's going on inside them. The reason is that people are often not aware of the meaning they give events and how that shapes their own self-image. Additionally, people are not aware that their identity and personality predispose them to being able to manage certain types of actions and situations better than others. That's one of the reasons I have been working with profiling tools as a compliment to the in-person work I do with athletes and executives, as it gives me insights that allow me to help my clients unblock some of the deep, unconscious models and beliefs that drive their behavior without them being aware of why.

The only brief I got on this client was that, when she stepped on the court, her anxiety and tension shot through the roof and she even had trouble breathing due to the accelerated state she found herself in.

I asked her if she would be open to taking a few profiling tests that feed into a proprietary model I designed (called *Unleash Sports*) as I felt that would give me insights into her motivations, intrinsic strength, and potential points of improvement. She accepted, and when the tests came out, I had a pretty solid hypothesis to work with her. Here's a summary of how the conversation went.

Me: *From the results of your Unleash scores, I'd like to explore some topics with you. When you feel under pressure, would it be correct to say that you get very anxious, you complain a lot when things don't go your way, you beat yourself up for any small mistake, and generally find it hard to feel grounded and centered?*

Player: *That's exactly how I feel. As soon as I miss a shot or lose a point I shouldn't, it's like I go into a spiral. I get really mad and emotional and I feel I'm an imposter and I don't belong on the court.*

Me: *Okay, let me check a couple of more things before we try to work through this. When you get into that spiral you mentioned, how do you react? My understanding from the data I've gathered is that you feel like you don't have a plan, you feel very emotionally and mentally scattered, and you feel an overwhelming sense of disappointment and you just want to give up.*

Player: *It's so hard to explain. I feel like I'm in a whirlwind and everyone is watching me and shaking their heads in disappointment.*

Me: *Alright, one last thing I want to understand. Why do you focus on what other people think or do? If I asked you what factor is the one that most impacts you or most matters to you when you play, would it be (a) winning titles, (b) making money, (c) having fun on the court or (d) other people's opinions?*

Player: *That's an easy one. Other people's opinions. No contest. Especially my dad and my coaches, but also the fans.*

Me: *Just to be sure I understand you, if you had to choose what matters most to you, either winning a tournament and getting the prize money and ranking points, or not winning, but having everyone talk about how valiant you were and how much you are admired, you would choose the latter?*

Player: *I'd rather both, but having people's approval is what gives me peace. For sure!*

Armed with this information, I now had some solid insights into my client's profile in terms of managing stress and drivers she most valued. I was able to explain the dynamic she struggled with to her, and how that generated her anxiety, and diminished physical stamina. Her focus on worrying about others' opinions of her left her mentally and even physically depleted. This allowed us to explore the meaning she gave to events on the court, and she eventually realized how distorted her perception was, and in fact, she was still carrying the mental model she had formed as a child where pressure from coaches and parents led her to give negative, self-destructive meanings to mistakes. She even anguished about being less skilled and developed than people expected her to be at different points in her career.

Through a process of working through these beliefs, she was able to reset her evaluation of her current skill level and career success, and choose how she wanted to move forward and what she would focus her energy on. She understood that, if her success and happiness relied on what others thought of her, she really had no control over her life, because she would always depend on exogenous factors to be happy and satisfied with her progress or not. Together we defined a new series of measures for whether she was on the right path and were able to put her current standing in the context of a *Mastery*

Map, where she could see that she was still very early in her career and needed to adapt her expectations to allow her time to evolve over a few years.

BLOCK 3: MOJO

What we can control is our performance and our execution, and that's what we're going to focus on.

Bill Belichick

(Eight time Super Bowl champion as head coach and assistant coach)

After Black Belt Comes White Belt

*Only one who devotes himself to a
cause with his whole strength and soul
can be a true master. For this reason
mastery demands all of a person.*

Albert Einstein
(Theoretical physicist)

WHAT'S THE BIG DEAL?

As we enter the third and final block of *The Optimal Performance Formula*, you should now have acquired the *raw materials* necessary with all the elements in the *Mindset* block, and you have an in-depth view of how to properly program and *design* your journey using the elements in the *Maps* section. Now it's time to *build* your masterpiece by walking the path. At this point, it all comes down to exceptional execution, or *Mojo*.

In the previous block, we explored the process of skill acquisition and improvement, and how to program these stages in your *Mastery Map* as you go from the very beginning of the process, when you start developing interest in a craft, to advanced practice. As a quick reminder, the phases of skill acquisition are: Identify, Learn, Practice, Bridge, Perform, and Refine and Improve.

This chapter is focussed on advanced training principles for high performers in the final phase of skill acquisition: Refine and Improve.

We'll delve into the protocols of *Deliberate Practice* and how to ensure you execute in a way that consistently improves your skill level.

I'll also share a series of advanced principles I call *The Echelons of Excellence* that are only taught once you have arrived at what I call *the Black Belt level*. When I studied in Japan, my Sensei explained that, when you receive a Black Belt in martial arts, that is where your learning really begins. The legendary teachers believed that, only when the student has trained at a high level for many years—and the black of the belt wears off due to use and once again becomes a white belt—does the student see the world with a beginner's mindset. At that point is when you can truly start a new, deeper cycle of learning on the never-ending path of concentric circles that lead to true mastery.

As we delve into the details of how world class performers develop their extraordinary skills, I hope one of the key takeaways for you is that there is no mystery at all about how they achieved their levels of mastery. In most cases, they did not have better genetics than others who achieved lesser levels of proficiency. What they *did* have, that set them apart, is a better knowledge of the necessary and unique structure and programming of their training that produced the most effective type of practice. Also, they practiced more—a *lot* more, over extended periods of time.

We now know that the most effective practice works by harnessing the adaptability of the human body and brain to create the ability, progressively, to do things that were previously not possible. If you carefully write out those steps on a diagram, you'll have something that looks a lot like a *Mastery Map*.

Great On Purpose:
The principles of *Deliberate Practice*

Throughout this book you've seen me mention Dr. Anders Ericsson and *Deliberate Practice* often. It's time to break it down for you in as simplified a manner as possible, and give you the guidelines that will allow you to structure your training and work such that you get the maximum benefit from the hours you put in.

Let me start by giving you some background to Dr Ericsson's research, to help you understand some very important characteristics. The first thing you should know is that the findings apply not just to athletes, but the principles have been proven to work across different disciplines, both physical and cognitive. In fact, one of the experiments that helped set the foundations for the model of *Deliberate Practice*, was carried out by Japanese psychologist Ayako Sakakibara. Working with children between ages two and six Sakakibara wanted to establish if a specific skill that is highly valued by musicians, known as *absolute pitch*, was a genetic gift or if it could be taught to anyone with the correct training. *Absolute pitch*, or *perfect pitch*, as it is also called, is the ability to identify or recreate a given musical note by just listening to it. Statistically, only one in ten thousand people normally displays the ability of *absolute pitch*. In Sakakibara's experiment, after one year and a half of training, all 24 of the participants *demonstrated absolute pitch*, leading to the conclusion that it is not something bestowed upon the genetically gifted, but rather can be developed by anyone with sufficient hours of the right type of training.

In the light of these findings, researchers have revisited geniuses of the past to try and understand how much is nature and how much was nurture. For example, it is known that, by the time Mozart was six or seven, he had trained for much longer than the children in Sakakibara's experiment.

The implication for you—as an athlete or business leader or performing artist—is game-changing. It means that achieving mastery is much more a matter of sufficient, properly-structured practice than having won the genetic lottery. This aligns perfectly with Dr. Carol Dweck's findings on growth mindsets, that we saw in an earlier chapter, and allows you to apply the skill of being a *master of meaning* to turn every struggle you encounter into an empowering situation. So mastery, then, is largely a matter of improving your mental processes, including the cases of athletes and other physical disciplines where science has shown that it is those mental processes that control what the body can do.

Restating this in the words of Dr Ericsson,

> "We now understand that there's no such thing as a predefined ability. The brain is adaptable, and training can create skills . . . that did not exist before. This is a game changer, because learning now becomes a way of creating abilities rather than of bringing people to the point where they can take advantage of their innate ones."

This exciting conclusion then begs the question: What exactly do we mean by the term *sufficient, properly-structured practice?* Let's have a look at the necessary characteristics for your training to qualify as *Deliberate Practice*, then I'll explain why those traits impact so dramatically on skill acquisition.

We've discussed most of these before, but here's a checklist of what qualifies your training as *Deliberate Practice:*

1. Training has to push you outside your current skill level, and thus requires you to be deeply focussed while practicing.
2. Your training has to identify the component parts of performance and have specific goals in each session to work them, and then stitch them seamlessly together for exceptional execution.
3. You need to have mechanisms in place to get timely and frequent feedback to modify or correct your execution.
4. You have to practice over a long enough time to allow the body and mind to adapt and hardwire the skills into your nervous system.
5. The focus is heavily weighted on execution, with less weight on theory.

Why are each of these factors so important? Don't take my word for it. Let's understand the science behind each one and why you should care.

ONE: Training beyond your current skill level

Most people hate to feel uncomfortable. Elite performers understand they need to push themselves beyond what they already know how to do, because in the mind of a world class performer, plateaus are taboo. Why do the best of the best push themselves so hard? Are they masochists? No, they just understand how this complex and sophisticated combination we call mind and body works, and they use that knowledge to drive performance. It all starts with getting your head around homeostasis.

Homeostasis is the tendency of an organism or cell to regulate its internal conditions, with the goal of stabilizing health and function, despite variations in external conditions. In other words, if nothing in our environment stresses the homeostasis regulation mechanisms, our organism sees no reason to change because it is capable of managing the situation. However, if something outside our organism changes, be it a physical or cognitive change, we are wired to activate DNA in the genes to generate changes that allow the organism to meet the new demands, and a new comfort zone is established as homeostasis is reestablished.

Most people understand how this works in the body when lifting weights or running long distances, but research has shown that the brain works in the exact same way. Both the structure, and the function, of the brain change in response to mental training, in the same way your muscles and cardiovascular system respond to physical training. If you want to drive more improvements, you need to modify the stimulus to trigger the whole process again. This method in physical training is known as progressive overload, and even if most people don't understand how the mechanism works, many have seen or applied it in an attempt to shape their bodies with more muscle and less fat.

Thus the importance of structuring training that is consistently beyond a performer's current skill level, keeping in mind that it is a moving target because skill will evolve with each cycle that triggers the homeostasis reaction. This is why so many people do the same thing over and over for many years without improving. As we discussed in an earlier chapter, they get to *good enough* and flatline. Notice that I said we need to change some demand to trigger the adaptation response, but that does not necessarily mean a greater volume of the same training. Many times it's not necessary to *try harder* but rather we just need to *try differently*. Experimenting with different variables can trigger a positive adaptation response without overstressing the organism. Many times the most effective way to get past a barrier is to come at it from a different angle. Here again, an expert mentor or coach can accelerate the process by being familiar with the type of obstacle you're facing and having developed a toolkit of alternative ways to overcome it. Since you are always being pushed to perform at a level above what you have mastered, successful progress requires a zen-like focus when doing your sessions. We'll talk more about the power of focus in an upcoming chapter because it is such an essential ingredient for driving optimal performance.

An important point to keep in mind is that the challenge lies in programming the practice at a level *just beyond* your current skill level. The *just beyond* part is key. When you properly program your progress, you set training levels just above where you are competent and comfortable, and that stress is what stimulates growth—be it improvement in skill or building more muscle or whatever. Your body and mind identify the need to improve certain variables and they get busy doing whatever is necessary to get you there. So here's where that little qualifier *"just beyond your current skill level"* kicks in. A common mistake of highly-driven individuals is to try and make too big a jump in skill, and that has the opposite effect, where you don't improve skill, get discouraged, and run a serious risk of getting injured. The most common example here is trying to jump up too fast on the weight you lift and injuring yourself. This is very common to see with weekend warriors in most commercial gyms, as proper form goes out the window, and you end up getting less benefit from the work you do than if you went with a lower weight.

Another example to illustrate the importance of proper increments in difficulty is the following. I may want to improve my tennis game, so among other variables, I'll try to train and play against players a little better than I am. Now, if I jump too far and try to play against Roger Federer, I won't even see the ball. I probably won't even score one point. Even now that Roger is retired, I still wouldn't fare any better. With this training, I won't improve because the jump is too big, and after a few minutes of enjoying just watching how great Roger is, it would become boring watching him swoosh shot after shot past me. I joke a little with this, but it's a good illustration of the futility of jumping too far, too fast in your programming.

Likewise, you have to make sure you have the right components in the right order. In other words, I may be in great physical shape and able to match Federer in a four-hour match in terms of stamina and running all over the court, but that doesn't add anything if I don't have the technique to be able to keep the ball in play with him. So I'd need to get those skills down before being able to play with someone that much better.

One last point on this subject. Often, even in physical training, it turns out that the variable that needs to change in training is psychological. Dr. Ericsson's research showed that it is surprisingly rare in any field that a person has reached some immutable limit on performance. What happens most often is that people just give up and stop trying to improve. Here again we see the importance of *CAGE-mode,* as maintaining the focus and the effort required to break through barriers is hard work and requires great doses of motivation to fuel the necessary grit to keep driving forward.

Training beyond your current skill level is a secret that has been practiced by all elite performers. As the great Pablo Picasso said,

"I am always doing things I can't do; that's how I get to do them."

TWO: Work specific parts, then stitch them together

If you remember, in the *Maps* block, we talked about practice having two potential objectives: hardwiring the skills you already have vs. increasing and expanding your skill in your craft. In order to focus on the latter, it's important that you break down performance into smaller chunks and improve each one of the pieces, then stitch them back together in one smooth performance. It's about putting a bunch of baby steps together to reach a longer-term goal, because *Deliberate Practice* involves building on previously acquired skills by focusing on particular components of those skills and structuring practice to specifically improve them. When those component parts are mastered and eventually stitched together, over time this leads to elite performance.

Dr. Ericsson's research marked a clear distinction between *Deliberate Practice* aimed at a particular goal and generic practice. Only specific forms of practice that are designed to achieve a certain goal, devised specifically to improve particular aspects of performance, have been shown to drive the most significant improvements in skill.

As a result, your training must have specific objectives that are measurable and linked to your overall *Mastery Map*. For example, if we look at a martial arts student, instead of having a generic goal to *just practice kicks*, a properly designed training program could include the following steps to work on specific components of technique:

√ During one cycle, be it a week or a month depending on the student's level, they would practice strength by performing sets of chambering the knee high, holding for three seconds, then extending the kicks, holding for two seconds, then re-chambering the leg

√ The next cycle, the student would practice the same kicks with maximum speed, then return to the starting stance

√ The following cycle would focus on introducing drills to improve footwork, to close the gap with the target

√ Finally, you would combine the three above components, by practicing the knee chambering while executing the footwork and then firing the kick off quickly

Notice that each small step requires extreme focus on the fine points of execution. You are giving each step your full attention, in order to refine and optimize your execution, then you add components to keep stimulating the adaptation response. This is the only way to develop your full potential, and it is why elite performers in any field structure their training and work sessions in this fashion.

THREE: Timely and instructive feedback

When striving to optimize your performance, it is essential that you receive feedback to identify exactly where and how you are falling short. We saw previously that you can get feedback from many sources: expert coaches and mentors, objective data measures, recordings, etc.

We don't know what we don't know and, without feedback, it's hard to figure out what you need to improve. Even if you realize the final outcome is not up to par, you may struggle to identify what you need to fix in order to improve, or how close or far you are from the level you aspire to. Often, the major breakthroughs come from minor adjustments, and having fresh eyes giving you the awareness you lack—and the knowledge you have not yet accumulated—is priceless. Likewise, having a guide to continually provide you with specific feedback accelerates the learning process until you integrate those technical details or cues into your technique. If you observe aspiring athletes in training, you'll hear their coaches remind them many times per session of specific fundamentals that they may be forgetting to execute and that impact their performance potential. Useful and applicable feedback is one of the crucial factors in maintaining motivation. It makes a huge difference in maintaining the consistent effort necessary to improve over time.

There's one thing you should keep in mind. Feedback becomes much easier to find—and much more useful in getting you up the mastery curve—if your craft has highly-developed, broadly-accepted training methods. Disciplines like classical music, math, and gymnastics are examples of established fields. Trading Bitcoin would be the opposite, as it's a new field with yet undetermined standards of excellence. In established disciplines, you can leverage experts for more insights and performance cues because there are clearly defined skills, developed over long periods of time, and sophisticated sets of training techniques. These fields generally also have consensus on what great looks like and how to measure performance.

FOUR: Practice long enough to ingrain skills

One of the most significant findings from Dr Ericsson's research actually remained relatively unknown until Malcolm Gladwell's book, *Outliers*, coined the famous 10,000 hour rule. That slightly incorrect take by Gladwell was influenced by Dr. Ericsson's studies of violin players, ballet dancers, and other world class performers, tracking them from the age of initiation in their crafts, to determine what factors influenced who became the best performers. Although there is nothing special about the number 10,000 in terms of hours of practice, it serves as a proxy to convey the key conclusion with regard to developing elite skills.

Dr. Ericsson's research concluded that the *only* major difference among the best performers and their peers was the total number of hours that the students had devoted to solitary practice. Even among the most *gifted* students, those who had spent significantly more hours practicing their craft were, on average, more accomplished than those who had spent less time practicing. Thus, the conclusion time and again, across different disciplines, was that to become excellent at a skill requires several thousand hours of practice. As a result, Dr Ericsson concluded that there are no shortcuts and no prodigies, only those who had spent more hours on solitary, *Deliberate Practice*.

It's important to point out that the key factor was the number of hours of practice, not the hours spent performing. More importantly, performing isn't the same thing as practice. In Dr. Ericsson's own words, when specifying the relevant variable of hours of practice from the violin study, he stated,

> "An hour of playing in front of a crowd, where the focus is on delivering the best possible performance at the time, is not the same as an hour of focused, goal-driven practice that is designed to address certain weaknesses and make certain improvements—the sort of practice that was the key factor in explaining the abilities of the Berlin student violinists."

One of the most exciting findings for driven individuals passionate about achieving optimal performance is that although approximately 10,000 hours was required to achieve a level of mastery, there is no point at which performance maxes out and additional practice does not lead to further improvement. So it would seem that Harvard psychologist James William was on the mark back in 1907 when he said,

> "The human individual lives usually far within his limits ... [individuals] the world over possess amounts of resources,

which only very exceptional individuals push to their extremes of use."

FIVE: Focus on execution of skill vs. theory

As opposed to the early stages of skill acquisition, where the focus is on discovery and understanding, in *Deliberate Practice*, the emphasis is on *doing*. Although you still receive coaching and insights in this stage, they are much more specific and focussed on practical details of execution.

This distinction between knowledge and skills is especially prevalent in the corporate world and highlights a stark difference between traditional paths toward expertise and *Deliberate Practice*. In most corporate training programs, the focus continues to be on transfer of knowledge, providing information about the right way to proceed without structuring any embedded practice that allows the team to become efficient at applying that knowledge in their day to day. *Deliberate Practice*, by contrast, focuses solely on performance and how to improve it.

Dr. Ericsson illustrates this difference with the example of how doctors receive medical training. During their schooling, the lion's share of the focus is on learning theory. Only when medical students become interns and residents working under the supervision of experienced doctors, do they finally learn many of the technical skills they need for their specialties. It seems evident that there is a lack of sufficient focussed training designed to teach execution skills, but the process gets worse after they graduate and begin working as full-fledged physicians.

The assumption is that doctors have developed all the skills they need to treat patients effectively. However, proof that this assumption is clearly flawed was provided by a study released in 2005, conducted by researchers at Harvard Medical School, that looked at how the quality of care that doctors provide changes over time. It concluded that doctors' performance stayed static or grew worse over time. The reason is that doctors do not gain expertise from work experience alone, as they are merely reinforcing the skill levels they have, but there is nothing in their jobs that allows them to continue to improve their skill base. Likewise, the traditional training activities that are offered, such as attending lectures, mini-courses, etc, contain none of the traits of *Deliberate Practice*. In other words, the only training they receive is theoretical, outside of an environment where they can try something new, make mistakes, get feedback, correct the mistakes, and gradually improve their skill level or develop a new skill.

This brings to life the story we reviewed in a previous chapter of how Dr. Gawande sought out one of his former teachers, Bob Osteen, specifically because he knew he had not improved since he had graduated, and even felt he'd gotten worse in some areas. Gawande intuitively understood what *Deliberate Practice* research has proven, that mastery requires long-term practice just beyond your current skill level, timely feedback, and more practice with adjustments. In other words, the high level of mastery exhibited by top performers seems like magic or genetics, but is really comprised of many little, hard-won steps, achieved over a significant period of focussed practice.

Why it works: how specific, focussed practice generates changes

The principle of plasticity—the idea that the human brain and body respond to challenges by developing new abilities—is the key to why focussed practice is so powerful in developing skill.

Studies have shown that, when you recruit your mind or body in certain specific tasks, the brain actually changes, and this produces improvements not just in cognitive abilities, but also in physical abilities. For example, a study of musicians showed that years of practice on a stringed instrument caused the area of the brain that controls the fingers of the hand to gradually expand, resulting in a greater ability to control those fingers. In other words, the practice not only increased musicians' skill in playing; it literally increased their resources and thus their ability to play.

Another similar study discovered that the inferior parietal lobule—the part of the brain involved in mathematical calculations and in visualizing objects in space—has significantly more gray matter in mathematicians than in non-mathematicians. In particular, Einstein's inferior parietal lobule was significantly larger than average.

The discovery that focussed practice can physically alter the relevant parts of the brain for the specific skills you are practicing should fascinate you also if you're an athlete. By consistently training in the correct way, you can enhance your physical skills by increasing the ability of the specific parts of your brain that you recruit to perform. For example, studies have shown that competitive divers have greater cortical thickness (i.e. more gray matter) in three specific regions of the brain that play a role in visualizing and controlling the movements of the body.

One of the most fascinating changes that *Deliberate Practice* produces in experts is what are referred to as *mental representations*. In essence, *mental representations* are pre-existing patterns of information or facts, that are held in long-term memory and can be used to respond quickly and effectively in certain types of situations.

Mental representations for an athlete can be a clear mental picture of what performance should look like at every moment and, more importantly, what it should *feel* like in terms of body positioning and momentum. However, it goes much further. *Mental representations* allow experts and masters to process extreme volumes of information and make decisions on how to respond at what seems like supernatural speed. A clear example of this is how chess masters structure data. As they practice and advance over the years, they develop *mental representations* of how a chess game can evolve. Once they are advanced, chess masters do not see individual pieces on the board; they see patterns or standard situations. These patterns are like *chunks*, and the important thing about them is that they are held in long-term memory, thus allowing the expert to identify that a given situation has only one or two possible best moves, and this enables them to process the options and make decisions at lightning speed.

Another example, this time in the physical realm, is how tennis players return serves that are traveling at 250 km/hour. The answer is also *mental representations*. Over thousands of hours of practice, the player's mind develops and organizes information about how different details affect where and how the serve will bounce. Details such as the opponent's tossing motion, body positioning, and flight path all get processed in the subconscious mind of the expert vs. thousands of data records at a speed so great that the conscious mind is not aware of the calculation, but the body is provided with a command that says *based on all these variables, the ball will probably land here and you can strike it if you put your racket head about here.* Without time to think about it, the body responds and to the untrained spectator, it seems like magic.

Over my decades of seeking mastery in the martial arts, I have been delighted by this process. At one point, without knowing how, I realized I was able to respond to my opponents' techniques before becoming fully conscious of what they were doing. My *mental representations* allow me to know, based on body movement, weight distribution and other cues, what was coming. It's not supernatural, just the result of thousands of hours of training in pursuit of mastery.

In summary, what sets expert performers apart from less skilled performers is the quality and quantity of their *mental representations*, developed from years of practice that have changed the neural circuitry in their brains, making possible the incredible pattern recognition that leads to reaction time speed. Since mental representations are extremely craft-specific—and they develop not by thinking about something, but by training, failing, revising, and trying again—the extra bonus is that honing your craft improves the relevant *mental representation*, and those improved *mental representations* further improve your skill.

The implications of the research on focussed practice methods such as *Deliberate Practice* are inspiring at the very least. If you wish to become significantly better at something, you definitely can, irrespective of your genetics. This realization can empower any performer because, as Dr. Ericsson stated,

> "...learning is no longer just a way of fulfilling some genetic destiny; it becomes a way of taking control of your destiny and shaping your potential in ways that you choose."

The Echelons of Excellence

Now that you have a good understanding of how to restore your *Mojo* with focussed practice, it's time to see how to apply the concepts of *Deliberate Practice* to work your way up the *Echelons of Excellence*. This is an advanced version of the *refine and improve* phase of constantly starting new, deeper cycles of learning on the never-ending path of concentric circles that lead to true mastery. The difference here is that each circle is focussed on a different attribute or echelon. The nature of the *echelons* is that each one is dependent upon mastery of the previous level. Thus the order is...

CONSISTENCY, then...

ACCURACY, then...

SPEED, then...

POWER

Without consistency, accuracy is just a pipe dream. With no accuracy, you can't aspire to develop real speed, and without speed, power is impossible, because speed is an essential component of power. Let's delve into the four echelons so you can understand the extreme importance of each one and how they are non-negotiable if you aspire to reach mastery.

CONSISTENCY

Consistency may sound insignificant, but it is one of the biggest weaknesses that keeps performers from stepping up to elite levels. When I used to train to compete in tennis, one of the most fundamental drills my coach would insist on every practice was focussed on consistency. He would set up at the net and I had to get at least 50 straight strokes over the net that he would volley back, with no break. If I missed one, either in the net or if I didn't get to the ball in time, we would start again at the beginning. The whole basis of the exercise was that you can't be considered even a mid-level player if your technique isn't *consistent*.

If you see great baselines like Juan "Pico" Mónaco (who I worked with), or David Ferrer, they based their game on getting the ball over every time, resulting very often in the other player—even top ATP pros—making unforced errors. It may sound too simple to be effective, but it works because so many competitors suffer a sort of *Dunning–Kruger effect*. Remember that the *Dunning–Kruger effect* is a cognitive bias in which people overestimate their skill level in a particular domain. You may be able to hit the ball very hard, but if you can't consistently get it over the net, you are not at the elite level. This, by the way, is how moonballing club players defeat better opponents, by returning everything—even if it's soft and with float-ers—but eventually the player, with what appears to be better strokes, ends up failing.

In the martial arts, consistency is also an absolute essential for mastery. You need to trust that you can execute your techniques with confidence at any given instant. If you only trust that you can be consistent with certain techniques, which is what happens to most practitioners, you end up using two or three bread-and-butter tech-niques when fighting. This may work against an opponent with a similar level, but a skilled fighter will quickly figure out your limited arsenal and it will be very complicated for you to successfully win a match, or more critically, a street fight. When we extrapolate this to professionals like the Navy SEALs, you can understand why they demand that every team member be extremely consistent in terms of world class execution—otherwise, lives can be lost.

In business, the same holds true. Businesses that consistently provide a magnificent client experience, in terms of high-quality products and exceptional service, have a competitive advantage in the market. I've heard many people mention this about Apple. Whether you buy an iPhone or a Mac, the experience is always similar from the opening of the box to setting up of your device, and you know Apple is built upon creating exceptional user experiences. It's no accident that, at the moment of writing this chapter, Apple has the second highest market capitalization in the world, valued at a whopping $2.793 trillion.

The simple formula is as follows:

Consistency = Correct fundamentals + Focus

You need to be present, in the present, to be able to execute consistently. That ability to be focussed on the task and your execution sounds easy, but it is rare and is the mark of top performers. Before even considering moving on to the next echelon, *accuracy*, it is required that you have mastered consistent, world class execution of technique. If we go back to the tennis example, how can you aspire to put the ball where you want during an intense rally if you are unsure you can even get it over the net and in the court? It's impossible and naive to even try it.

Likewise, if your spinning back roundhouse kick only works sometimes, and other times you lose your balance or forget to chamber your knee, you can't trust your technique when you need to perform and not fail. You may score the blow, or you may end up on your butt, and that's not a scenario that generates a lot of confidence in your abilities. And it's definitely insufficient for the level of performance elite performers aspire to.

Again, the application to business is also direct here. I'm sure you've seen a company with that one employee whom everyone asks to do the important things, because everyone knows that person will consistently step up when asked and get things done on time. That person becomes ultra-valuable. As I often say to clients in corporate settings, if you want a raise, then become so valuable that the company will gladly pay you more to make sure you don't leave. It's that simple.

What does *Deliberate Practice* look like for CONSISTENCY?

Athlete example: Imagine we are working with a quarterback. A focussed practice protocol might include drilling the player until his mechanics are consistently correct. For example, drills might include challenging the player to consistently produce the proper footwork, hand and head placement, eye movement for scanning the field, and proper release mechanics. As the player becomes more comfortable reproducing the correct technique, the coach would introduce variables to up the complexity. For example, the player might be required to execute in an accelerated time frame because they let a rusher through the line. Other examples of progressively pushing the player outside of his current level might include advancing the drills to throw on the run or across his body or even while purposefully off balance to learn how to make the proper body adjustments in case this happens in a game. At every stage of the training, the player will receive immediate feedback from the coaching staff, as well as film to later study dimensions of his execution he cannot see, like his footwork or ball release.

Business example: An easy-to-visualize example here is a sales professional. They must be able to explain product or company features and advantages consistently and clearly. Also, they would have to master the base skills of active listening and open questions, as well as be adept at industry and client research before engaging with prospects. As they progress, the training protocol would introduce variables to increase the complexity, such as a roleplay with an aggressive client, reduced time to respond, simulated loss of printed or digital sales collateral, or having the make-believe client introduce unknown variables that the sales rep must adapt to on the fly.

ACCURACY

Achieving pinpoint accuracy is a prerequisite before moving to the third echelon: SPEED. Without accuracy, speed becomes a liability instead of an asset. You can only go as fast as you can while being accurate. To paraphrase the classic Pirelli tire commercial: *Speed is nothing without control.*

My experience in the martial arts has taught me that developing accuracy requires clear intention. The biggest mistake I see with fighters is that they throw strikes in the general direction of their opponent. When I see that, I realize they do not understand the deeper meaning of accuracy. It's not just about aiming for the liver or the jaw, but also the target you are choosing will impact the angle you need to apply when approaching with your strike, and the amount of follow-through you need to include in your calculations. Elite strikers know that their techniques need to strike the target several centimeters before full extension, otherwise you don't have any power to strike through the opponent. If you are not including all these factors in your calculations of accuracy, at best, you'll get lucky with a strike, but elite performers are like skilled surgeons and work on clean, meticulous technique.

Accuracy applies to cognitive tasks too. The most sought-after businesses are those who have a reputation for guaranteed quality outcomes. Think about it—do you prefer the restaurant that remembers your preferences and cooks your food exactly as you like it, or the one that produces varied food and service quality depending on who's working that day? Most customers will gladly pay a premium to ensure they get the experience they expect.

Going back to our example of the reliable and valued employee, you not only want someone who is consistently there and willing, but you value them even more when everyone knows that person will do a great job that you won't have to fix because they will meet expected standards. If you need to take advice from someone, you will surely prefer the person who you believe has greater expertise and will give you the best advice for each challenge. In other words, you prefer the person who will give you the solution that most accurately solves your problem.

What does *Deliberate Practice* look like for ACCURACY?

Athlete example: Staying with our quarterback example, once the player has all the mechanics mastered to the point where he consistently executes them properly, the focus would be on being able to throw the ball at will at specific targets. As the player develops the accuracy to deliver simple throws, the practice protocol would introduce complexity with such changes as having to throw at a moving target, having to throw before the receiver makes his cut and thus calculating where he will have to place the ball, and executing accurate throws under pressure or on the run. Each level introduces a greater level of complexity, and the player will most likely struggle at first, requiring feedback and then having to work specific variables. For example, a player may find that, to throw accurately while off balance, he needs to strengthen certain parts of his kinetic chain. This *feedback* results in a mid-term work plan to develop the foundational strength necessary (specific strength training) while practicing the technical skill (throwing off-balance) and discovering the finer points of technique to achieve the desired result (accuracy while throwing off-balance).

Business example: As our sales rep achieves consistency, we'd focus on developing the ability to accurately read the verbal and non-verbal cues from potential customers, together with the answers to the probing questions that they developed the ability to structure in the consistency phase. The objective would be to use the tools developed to structure winning proposals for each specific client. The progressions of challenge could start with a case where there is ample information available on the buyer and the target company, and could progress to simulations that require the rep to extract and process the limited information available from an aloof client to still accurately find a successful way forward to close the sale.

SPEED

Once you have consistent and accurate fundamentals, you can work on speed. The seemingly paradoxical trait of speed is that you need to be relaxed to achieve it. This implies being equally relaxed physically, as well as mentally. From a physical standpoint, if you are too tense, your own muscles and nervous system will limit the generation of speed. One of the reasons for this is that your body is an amazing machine and to use it to its maximum potential, you need to leverage the biomechanical advantages it offers through optimizing the kinetic chain for any movement. In other words, martial artists don't strike exclusively with the force of the leg or arm, but rather they start by generating force through the legs by rooting to the floor, then adding the movement of the hips and torso, then finally, as the weapon (foot or hand) travels toward the target, adding the power of the leg or arm muscles, and finally the wrist or ankle at the instant of impact. This kinetic chain can only be accessed if the body is sufficiently relaxed, otherwise it would move as one block, instead of a synergistic succession of pieces of the kinetic chain.

Other athletes, such as tennis players or baseball players, use the exact same principles to accelerate their rackets or arms when pitching and generate tremendous power. So, given the extreme level of complexity necessary to generate that speed, you can better understand why consistency and accuracy are prerequisites. Without the first two echelons, you would end up losing energy along the way due to improper technique and non-optimal flight path. Additionally, the faster you go, the harder it is to make sure you hit the target, so accuracy needs to be burnt into the nervous system beforehand so that your body automatically knows where it has to place the hand, foot, racquet or bat, whatever the case may be.

Again, the echelon of speed is essential in business and other cognitive settings also. We mentioned before how everyone loves the person who guarantees a great outcome. Well, a *great outcome* requires accurate results *and* timely execution. If someone is technically good, but takes an eternity to carry out a task, it will not be practical. And likewise, if the person is fast but careless, no one will trust the outcome. So speed is equally essential in business settings where performance aspirations are high.

One more important consideration on speed. One of the most often misunderstood elements of speed is that it is, in fact, made up of two components: reaction time and execution time. Up until now, we've been speaking of execution time—in other words, the time it takes you to execute something, be it a physical move like a kick, or a cognitive task, such as solving a problem or processing something in a business setting. However, reaction time—in other words, the time it takes you to process the situation, access your database of possible optimal reactions or actions, and execute—is also an essential component and is one of the key superpowers of top performers.

When I refer to superpower, don't be discouraged thinking it's something genetic; rather, it comes from the evolution of *mental representations* that result from long-term focussed practice, as we saw earlier in this chapter. Whether you're discussing a chess master who is able to evaluate complex patterns quickly, a tennis player who is able to process multiple cues at lighting speed to guess where a serve will land, or a senior sales executive who is able to pick up unconscious signals from a prospect and drive a sale to closure, *mental representations* give the performer a huge advantage when deciding the course of action, freeing them up to focus on fast execution of the chosen technique or tactic.

What does *Deliberate Practice* look like for SPEED?

Athlete example: The next stage of programming for our quarterback would be requiring the player to increase processing speed (e.g. reading defensive formations and deciding audibles to adapt the play based on what he sees), as well as working on reaction speed (e.g. quicker release of the ball). Again, as the QB begins to master the basic skills, the levels of increased challenge can come from introducing defensive shifts at the line, eliminating the main target of a play to force him to go though his progressions, and limiting the time he can hold onto the ball.

Business example: Our sales rep at this stage would start to develop and use *mental representations* to quickly process all the complex variables in the sales process and be able to choose the optimal path forward to drive success. Progressions could include having simulations where clients suddenly change criteria due to some internal change and require a reworked proposal on the fly. This is the stage where a rep begins to show mastery of all the fundamentals and mixes in all the tools, techniques, and experience they have accumulated to be able to keep the client's attention and buying intent in real time as the situation evolves.

POWER

The final echelon is power. I really like the definition of power as a means to be able to accomplish something, and we'll explore this in a couple of different contexts.

In terms of generation of physical power, such as the explosive characteristic of a punch or kick or a tennis serve, the connection with speed is very easy to see by just remembering basic physics. We know Force = Mass x Acceleration, remembering that acceleration is proportional to speed squared. So a one-unit increase in speed drives a greater increase in power than a one-unit increase in mass because kinetic energy increases as the square of speed. However, speed is not enough, because you need to be grounded so that, when you impact your target, you can transfer that power where you want it, instead of having it turned back on you. This again is why consistent and accurate fundamental technique is so important before attempting to develop effective speed and power.

In the realm of cognitive tasks, I think it's useful to use the definition I just mentioned of power as the ability to accomplish something. So, if we go back to the key team member example in a company, the person able to provide speedy resolution gains power in terms of the ability to influence and make things occur in the company. Power then—that so valued and sought-after trait—really requires that you move up the other echelons of excellence first in order to be able to have the speed, accuracy, and consistency necessary to generate power safely and centered on a focussed target.

What does *Deliberate Practice* look like for POWER?

Athlete example: At this stage, we could start to work with our quarterback to vary the additional tools that drive positive outcomes. Remember, we defined power as the ability to accomplish things, and here the quarterback may need to make more difficult and high-risk throws (e.g. fast bullets into tight windows) or find a way to make gains on a broken play. This is only sensible to train once the player has progressed through the other echelons and is able to consistently, accurately, and quickly execute the fundamental plays. At that point, we can help the athlete work on developing exceptional play-making ability.

Business example: For our sales rep, we can broaden their range of influence by allowing them to input into product design and innovation decisions or service levels, leveraging the mastery they have achieved and the deep market knowledge they have gathered, together with unique insights into the customer journey for their clients.

This chapter has given you the fundamental protocols of how to structure focussed and powerful practice to develop exceptional levels of expertise and mastery. You can use these guidelines when designing the training protocols and programs to deliver the skills identified in each phase of your *Mastery Map*.

And remember, perfect performances can't exist without perfect practice, so don't practice until you get it right; practice until you can't get it wrong!

Note: I consider this chapter an advanced extension of the chapter "How Humans Learn: Programming The Skills Roadmap" from the Maps section and have opted for the same format of including examples in each step for easier understanding of how each one applies. As such, this chapter does not contain Coaching Case Files, as it would be redundant and would add little or no additional value.

Slow is Smooth
and Smooth is Fast

*It is not a question of skimming the surface
of the art, it must be probed to its depths,
for to seize upon superficial things only is to
degenerate into mediocrity and obscurity.*

J.G. Noverre
(French choreographer and dancer known as "The Grandfather of the Ballet")

WHAT'S THE BIG DEAL?

One of the concepts that I always work on with clients is *slowing down to move faster and more powerfully*. Very often, this seems counterintuitive to most people, yet it is a fundamental lever of productivity and performance.

When I say *slowing down*, I mean *centering* or *rooting*, as it's often referred to in martial arts. It's about being mindful of your movements, decisions, and thoughts. It's about slowing down to see where you are and taking stock of the fine details. It's about transitioning from frantic, high speed running on autopilot, to slow, mindful focus on what you are doing, and how you need to adjust or change to improve. In our fast-paced world, slowing down is a superpower. It gives you the ability to reset and to act, instead of just reacting.

Contrary to popular belief, slowing down is *much* harder than doing things quickly and frantically. Slowing down requires you to up your level because you can't ignore or compensate for your weaknesses.

Fast and frantic allows you to be less effective, because it looks like you're doing so much, but it covers up your weaknesses. Don't believe me? Try this simple exercise. Slow down your walking speed to super slow motion. Take 20 seconds between the moment one foot leaves the ground and when it lands again. To do it properly, actually time yourself and ensure your foot is off the ground for 20 seconds. What you will most likely discover is that you feel much less stable than you would expect during those 20 seconds. The reason is that, when your gait is normal speed, you compensate for the lack of strength to properly stabilize your legs and hips, but when you slow it down, the weakness is exposed.

The same occurs if you slow down a fast talker who spouts nice-sounding platitudes and buzzwords while trying to convince you of something or sell you something. Stop the person and drill deep into each phrase. Ask what exactly that means, and how it links to the overall theme. You will find more often than not that they lose their aura of enchantment and ability to sound convincing. Again, the speed, cadence and intonation the orator uses compensate for fundamental flaws and deficiencies in the core content.

The key point to realize here is that we all fool ourselves with speed. And we do it often. It's convenient because it allows us to ignore areas we should improve, and gives us the impression that we are better at a task than we, in reality, are. This is why feedback is so important. The expert eyes of a coach will mentally slow down your technique and identify flaws, just as you can do by watching yourself on a slow motion recording. Experts know this, and it is why one principle to structure into your training is phases of slowing things down to fine tune and optimize them.

I used to use video recordings of my clients on the ATP tour to later show them how their process cues and body language were different when they performed well vs. when they performed poorly. Without fail, they were shocked to see how evident it was, but they had never noticed it before.

The three dimensions of slowing down

For me, slowing down is key in three dimensions:

Slowing down mentally
Slowing down your emotions or state
Slowing down technique

Let's look in more detail at each of the three.

Slowing down mentally

This is probably the most talked-about form of slowing down. Whenever I work with clients, I slow them down before they step into the area where they perform, be it the dojo for martial artists, the court for tennis players, or the board room for executives.

I ask them to remain silent and calm their minds. This involves leaving all their concerns and thoughts not related to their craft in the locker room (or in the case of a business, on the coat rack in the entrance). I teach them to visualize as they take off their street clothes and hang them in their locker, that they are leaving the thoughts and emotions about the rest of their lives in that locker too. They can pick them up later, when we're finished training or competing, but when they're working on their craft, I want all their energy. That's a nuance that often catches people off guard. I tell my clients that I don't want their *time* when we work together; I want their *energy*. I need their *focus*. Let's face it—if your mind is somewhere else, and you're executing with less than full effort, we're both wasting our time. So, before we even begin working, I teach them to clear their minds, slow things down, and focus exclusively on the work we're going to do.

At the beginning, the problem lies not only in that they do not know how to do it, but rather that they don't even understand what it really means to quiet the mind. And they feel it's a waste of time, until one day it clicks, and it becomes one of the most essential parts of their preparation. During the hours we're working together, they are free from the exhausting monkey mind and stress they carry around all day, and as a result, they come out refreshed and stronger after the session. By the way, this happens not just with clients who are pro athletes, but also senior executives admit having the same experience and benefits.

The title of this chapter, "Slow is Smooth and Smooth is Fast," is a mantra used by elite performance groups like the Navy SEALs. The idea is to focus on accuracy over haste. Second-order thinking allows you to make better choices that result in smoother operations with fewer errors. In high-stress situations, slow and deliberate actions prevent negative outcomes. SEALs apply this to tactical scenarios like weapons handling and mission planning. Careful checks of gear and meticulous studies of maps are mandatory because, when it counts most, accuracy is necessary for speed, as you saw in the previous chapter.

One of the really cool insights I've learnt about how the brain works when you force it to slow down is illustrated by the Coffer Illusion. The Coffer Illusion was created by a Stanford University psychologist, and is an image made up of a pattern of black, white and grey lines of various shades that create the illusion of rectangles. If you've never seen the Coffer Illusion, Google it to see the image so you'll better understand the example.

Here's where this links into performance. If you stare at the image long enough, you will see circles begin to appear. This is a great illustration of how our brains work. For the sake of efficiency, your brain captures information as you grow and it learns and classifies this information based on your experiences and interpretations. It then builds express routes, similar to macros in computers, that are meant to identify patterns and jump straight to the response. So, what the brain tries to do as often as possible is to link sensory inputs and other data you encounter to something you have already experienced, in order to quickly understand it. A curious example is how the brain creates groupings based on concepts. For example, an apple is put into a specific grouping called *fruit*, and your siblings get put into a grouping called *family*. If you've ever seen your mother or a grandparent call you by the name of another family member, or run through all the names of your siblings and cousins before hitting yours, this is why. Their brain goes to the *family* file and starts pulling out data, and may pull out the wrong name. However, it is rare that they will call you the name of their banker or physician, because those names are stored in different categories.

The point is that, when your brain thinks it knows the answer, it stops analyzing and jumps to the conclusion. This is why, if you change all the letters in the words of a paragraph, except the first and last letters of each word, you can read the entire passage easily, because your brain fills in the blanks. This is very useful for many advanced skills, such as we saw when we discussed *mental representations*.

Okay, so this is great, right? Well, yes, but like everything, it can have a couple of downsides. The first problem occurs when your brain leverages this fabulous ability and automatically jumps to an answer that is *wrong* and then stops thinking about the problem. This challenge has been long studied in cognitive psychology because of the impact it can have on the meanings you give to events. As we saw when we discussed the power of *meaning*, many of the beliefs we have were programmed into us when we were young, and may not be applicable anymore or, even worse, may just be dead wrong. If we never revisit them, we are held hostage to limitations that are not real.

A second and related problem that results from the brain jumping to what it thinks is the answer, is that it stops analyzing other options and, as a result, you miss new answers and other possibilities. This is exactly what the Coffer Illusion illustrates. When you first look at it, most people see squares because your brain arranges the images, lines and shades and thinks it knows the answers. Well, it actually knows *one* answer. The most common one or obvious one. Now, when you keep staring at the picture for a period of time, you are essentially forcing your brain to slow down and look at this information differently. As you force your attention on the picture, the brain starts to reconfigure the data to see what it can come up with. When it does, it realizes these lines and patterns can create circles, and it shows you that.

The Coffer Illusion teaches us a valuable lesson in slowing down to drive performance. When you work the basics of your craft over and over, you start noticing things you missed before, and you start exploring new tweaks you've never tried. Over time, you start finding little details that make a huge difference in performance. But to get there, you need to drill the basics so they are hardwired into your nervous system, and then practice with full focus and intention to see how you can improve. I believe this is the reason that certain famous innovators in business such as Steve Jobs or Elon Musk have been able to revolutionize industries. They may not be smarter than everyone else, but they have simply thought deeply about, and worked on, certain problems much more than most people, which led them to make breakthroughs others did not. If you're of average intelligence, but study, practice, and work on one subject obsessively, you will probably outperform the vast majority of people. Remember, Dr. Ericsson's research showed that it is the number of hours of focussed practice that produces elite performers.

Slowing down emotionally

Although your thoughts affect your physiology, and vice versa, I like to distinguish between the two because it gives us a second set of tools to drive performance.

At this point, I'm sure you've heard of the fight-or-flight response. This is hardwired into us from millions of years back, and is basically a survival mechanism from the time when threats came in the form of saber-toothed tigers instead of corporate raiders or too few followers on social media. If you believe you are under threat, adrenalin spikes, your heart rate goes up, and you get physiologically activated so you can spring into action to stay safe, be that by running away or fighting back. Either way, your body focusses all your resources to the most critical task—in other words, it prioritizes whatever physical tools you need to stay alive. That same reaction still happens; it's just that the program hasn't been properly updated in your nervous systems, so whenever we feel a perceived threat—which may be to our egos, our careers, or any other social variable—our body activates the same neuro-chemical cocktail. Actually, many ambitious and successful people live in constant fear, even though they prefer to call it stress, angst, or anxiety, but it's the same base process meant to keep you alive when threatened.

So, where's the problem? Well, to massively simplify this, there are *two* big problems. First, the fight-or-flight response is designed to be a short-term *turbo boost* to get you out of trouble. You might need to run for 5 minutes from a tiger, but not 50 days. Unfortunately, our bodies activate this response when we are under stress, be that a less than ideal work environment or anxiety over an upcoming competition for an athlete. And that response can become almost a constant state for many people with ambitious goals. This chemical cocktail, while valuable in short, infrequent bursts, is deadly if it becomes your chronic medium. Health suffers, mind and body burn out, and performance goes down. In fact, medical research estimates as much as a whopping 90 percent of illness and disease is stress-related. Stress can interfere with your physical functioning and bodily processes causing high blood pressure, cardiovascular disease, ulcers, allergies, asthma, and migraine headaches. The American Psychological Association has declared that chronic stress is linked to six of the leading causes of death including heart disease, cancer, lung ailments, accidents, cirrhosis of the liver, and suicide.

This leads me to the second problem: if you don't know how to regulate physiologically, your body and mind will not respond when you need to perform. Your body takes your resources and sends them to the key functions necessary for a very short-term physical burst. It doesn't care if you are burning muscle, filling up with cortisol, limiting your ability to access technical skills, or inhibiting your ability to think strategically. It just wants you to solve that tiger problem.

As a result, it's so important to learn to slow down your heart rate and state in order to be able to think clearly and access all your training during high pressure moments. We'll explore in detail in the next chapter how pressure is generated by our fear of the perceived negative consequences of a situation, be that a game-deciding penalty kick, making a big sale, or piloting a plane to an emergency landing (and we'll see ways to mitigate the negative effects of pressure).

Here's where mind and body interact. Your thoughts define the meaning you give to events, and these meanings affect your emotions and state, which in turn affect your ability to access skills and perform at your maximum level. However, the process also goes the other way—your physical state affects your emotions and your thoughts. If you are in a slouched position, you'll find you are more prone to feel blue, and as a result, will be less active and aware.

This back and forth between thoughts and state occurs often in the world of tennis and provides many clear examples of the struggle. When a player is battling at a critical point in a match, if they have not practiced slowing down the mind, emotions, and state, then a potential failure or mistake in a given moment can lead to the player freezing with fear and worry, thus turning those anxieties into a self-fulfilling prophecy. The internal conversation could go like this after missing a point:

> OHHHH, come on, you can win this. For the first time, you can beat this rival. Come on, you can't miss a shot like that. You gave the point away and now your rival will grow confident and start pushing you more. And then you will feel really stupid. How could you give up this lead? You are pathetic . . .

This thinking generates more anxiety, so physiologically the player goes into fight-or-flight mode, breathing becomes shallow, heart rate goes up, which makes performance go down. This leads to more negative thoughts that take critical energy and focus away so the player is not 100% focussed on each point. This leads to more mistakes, more anxiety, and on and on. This *hemorrhaging*, as I call it, continues until the player is unable to make even simple shots, starts cramping out, and often gets injured. We've seen this happen recently to Carlos Alcaraz as he struggles to manage the huge expectations placed on him.

There's another great player who had this problem, and later learnt to slow down and, well, the rest is history. Flash back to the 2007 US Open final between Novak Djokovic and Roger Federer. Novak, at that time, was considered a mentally weaker competitor, as he had quit matches when he was losing or was out of breath and seemed physically unable to continue. In the 2007 US Open final, he was pushing Federer, but anxiety got the best of him and he did not know how to slow down. He then made three consecutive double faults in the tiebreak. Despite all his talent, technique abandoned him because his mind and state were out of control. He lost that match. I love this example because it shows that even elite performers struggle with this and need to learn the skill of slowing down. Novak has since learnt how to slow down his mind and manage pressure; he slows down his state and no longer cramps up; and he did the hard work of improving in all areas—including his conditioning and his diet,—to drive his performance to the legendary level he now exhibits. So keep faith. Even if you've made this mistake—and most people have—you can always drive your performance to new levels by practicing and implementing the skill of slowing down to become more powerful.

Slowing down technique

This is by far the least-understood performance driver and the hardest one to do. It's hard because it requires you to take what feels like a step backwards in your skill level, and it will reveal your weaknesses and deficiencies in technique. The compensations and flaws in your technique that you will discover when you slow it down are usually foundational, and thus will take time to improve, so you need to commit to feeling comfortable with feeling uncomfortable over an extended period of time. For these reasons, most people won't ever go here, but the greatest performers do.

It is worth repeating and emphasizing what I said earlier. Slowing down technique is much harder than doing it quickly, especially if you've gained a certain level of proficiency. Why is that? Speed allows you to cheat and compensate. Going slow forces you to develop the skill, strength, flexibility, or whatever traits you need for each part of the technique. The slower you move, the more likely you are to notice small jerks or twitches in your techniques. These small glitches are blind spots in your proprioceptive map (the areas of the brain responsible for sensing movements). After years of repetitive training, your central nervous system tends to block out parts of movements, a phenomenon known as *sensory motor amnesia*, due to your compensations while executing the technique fast. Cheating has literally become carved into your neural pathways. Slowing down technique allows you to explore, identify, and eliminate these cheats in your technique. Also, when you slow down, you'll notice other things like excessive force, tension, weakness, and muscular imbalances.

For me, one of the best references for slowing down to achieve mastery are dancers. They work until they can do each move slowly, and then they combine them at full speed to create a fluid masterpiece of perfectly executed techniques. The result when dancers don't embrace the suck of doing it slowly is usually more impactful than just staying stagnant in your skill level. Since they inevitably end up doing the techniques with all types of compensations, because they are focussed just on the end output, they end up being a prime candidate for serious injuries that set them back even more. This is very common, not only with dancers, but also martial artists (myself included). I shared in an earlier chapter how I tore my hamstring because I hadn't worked the fundamentals properly.

During the journey of fixing my alignment and flexibility with my mentor Donna, whom I mentioned before, I realized that I needed to swallow my pride and fix what was weak and not moving properly. To do this required that I journey down the hard path of slowing down technique. I began focussing on the deep muscles of the hips, both in terms of range of motion, and of strength and stability. I'll be honest, it was really tough. I went from feeling like a world class competitor (which I'd been), to feeling clumsy and weak as I trained my body to move more biomechanically correctly. I no longer allowed myself to use my speed to generate force to lift my leg high, but had to start developing the strength to slowly raise and hold my legs high. I had to reiteratively tell my ego to shut up as I struggled with the most basic, baby level exercises that little children in ballet do. It's still a work in progress, but my performance has already improved exponentially and I now know that, when I achieve the proper level of slowed-down technique, I can improve even further. Only then will I be able to optimally leverage my strengths, my speed, and my power because I'll have raised my fundamentals to world class level.

This is a theme you'll see if you study great competitors like Kobe Bryant, who restructured how he moved and shot after a serious injury, coming back stronger and faster. Tiger Woods also famously changed his swing halfway through his career, when he was already considered a top player.

I recently heard a swim coach talk about slowing down his swimmers' speed to 50% to improve technique. He pointed out that, when people, even very advanced swimmers, slow down, they often still rush their arm through the underwater phrase, especially on their breathing arm. This is usually due to the lack of momentum keeping their bodies afloat and this can then often lead to a "timing limp" in their stroke. He uses the slowing down technique to help his athletes find their stability and balance through their core, which will make them stronger swimmers.

In the world of business, I see so many people who get by on their strengths, but they don't slow down to learn the basics that could take them to a new level as leaders because they feel it is humiliating. Very often, people in executive roles are promoted because of some functional success in the past, yet their new role requires that they learn other skills that they were able to get around in the past while still producing results. Skills like coaching to develop team members, teamwork, active listening, and understanding how to create a culture of psychological safety are common gaps in the current skill set of most corporate leaders. The sad part is that most will be unwilling to do the hard, unpleasant work to slow things down to learn these skills.

Rest and the Triangle of Performance

A simple model I use to help clients keep track of the balance necessary to drive performance in the long term is what I call the *Triangle of Performance*. It's actually very simple and logical, but also greatly underutilized. Most of my clients are ambitious people—Type A over-achievers. That's great in terms of drive and desire to work hard, but that's only one-third of *The Performance Pyramid*. Like the geometric shape that gives this model its name, stability comes from the sum of the three strong vectors that work synergistically to give you a solid and resilient structure. *The Performance Pyramid* requires that you plan and optimize all three of the dimensions that comprise it: Work, Nutrition, and Rest.

Work is the easiest to understand, and you've probably picked up this book because you are looking for smarter and more efficient ways to structure that work. The chapters of this book contain tools, techniques, and principles to optimize your work. However, let's look at the other two dimensions, as they represent specific ways to *slow down* that will improve performance.

Nutrition

When you're working beyond your current skill level to improve, as we saw in the explanation of *Deliberate Practice*, feeding your mind and body with the highest quality fuel is essential. Whole foods that will give you the physical and cognitive stamina you need are not merely recommended, but they are essential to repair and recover from the work you do. Proper hydration is also incredibly important. Research shows that water loss of as little as 2% of body weight can impair performance, whereas losses of 5% can decrease capacity for work by up to 30%!

Most people will admit that what and when you eat and drink can affect your performance, but when I refer to nutrition, I'm not just referring to food and hydration. I mean anything that can enter your mind, body, and soul and affect your performance—and that includes the environment you work and live in. The people who surround you can have a huge impact on your performance and your mental and emotional state. A toxic environment can not only drain your energy to unsuspected levels, it can plant doubts in your mind from all the negativity surrounding you day in and day out.

Even well-intentioned people, such as family members, can often be unconsciously influenced by their own biases. People have a tendency to extrapolate their limitations and frustrations onto you. If they did not achieve their dreams—or worse, if they did not even attempt them due to fear—they will be more propense to try and discourage you on your mastery journey. I honestly believe that, many times, these people do not have hostile intentions, but the ego is tricky and often drives behaviors meant to protect its fragile self from feeling inadequate. People generally do the best they can, given the resources and level of evolution or awareness they have at any given moment. As a result, well-meaning people close to you may be the biggest naysayers who try to get you to give up on your dreams. Often, they may remember the pain of having not achieved their goals, and are trying to spare you that experience. Of course, that's not their decision, and it doesn't help you, but again, people do the best given where they are at the moment. That doesn't mean you should listen to them. As a matter of fact, you should eliminate them from your environment, at least as far as your mastery journey goes. I'm not suggesting you stop seeing your close family members, but you can set a rule that you won't discuss anything related to your dreams or goals with them. It's perfectly acceptable to set barriers. Your family and friends will continue to be important members of your life, but it is perfectly legitimate if you choose to construct a carefully curated network to support your mission that does not include them.

Choosing that support network carefully can have a greater impact than just having people believe in you and support you with positive words. It also provides a valuable benchmark for you. They say you are the average of the five people you spend the most time with, and I believe there is truth in that. I think the biggest impact comes from how your inner circle sets a standard that you can rise or fall to. The people who surround you while on your journey can make a huge difference to the ambition you set for yourself—and whether you believe more is possible or you let yourself off the hook based on what you see around you. If I want to feel in shape, I can hang out with five clients who are top executives and have successful careers, but are in quite poor physical shape. By comparison, I feel great. I'm the fitness icon of that group. Alternatively, I can spend more time with five of my clients who are professional athletes, and compare my level of fitness to theirs. In the latter case, I realize how much I could improve if I aspired to reach the skills and abilities they have.

The key point I want to get across is that not choosing all aspects of your nutrition is also a choice. It means that you let circumstances shape the quality of what raw materials you use to regenerate your mind, body, and soul. Thus, slowing down to plan and curate your food, your hydration, and your environment is essential and will catapult you along your mastery journey in the mid and long term.

Rest

The third variable of *The Performance Triangle*, rest, is such a powerful performance lever, yet most people get it wrong. This is an especially common pitfall for highly competitive athletes and type A business leaders. Rest needs to be carefully designed and programmed according to each phase of your training and development.

This topic feels especially personal to me because it's a lesson that I took a long time—too long—to learn. In every area where I've chased mastery—and especially where I've excelled—my *superpower* has always been the time, focus, and energy I dedicated to working on my craft. The nice part of that story is that I'm proud I am able to leverage the best of myself by focussing on the variables I can influence and control.

Now, the dark side of the Force, as it were, is that when you come to believe that your superpower is outworking your competition, you tend to base your work plan on doing more, with more intensity and more focus, for longer. That works pretty well, *up to a certain point*, but there is a very dangerous, fine line you need to understand and not cross. Pushing yourself beyond the threshold for that given moment of your training can have a significant negative impact on your performance journey. Your mind and body absolutely need the proper rest in order to recover from the hard work you put in and to allow your organism to adapt and grow in response to the stimulus.

When I speak of programming rest, I divide it up into three different, but very relevant, dimensions: sleep, mental rest, and recovery time after training stress.

Sleep

Let's start with the first one, as it's the most straightforward. Sleep is considered by many experts as the most underused performance enhancer available. People grossly underestimate the importance and impact of proper rest on their performance. This is true from professional athletes to top CEOs. Sleep is so important that top names in professional sports like Roger Federer and Cristiano Ronaldo have openly admitted to hiring sleep coaches to help them optimize their rest. Most professional athletes who work with a sleep expert have found that they need at least 10—and up to 14—hours of sleep a day, sometimes split between nighttime sleep and mid-day naps, to perform at their best.

The corporate world, in large part, is still living in the Stone Age in this regard, pushing the hurtful fallacy of *face time* being a great indicator of employee performance. I have seen so many corporate teams performing far below optimal levels because of lack of sleep and overall rest. The mantra that *more is better* needs to be reviewed in corporate settings because there is a clear diminishing return—and even negative return in the extreme—on working more hours past a certain point. You may be able to push through during a short window, for a specific event or deadline, but sustained over time, teams that do not get enough sleep perform way below average and definitely below potential.

Mental rest

The second type of rest, mental rest, is just as important as sleep. *Deliberate Practice* requires extreme focus, energy, and effort, and as you've seen, that's part of why it works so well as a training protocol. However, humans aren't wired to consistently throw the throttle to 100 in any dimension. Just as you can't sprint for five hours in a race, you can't focus at peak level for 14 hours a day, every day. It just isn't possible. So, whenever I see excessive hours of work, I know clients are mentally just going through the motions over half the time, and that defeats the whole point of working harder, because you aren't getting the returns for the effort. It's as senseless as throwing more money at an investment with diminishing returns in the hopes that it improves.

Again, in business, this is especially prevalent. Team members, especially executives, convince themselves that they can work marathon hours and remain sharp as a tack the whole time. It's sad that I even have to say this, but there's no way that's possible. It's pure fiction. It's pure ego talking, and not very smart if what you want is truly to drive towards mastery and improve performance. Unfortunately, in many environments, it's about politics, not performance, but that's a subject for a separate book.

Recovery time after exposure to stress

Let's look at the third type of rest, which is recovery after exposure to stress. So, just to refresh your memory, when we talk about stress, we mean any demand put on the organism, physical or mental, that is beyond your current level of resources. I define resources as skills or physical capabilities like strength, stamina, etc. So, that stress can be lifting a heavier weight (demands) than what you can comfortably manage with your current muscle mass (resources), or working on a new skill (demands), physical or cognitive, that requires you to learn and develop new capabilities (resources). As we saw before, stress takes you out of homeostasis and triggers an adaptation from the organism. Now, here's the key: it's during rest that you actually improve. Let me repeat that again: it's during the *rest* phase that you create the improvement in motor skills, strength, endurance, or cognitive skills.

This has long been known by elite bodybuilders. They know muscles don't grow when you're lifting. That's what breaks them down. Work causes micro tears that are exactly what need to be repaired in order for more muscle fibers to be produced in response to the load demands. That whole process occurs *after* you finish your lifting workout. If you don't stop lifting—in other words, if you don't rest—the body can't repair and improve, and what you end up doing is weakening the muscles by breaking them down until you suffer an injury and loss of strength.

The exact same process occurs with technique or skill movements. You drill a free throw or a spinning back kick, but it's during *rest* that the body generates more myelin and deepens those new neurological pathways that drive that skill. My flexibility coach, Donna Flagg, often says that, when working flexibility in extreme ranges—for example, full front or side splits—it's necessary to give the body a day or two to repair, but also to *figure out* what you're asking it to do. Deep flexibility requires training, or for most people, *retraining* the body to move in a certain fashion that you're not used to and recruiting certain deep muscles you don't currently know how to control. It takes a while for the body to *get it* and start making the physical and neurological changes necessary to consolidate that skill so you can access it anytime. Again, that adaptation occurs during rest.

Although we all cognitively understand this, you'll find that most overachievers—in both sports and business—do the exact opposite when working their craft. The overriding belief is that, the more you work, the faster you'll advance, and that's only true up to a point, after which the returns are negative.

As we've seen, mastery of anything takes a long period of sustained, consistent, focussed practice. So, if you remember what we said in the *Maps* block, you need to plan and phase your training over a long time, building on the component parts in the correct order. To do that, you need to be able to train long and hard, over a sustained period of elapsed time. Pushing too much or resting too little leads to burn out, physically and mentally, and can easily result in injury. If you do get injured, it will set you back in your evolution, because you then have to recover, rehab, rebuild, and get back to the level you were at. It is a lot more intelligent and productive to ensure you continue to improve consistently over the long term.

I know it's not easy. I have committed this mistake myself many times, but over 35 years of training, I've fortunately gotten some things through my thick head, and since I've started programming adequate rest and recovery, my training has actually gotten more pleasurable and my results have skyrocketed. The best part is that I not only perform better once I warm up, but I now warm up faster and have more stability in my execution. So, the lesson is that proper rest also produces better long-term and sustainable performance gains.

I read a really wonderful post from Caroline McMorrow, a former college athlete that captures the essence of what we've been discussing, and I would like to share an excerpt with you. Here are a few lines from Caroline's post:

> "When I was an athlete in college and years prior too, the focus was on 'ignoring' my body at the cost of performance. Instead of learning to work with it. . . . it was about pushing through no matter what. That was the ultimate sign of strength and commitment. . . Sometimes I think about how much better of an athlete I could've been had I learned to work with my biology. Rather than against it . . ."

Let me stop here and highlight that last part. I have heard that sentiment from many professional athletes and have said it myself. So, a key takeaway here is to reframe what smart and dedicated training looks like. We need to break long-held paradigms that you need to push yourself and your teams to exhaustion and beyond. That may develop resilience, but it comes at a very high cost in terms of performance. Caroline's post finishes with the following thoughts:

> "The irony is, as an athlete, I've always felt quite in tune with my body. But at the same time, propelled to shut down the signs it shares with me—especially those to 'slow down' . . . Mind over matter. I can overpower my body with my mind. As competitive, hard charging people, it's so easy to silence those internal signals as your default. . . . but in the long run, it only ends up hurting you.
>
> Learning to work with your body and give it what it needs when it needs it. That's the key to high performance. . . . Sometimes discipline is pushing through and sometimes it's pulling back."

The feeling of an athlete being connected to our bodies is something I know well, but the problem is you learn to compensate for weaknesses and imbalances, and that ends up feeling *right,* because you've been doing it so long and it produces the end results. That's why it's so invaluable to have fresh eyes from an expert mentor to help you see where you need to work smarter. It's so common to see business people who have climbed the corporate ladder by being the person most dedicated to the firm, or *the champion of working late,* and later they not only don't realize how performance has been hindered by that, but even worse, they demand it of others, driving overall performance down.

That final thought from Caroline's post—that discipline sometimes is pushing through and sometimes it is pulling back and recovering—should become your mantra. I challenge you to evaluate how you work your craft and find an expert coach to challenge you and give you valuable insights. Your performance will skyrocket if you have the discipline to learn and implement proper rest and recovery.

Coaching Case File: Working with a CEO to slow down and drive success

The funny thing about success is that sometimes it takes on a life of its own. I've seen this in business often, and this particular client was living a fairy tale success story, but he felt like Dalí's famous painting *Els Elefants,* that depicts elephants with spider legs.

The company my client led had grown exponentially and was a favorite for investors who offered funding for continued growth through acquisition. Each victory drove stock price and enterprise value up. Although slowing down the speed of growth of the business was out of the question, we discussed slowing down the frantic pace that the leadership team was running at, and working some fundamentals that would solidify their ability to keep growing in a healthy manner. Radical candor is one of my core values, and I tell clients what I believe, because that's why they hire me—to improve. I told my client that his team was drunk on success. Things had gone so well that each new deal was pushed through in a shorter timeline. In my opinion, they were neglecting some key fundamentals, including slowing down and properly integrating the acquired assets and businesses. Many companies acquire competitors, but mistakenly only integrate financial statements and legal entities.

I worked with my client on all the fundamentals of integration that weren't being addressed, such as implementing a standard homogenous operating model across divisions, restructuring supplier clusters to achieve synergies, and rolling out best practices to all parts of the business to drive efficiencies and simplify integrating future acquisitions or organic growth.

Likewise, the leadership had spent years working 100-hour work weeks, and I believed they'd lost perspective and time to look reflectively at their organization and how they could improve. Their organizational structure had not evolved to drive the new size and complexity of the business. Innovation was talked about but not incentivized or properly funded. We ran an exercise I call *kill the company* where the goal is to have the leadership team pretend they have all just gone to a competitor, and using the knowledge they have of the strengths and weaknesses of their company, design what they would do—if they were competitors—to kill the company. What services or unique features could competitors launch that you could not match with your current company structure and operations model? What processes are slow and costly because you haven't done the efficiency work that competitors could offer more efficiently?

The process was rough at the beginning, and we had to deal with some sensitive egos, but as we looked at components of the model in a slower, more critical way, the potential benefits identified were huge and worth the hard work to drive them forward.

This client was an interesting example, because on the surface, it was all about success, but if you slow down and look deeply at each piece of the organization that you should have, the potential for improvement was sizable. In these cases, the most important turning point is getting the organization to understand that improvement potential doesn't mean the work was poorly done; it just means you are raising the bar of an already successful organization another notch up towards true mastery.

Coaching Case File: Slowing down kicking speed to develop greater strength and power in a martial artist

Whenever martial artists come to me to improve their performance, we almost always end up working on slowing down movements to later speed them up. When I speak of ambitious performers compensating for weaknesses in order to achieve the output, martial artists are a classic case. People who study kick-heavy arts like Tae Kwon Do—and some styles of Karate—train until they are able to get kicks off and then they work on consolidating that technique. Remember: *practice makes permanent*, so most martial artists find a way to work with their limitations and develop acceptable kicks and hand strikes, but most never realize the power potential they could have if they worked on the fundamentals.

This client came from a background in Olympic-style Tae Kwon Do, and was starting full contact kick-boxing, but his first few fights had not gone well. When we started working together, it became evident that, although he was fast, he lacked strength in his deep hips and core to generate the power needed in a full-contact environment where bouts are not usually decided by points, but by power. In Tae Kwon Do tournaments, he had been able to get by with kicks that were quick, but not powerful; however, they served to score points and win matches.

After preparing him for the road ahead, we began working on his balance first. The first pillar was developing the stability and strength to stand on one leg until he could push back a rushing opponent when he kicked, instead of being knocked over himself. This sounds easy, but it's a fundamental that few people work properly. From there, we worked breaking his kicks down into component parts, and strengthening each one. First the chamber, then the extension... each step slowly and meant to develop the same dexterity in his legs as most people have in their arms. We then worked on generating speed in smaller intervals of the technique. In other words, instead of using the momentum of stepping in and winding up to then throw the leg up, he learnt to raise his leg into a chamber, stop the technique there, then without momentum, generate speed to full extension.

Effectively what we did by slowing down the technique was to improve his execution and strength in each segment of the move, and then we weaved them all together, generating the synergy of increased power from each sub-component. Without slowing down, we never could have corrected his errors in technique, and he would have continued compensating for his lack of strength by using momentum. It took several months, but when he got the hang of breaking down technique and slowing it down to perfect it, his results in the ring began to improve significantly, as did his confidence.

By the way, slowing down is a tried and true technique in many domains. Bodybuilders have long since discovered that slowing down their reps generates more time under tension and prevents you from cheating reps with momentum to move heavier weights, resulting in more strength that they can later use for bigger lifts. Dancers similarly work balance and slow technique to develop exceptional strength, stability, and fluid movements.

Even though slowing down feels like going backward, because you are stripped of your compensation mechanisms, it's essential if you want to build the best technique you can to drive your maximum performance potential.

Stress and Pressure:
The Children of Fear

"Pressure is a privilege.
It only comes to those who earn it."

Billie Jean King
(World Number One
39x Grand Slam champion)

WHAT'S THE BIG DEAL?

Whenever I work with clients, no matter what field they specialize in—be it professional sports, high stakes business, or the performing arts—the discussion around stress and pressure inevitably always comes up. When it does, the first order of business for me is explaining that, although they are usually lumped together, stress and pressure are fundamentally different animals that require different approaches.

Knowing how to perform optimally necessarily requires an understanding of both stress and pressure, and the underlying F-word: *fear.* More specifically, optimizing your performance requires that you learn how to properly manage stress, pressure, and fear to mitigate the potential toxic effects they can have on your mind, emotions, and body.

Let's start by understanding each one; then we'll delve into tools and techniques related to each that will help improve your performance. Finally, we will look at what leaders can do to help their teams manage stress and pressure.

Stress: the good, the bad, and the ugly

In essence, stress occurs when demands exceed current capabilities or resources. This may sound familiar from when we discussed how to structure *Deliberate Practice* so that it pushes you just beyond your current skill levels to trigger the homeostasis reaction. This is the *good* type of stress. You program a stress that is slightly greater than your current abilities, and that triggers your organism to create the changes necessary to meet the increased demands. This is all good, as long as you can program the increases in stress and progressively manage them to generate the required improvements.

However, when most people speak of *stress*, they are referring to a situation where the *demands* seem to far outweigh the *resources*, no matter how fast you adapt, and this causes psychological, emotional—and even physical—*distress*. This is the *bad* type of stress. The dictionary definition of *distress* is the negative impact caused by excessive or prolonged stress. Keep that definition in mind as we look at how this plays out.

In a work environment, distress can arise from not having enough people for the volume of work, resulting in the backlog accumulating continuously until it feels unmanageable. Likewise, if you're asking people to take on new functions or enter new markets, they may not have the necessary skills, and again they may feel negative stress as they do not feel fully in control of the situation or unsure if they can deliver up to expectations.

For an athlete, say a gymnast, distress can arise because they are unable to master a specific move that they need to display in competition, creating a sense of frustration and anxiety.

Now the important point here is that not being able to meet all demands is not usually a hard stop in the short term and mid term, and the negative effects are not immediately visible. We've all seen teams or departments that struggle daily to manage the volume of work, but the company seems to continue forward. The impact on the team is less overtly visible, but progressively burns them out and, as a result, performance goes down over time and employee focus, productivity, morale, and health all suffer.

This is exactly what can happen with excessive physical training. In the last chapter, we saw that in *The Performance Triangle* model, if work is not properly balanced with rest and nutrition, the body and mind will not be able to recover, and you will start to burn out over time. Performance will actually get worse as a result of overtraining, and all too often, the result will be an injury.

So, when you're dealing with stress, you're not facing an immediate threat, and you may not see the impact in the short term, thus it's easy to assume people can just give *one more push*. However, you must consciously improve the equation of *demands to resources* over time, or performance will come crashing down at one point when the system—be it the human body or a department—can no longer sustain the excessive demands.

To understand the impact of not adapting resources, imagine moving the finish line in a 100-meter race. If people arrive at the finish line, and see you've moved it 10 meters further, they can put in an extra effort. Yet, when they get there, it's moved another 15 meters. They can push again, but each time, physically and psychologically, you are draining resources and pushing the system beyond what it was designed for. At one point, if you keep pushing, the system will break. If you let it get that far, you'll find recovering from there is infinitely more costly and difficult than having put in place the necessary changes to rebalance the stress equation.

Before we talk about how to attack and reduce stress, let's define pressure. Then we can look at how to deal with each challenge.

Pressure and what it really means to be "clutch"

The first and most fundamental point about how pressure differs from stress is one of capabilities. In the case of stress, you don't have sufficient resources to respond to the demands, whether that be a volume/capacity gap or a lack of specific skills necessary. When you are under pressure, however, you generally *have* the skills necessary, but the perceived cost of not performing well is so high that you freeze up and cannot access those skills properly. As opposed to a *demands/resources* imbalance that can build up over time, but does not create a threat in the short term, pressure situations occur when the stakes are high and impact is immediate. Or rather—let me nuance that— pressure occurs when your *perception* of the stakes is high. You feel pressure when you believe that the outcome of your activity has a very high value—either great reward or tremendous negative impact in the case of failure. The easiest example to illustrate this is the emergency landing of an aircraft. If you succeed, everyone survives. If you fail, many people—including yourself—may die. That's a high-stakes outcome and a pressure situation with a pretty immediate impact.

Note that there's no mention of lack of resources vs. the demands (i.e. skills or abilities) in the plane example. In other words, you may have the skills to fly and land an aircraft, and you may have done so successfully many times. The problem is not that you don't have the resources, or skills in this case, but rather that the gravity of the situation hinders you from accessing the skills you already have. This is why performers who do well under pressure are rare and considered *clutch*.

Again, we are talking about your *perceived* valuation of the potential outcome. In the plane example, most people would agree that the stakes are very high, but it's not always so objectively clear. A pro athlete who is taking the deciding shot in a championship game can feel the stakes are extremely high. The athlete won't die if they fail—at least not physically—but emotionally and psychologically, the threat feels very real. One failed shot will most probably not derail their career, but as long as the player believes that it will, their emotional state will enter into fear or anxiety mode, and their physiological reaction will be accelerated heart rate, tension, and usually, a steep drop in skill level.

It's worth stopping here to dispel a myth that is very prevalent in sports. When people talk about *clutch* players, there is a narrative that says they perform better under pressure. That has been empirically proven to *not* be true. Even a legend like Michael Jordan did not have a higher shot percentage under pressure. In fact, he had lower conversion rates in pressure situations, such as when the game was on the line. What made him *clutch* is that his performance dropped *much less* than the average player in these high-pressure situations.

Clutch does not mean better under pressure than without pressure; it means *marginally worse under pressure*. This may not sound like much, but it is very significant, because pressure situations tend to freeze people up, and they can not access their full level of skill that would normally be enough to complete the task, Again, this is a very different problem from the case of stress, where there is a real gap between demands and resources.

Types of fears and how to mitigate them

To simplify, I like to ask clients to separate fear into two broad categories. The most basic and easiest to recognize is what I call *survival fear*. This is the response when you fear for your life or safety. It's characterized by an adrenalin spike and accelerated breathing and heart rate. This is the kind of fear that is wired in your limbic brain and kept your ancestors alive long enough to pass on their DNA. If someone pulls a gun on you in an alley, this is the fear that it can generate because you believe this may put your life at risk. *Survival fear* is usually a short-term event. You are confronted by a danger that you need to mitigate quickly, and then it's over. This is the main fear you will encounter in pressure situations. Whether it's emergency-landing a plane, or taking the game-deciding shot in the seventh game of the NBA finals, you have a short window to react, and your challenge is accessing your maximum skill level to face it.

The second type of fear is what I call *first world fear*. Although people may feel like it's life-threatening, this is much more about feeling inadequate and socially in danger. This type of fear may keep you from innovating or standing up to an abusive boss for fear of losing your job. It can keep you from doing things you really want to try because you fear other people's opinions. This type of fear is a long-term, nagging fear that is background noise in your life and influences your choices and becomes an obstacle to feeling fulfilled. This is the fear that activates your fight-or-flight response under stress situations, despite there not being an immediate threat to your physical survival. This fear is linked to your need to be successful, your drive to beat others in order to prove yourself, and your fear of not being enough. All these drive the stories you tell yourself about why you can't reduce demands or increase resources that keep you stuck in chronic stress.

Let's look at how to manage *survival fear*, which is what you need to control in order to better manage *pressure*. As opposed to *stress*, that requires reestablishing new levels of resources or demand to achieve a healthy balance, *pressure* requires strategies to allow you to access as much of your existing skill level as possible. It's not the task that is overwhelming; it's that the fear generated by the perceived magnitude of the potential outcomes does not allow you to access your full skill level. The following are some of the most powerful techniques I teach my clients to manage *survival fear*.

Manage Meaning

Your first line of defense is being a *master of meaning*. Remember that nothing means anything, per se, except the meaning you give it. If you remember one of the coaching case studies I shared earlier, when one of my ATP players changed the meaning of converting a break point, he freed himself from the performance-inhibiting tension of believing the outcome could have a catastrophic impact. Once he realized that failing to convert *one* break point was not, in isolation, statistically significant, he was able to play with confidence and leverage his full skill set.

If you find yourself in a decisive moment where making a shot can decide a championship—and this generates *survival fear*—you can also reframe the situation by remembering the words of Billie Jean King that opened this chapter: "Pressure is a privilege." This means that you're fortunate enough to be competing in the most coveted circles, so whether you win or lose, you will always have the satisfaction of knowing you arrived where very few ever have. One player I worked with used this technique every time he stepped on court and felt the physiological response of *survival fear*. He would remind himself that this was what he had trained blood, sweat, and tears for his entire life, and he was going to let go of fear or expectations about the score. He was just going to experience the *autotelectic* experience of doing what he loved, in the most coveted arena in his sport.

The vast majority of the challenges you will encounter are really not as devastating as your uncontrolled mind can make you believe. However, what if you don't manage to convince yourself that the threat is anything but life-altering? When this happens, we need to leverage a toolkit of cognitive techniques to allow us to manage the survival fear that we can't diminish through managing *meaning* alone.

Focus on Process Cues

One staple technique I work on with clients is to focus on process cues, which is all you can really control. The outcome may be influenced by many factors outside your control, but your effort and your technique is completely under your scope of control. In fact, focussing on process cues is the best way to ensure optimal performance. It's logical if you think about it. What do you think will bring you better results—thinking *I want to win this point* or thinking *I know I play best when I keep active, relax my body, and shoot with no fear*? In case the answer is not obvious, it's the latter. Process cues are like the ingredients in a fine dish. If you focus on putting in the best ingredients, and cooking them in the way you know brings out the best taste, you've got a much better chance of making a wonderful meal than if you just think *I hope this meal tastes great*.

Prepare better than anyone else

Another very useful technique to help you manage pressure like an elite performer is to prepare so meticulously that you can rely on your training in the moments of most pressure. Besides the confidence that comes from knowing you worked harder than anyone could have expected, there are things you can do to improve your actual tolerance to pressure. One technique I use with players is what psychologists call *systematic desensitization.* This technique, used often to treat phobias, is based on exposing yourself to small, controlled doses of what generates your *survival fear* and progressively increasing the stimulus as you develop a higher tolerance. Although it may seem counterintuitive, the more you are exposed to the stimulus that generates your fear, the higher your threshold to tolerate that stimulus without freezing up or dropping your skill level.

I had a friend I met when doing my graduate degree at Yale who personified this principle. He had been in the Israeli army for years, and had become desensitized to the noise and fear of gunshots and explosions. This was put on display when he was interviewing with an Investment Bank near the World Trade Center in 1993, when the bombing occurred. The interviewer, an aggressive banker, cowered as he looked for someplace to feel safe (under his desk seemed a little childish). The conversations went as follows:

Banker: *What was that?*

My friend: *That was a bomb.*

Banker [nervously]: *How do you know that?*

My friend: *I've had bombs explode around me for many years. Trust me, it's a bomb. By the sound, I think it's not near enough for you to have to worry.*

My friend had become desensitized and was able to calmly assess the situation. By the way, he got hired because of that incident and his calm demeanor during the situation.

Research shows that desensitization works even when the stimulus is not identical or proportional to the one you may find when performing. For example, to help desensitize a player to the pressure of match play at Grand Slam events, I could not simulate a Grand Slam event, but I devised a series of anxiety-evoking stimuli during training. For example, I invited a former world number one to come watch him train. The pressure of knowing he was being watched by someone he admired, served as practice for him to focus on his process cues and become accustomed to accessing his full skill level despite feeling pressure.

Another great way to prepare and reduce fear when under pressure is to preplan responses to unexpected deviations so that, when things don't go as planned, you have already practiced adapting and finding solutions. Bill Walsh, former head coach of the San Francisco 49ers, used to run his players through different scenarios in training and in the film room, until they developed the habit of adapting to unexpected events and applying a predefined strategy to each one. The roleplay technique I use with sales teams, that I explained in a previous chapter, is a variation on this technique.

Stay in the present

One of the most performance-inhibiting habits people develop when under pressure is to time travel, as I call it. Performers begin either thinking of the past or the future and lose control of the only moment they can really influence—the present. People either think of past failures and feel anxiety about whether these outcomes will repeat themselves in the present situation, or they think about potential future outcomes that scare them. Neither the past nor the present are real or add any value to your performance in the present. The past is, well, *past*, as its name suggests, and there is no reason to believe it influences the results of the present moment. That's just your fear talking. Likewise, feeling anxiety over potential future outcomes is senseless because you don't know the future, so you are actually diverting focus and energy on one of a multitude of possible outcomes. Most often, the outcome you are fretting about never comes to pass. As Mark Twain famously said,

> "I've lived through some terrible things in my life, some of which actually happened."

The power of staying in the present is truly under-valued. When you find yourself traveling to the past or the future, take a few deep belly breaths and ask yourself the question: What *is real, right now? What problem do I have now, not what problem might I have in an hour or a week, but what is the situation right now?* Think about it: if you are worried that, if you don't make a sale you will lose your job, you're taking focus and energy away from the goal, closing the sale, and thinking about a potential outcome. *Have you been fired right now?* No, so don't think about it. It does not help.

The same technique can apply if are serving in a tennis match and have break point against you. *Has your serve been broken?* No, so focus on the process and unleash all your talent to win the present point. This is the only thing that is real, so eliminate everything else from your mind.

If, despite your efforts to stay present, you find yourself unable to stop thinking of past experiences where the result was negative, then at least challenge yourself and recall a successful execution in a similar situation before. This generates confidence because you remember you have the ability to manage this situation successfully because you have done it before.

Additional techniques to manage stress

All of the above techniques can be adapted to help you when dealing with the *first world fear* associated with stress. *Mastering meaning*, preparation, and staying in the present will all assist you in finding positive solutions to manage stressful situations. However, there is one additional dimension that we need to attack when the challenge is *stress*, not *pressure*.

Remember that *stress* is actually a good thing, if managed properly. The problem isn't stress, per se, it's the persistent existence of *excess stress which exceeds your current resources*. So, the first mistake you have to be careful not to make is to assume that, because you're a top performer, you can handle it. Although you may be able to endure the effects of stress in the short term, you absolutely must drive a solution that will rebalance the *demands/resources* equilibrium. That could mean bringing in team members with other skills that are missing (i.e. increasing resources), or directly reducing the workload of that team by reassigning it to another group (reducing demand). Likewise, if the resources you lack are specific skills, you need to put a plan in place to develop those skills, thus reducing the *demands vs resources* imbalance.

The key pitfall is that stress, as opposed to pressure, is not a short-term problem. It's the result of excessive stress over an extended period of time that can have devastating effects. So you need to ensure you start improving the situation as soon as possible. Don't make the mistake of thinking that, because you don't consider it as urgent, it isn't important.

One of the most obvious and powerful tools to manage chronic distress is to reduce demands. You might ask how you can do that if the demands are being put on you by others. Well, the truth is you can always choose to stop doing certain things. Seriously, you may be afraid of the costs you think those choices might have, but that doesn't rob you of the power to choose.

In fact, one of the traits of top performers is that they very clearly and firmly decide what to stop doing and what to focus on. As we'll see in the next chapter, focusing your energy gives power. If you disperse it, you lose power and effectiveness. Elite performance requires choosing your focus very deliberately. Being a perfectionist is just another way of saying you're afraid. Perfectionism is a cop-out. Fail often and fail forward.

Likewise, you have to worry only about what you deem important. If you think about what others would like, you'll wear yourself ragged, but the only person you have to be accountable to at the end of the day is yourself. Don't act like the printer queue, where all requests get processed as they come in. No one will console you if your choices don't drive you closer to your dream, so make sure you develop the strength to say no.

Tony Robbins has a great suggestion for how to frame this. He suggests distinguishing your *shoulds* from your *musts*. Musts are the ones that are non-negotiable. You never say you *should* feed your kids; it's a *must*. That's how you have to treat the activities that will take you closer to your mission. Discard the rest. A mastery journey is not about pleasing anyone; it's about fulfilling your soul's calling. Never sell out on that. The cost is too high.

One last and very important reminder. Fear will make you play *to not lose*. There is no way you can reach your full potential like that. You absolutely must *play to win*. The outcome really won't matter, because the real prize is not the titles you earn, the money you make, or the trophies you collect, but rather who you become in the process.

How leaders can make a huge difference (or be part of the problem)

Although all of the above techniques to mitigate fear and improve performance under pressure and stress seem like things that depend solely on the individual, as a leader you can greatly influence the environment and help or hinder your team members.

When something does not go as planned, great leaders first rally around team members, trying to understand the situation without laying blame. By doing this, you are changing the dynamic from an evaluation of someone to a problem-solving team exercise. When leaders start with *Whose fault is this? Who messed up?*, they automatically put team members in defensive mode, distracting their mental resources for the important task: finding a solution. That approach changes the perceived risk the person is facing. In other words, the leader is creating greater pressure, and as we saw before, pressure never makes people perform better.

Laying blame and speaking to team members like an angry parent would to a child is something archaic I see a lot amongst sports coaches and executives that absolutely needs to change if you want to drive optimal performance in your teams. For some misguided reason, people believe that, by screaming or otherwise pressuring team members, they will improve their performance. The underlying assumption there is that people need to be pressured or threatened to perform. *Do you really believe that?* If you honestly believe that, then you need to change your team. I have encountered very few people who require pressure to give their best. In fact, I have a very different and firm belief on this, based on three decades of driving performance.

First and foremost, most people *don't want to perform poorly*. Nobody goes to work thinking: *Let's see how poorly I can do my job today so I can be embarrassed in front of my teammates.* Think about it!!! And non-supportive reactions from supposed leaders are a big part of the problem. When poor performance does happen, it's usually not something the person or persons involved are happy about, so getting berated adds absolutely no value. In fact, it makes things worse. So, as a leader, be more concerned with driving performance and less concerned with giving your personal frustration and fears an emotional outlet.

Secondly, as we discussed before, performance always drops under pressure. So the more you make your team feel that the implications are very serious and it's life or death, the worse their performance will get, which is, paradoxically, the opposite of what you should be trying to achieve. And it is definitely not a positive leadership contribution, as you become a part of the problem instead of a support system and mentor.

The other toxic behavior I've seen many managers or coaches display is stepping out of the way and leaving the team member on their own to solve the issue. It usually sounds something like: *It's your problem. You need to fix it.* Well, that's a great way to make team members feel that the group is only a proper team when performance is high; otherwise, no one has their back. Feeling motivated yet? Probably not.

Let's be serious—no one performs perfectly 100% of the time, so creating the expectation that you need to never slip up, or you'll lose your standing with the leadership team, is a really stupid way of trying to drive performance. It just increases the pressure, because people feel that any mistake will be almost impossible to recover from. That's the opposite of what you want. You want teams that are resilient and who know the entire organization is vested in a common goal, and team members have each other's backs. Otherwise, that's not a team. It's a collection of individuals trying to get maximum personal benefit, even if that comes at someone else's cost.

Don't get me wrong: leaders need to give feedback—radically transparent feedback. However, feedback is meant to build a stronger team, not tear into someone who made a mistake. Great feedback serves as data to improve performance, not as a commentary on someone's character.

I often use the following metaphor to show corporate managers how absurd their behavior can be. Imagine your favorite sports team plays on any given Sunday. What would you think if they lost, and the coach walked into the locker room and said,

> "You really messed up. That was terrible. You'd better get your act together or you'll all be fired. Okay, I'm going home. I'll be back next Sunday to see if you've improved. Remember, I'm watching you."

Almost unanimously, people say that would be unacceptable, and what a shitty coach. Yet that's what so many managers do.

> "Hit your targets by next quarter or you're out. I'll be checking your numbers."

You would expect the coach in our example to evaluate what went wrong in strategy, tactics, and execution, to assess which skills need to be improved by each player and as a whole, and decide how to elevate performance. They might identify the need to work with specific assistant coaches on certain plays or improve physical traits in certain players like speed or strength. The coach may decide to bring in skills that are missing and integrate them in the team. And the most important part: on Monday, the coach and the team start working *together* on the plan to improve performance.

Now, imagine if managers in business applied the sports version of coaching leadership. The conversation would be more as follows,

> "How come you didn't hit your targets? Are you missing product support, market information, selling skills training, or sales support? Let's start on Monday working on this together and see if we can't get you back on track."

Any company that does that will have an engaged team that will go the distance for them, because they know they are part of a team and leadership is vested in their success. My experience is that people yell and attack when they feel insecure. A leader who blames others has no idea what to do to improve. By the way, it's okay to say you don't know the answer and work together with the team to find one.

Strong leaders don't lose their composure and always assume they are ultimately responsible for making things work. They learn to distinguish between stress and pressure situations and act accordingly as a leader. Most of all, they always remember they're trying to build a unique and high-performing unit, not find someone to blame if it doesn't work. That's how real leaders inspire and drive performance beyond what others can even imagine.

Coaching Case File:
How one ATP player learnt to unleash his talent under pressure

One curious thing I've noticed working with athletes is that different situations stress them in different ways. I've had players who play loose and relaxed when they're ahead on the scoreboard but freeze up when they're behind. This particular client was the opposite. When he was ahead in a match, his internal self-talk revolved around not losing the lead and the expectations that others would have of him winning the match, causing him to tighten up and skyrocketing the number of unforced errors he committed. When he was behind in a match, on the contrary, he seemed to feel that all was lost and nothing mattered, so he let loose and ended up playing some of his most amazing tennis.

The challenge then was how could I get him to feel loose at all times, no matter who he was playing or what the score was. The solution came from a series of tools we worked together, but the first one was to forget the score, *literally*. The way to do that was to change his focus exclusively to his process cues. In fact, we worked on having him focus so intently on the ball from when it came off his opponent's racket, that I wanted him to only see the ball clearly, and his rival should be a fuzzy image in the distance. To simplify things, the only self-talk he was allowed were things related to his process: *keep your feet active, relax to explode into the ball, breath deep, and release tension.* In essence, the goal was to get him to focus on himself, and his mental representation would take care of deciding the tactical responses of where the ball should be played. He knew all this and didn't need to think about it. His key success factor was getting out of his own way, and this allowed him to access the *zone*, that magical state where performance is optimal and things seem to slow down.

The additional benefit of not looking at the score was that he played with less fear. Since he wasn't allowed to think about how critical a certain game or point was, he played each point as if he were in practice. Likewise, since he wasn't focused on his rival because he was in the zone, he reduced the mental intimidation of facing higher ranked players. As a result, he ended up winning against several top five players in convincing fashion. This reinforced his belief that he was good enough to compete at the highest level.

His training intensity also increased as he was forced to apply the process cues model in practice as well. Eventually, this became his safe mental space, and he could access it during matches, allowing him to achieve the physiological state and level of activation that best worked for him.

Coaching Case File:
How a corporate client mitigated chronic stress

One large multinational had a very high-potential group that was suffering a progressive drop in performance. When I first sat with the team, it was crystal clear that they were feeling burned out from the chronic volume of demands that were way beyond their resources. The interesting part was that the volume of work corresponded not just to what their department should naturally do, but to a significant number of tasks that they picked up because other parts of the company were not performing up to the required level. This is an example of what I described earlier when I spoke of how ambitious individuals and teams over-stress certain links in the chain to compensate for others that are not meeting the fundamental requirements. Just like the example of an athlete who injures a hamstring because it is constantly called upon to compensate for rigid and immobile hip structures, this department was so dedicated to helping the company achieve its goals that they progressively took on new functions that others were not doing at acceptable standards, until their own performance started to suffer from the situation.

I helped them understand that they needed to rebalance the resources/demands equation, either by hiring new team members or by defining a reduced scope of work for the existing team. Since budget constraints and political factors made it impossible to increase the team, we needed to teach them to be focussed on the highest value-added activities. We reviewed the concept of *Area of Impact (AOI)*, those activities where each person has a disproportionately positive impact. When we mapped out their current time dedication, the average person on the team found that they spent around 5%-10% of their time working on activities in their *AOI*, and the bulk of their 12- 14 hour days managing the hundreds of other things that came across their desk.

We re-engineered each individual's activity list, ranking them from most to least critical, and then we drew a line at the point where they felt they could not manage more activities. The result was a significant list of tasks that the team lead took to the executive board and said that this department was going to stop doing because, either they were activities that corresponded to another area and were being covered, or they added little value. The team believed that the activities they were giving up would have a negligible impact on company performance.

The results were fast and significant. The team's time dedication to *AOI* activities shot up, the sensation of chronic stress and burnout decreased, and motivation and engagement went up. It sounds too simple to work, but knowing when to say no can be a very powerful performance driver. As for the activities that the team stopped doing, as Peter Drucker famously said,

"There is nothing so useless as doing efficiently that which should not be done at all."

High Heels and Martial Arts Masters

The successful warrior is the average man,
with laser-like focus.

Bruce Lee
(*Martial Arts Legend*)

WHAT'S THE BIG DEAL?

There are many lessons I have learnt from martial arts that have served me as powerful performance drivers, but perhaps none more than the concept of *focus*. In our current scattered, short-term-biased world, focus is a dwindling skill. People have been rewired to consume passive entertainment from electronic devices, and a growing number of people have lost the ability to focus long enough to read a book.

When I mention this to younger people, their response is usually: *Times change. So what?* It's true that technology has produced efficiencies in many areas, and it has opened up possibilities that we did not have before. At the same time, it has changed people's habits such that some truly essential skills and abilities have been lost. The introduction of a broader range of motorized vehicles, from cars to motorized scooters, combined with more sedentary jobs, more leisure time spent in front of computer or mobile screens, and diets loaded with processed foods, have resulted in a marked decrease in the physical activity that the average person does—with a corresponding increase in overweight and obese people in the population. In the same manner, the ability to focus intensely and consistently is becoming a lost art, and the *so what?* is that it has had a dramatic impact on human performance and the average performer's ability to realize their full potential. In fact, psychiatrist and neuroscientist Manfred Spitzer in his book, *Digital Dementia,* strongly warns of the consequences of excessive screen time and claims that his research has shown it can result in a reduction of grey matter in the hippocampus region of the brain.

The way I help clients understand the importance of focus is with an example almost anyone can relate to. If you've ever had your foot stepped on by a woman in high heels, you can attest to how painful it can be. If you haven't had this experience yet, find a friend with a pair of heels and ask her to step on your bare foot and you'll quickly get the point, both physically and metaphorically. If the same person takes off the heels and steps on your foot, you'll find the sensation is much less intense and less painful. That's a great illustration of focus. Explained in terms of physics, the more concentrated a given force is on a small area, the higher the pressure exerted against that surface with which it is in contact, where pressure is the force per unit area. So, the more focussed energy is, the more force it produces, and thus the more powerful it is. This is the secret by which martial art masters are able to break bricks with their bare hands by focussing all their power into a small striking area. If the same martial artist spread their arms as far apart as possible and pushed on a brick wall, the force would be much less because the energy gets dispersed and the bricks would suffer no damage.

That same principle happens not just with focus in terms of your physical body, but also in terms of your mind. The saying is true: *Where your focus goes, your energy flows, and whatever you focus that energy on, grows.* Since focus and energy are finite for any given person—you only have a certain amount to go around—then it's logical that, when you decrease the number of things you have to focus on, you increase the focus you can bring to that primary target, and thus you will have greater impact on those priorities.

Assuming I have convinced you that focus is, in fact, a performance superpower, let's explore the different types of *focus* that can most impact your results. I usually work on four different areas with clients who are serious about optimizing their performance.

I. Focus on staying present

II. Focus on eliminating multi-tasking

III. Focus on aligning priorities and decisions with your goals

IV. Focus on your level of activation

I.   Focus on staying present

In the previous chapter, we spoke about staying in the present as a technique to manage pressure. I'd like to dig a little deeper here about how to keep your focus on the present, as it's one of the most essential skills you can learn. It may sound basic and simple, but 99% of people are unable to do it consistently. This is a skill I've developed through my years of martial arts training and is one of the most valuable gifts I've received from walking the path of the martial arts.

I often refer to my training routine as my daily therapy. This is because it requires such absolute attention to technique, situation, and environment, that if you lose your focus, you can get hurt. That's easy to imagine if you think of when you're sparring, where loss of focus usually manifests as getting kicked or punched in the head (not fun). However, even when working alone on the heavy bag—which I do a lot—if you lose focus, you can strike incorrectly, and given the speed and power you're striking with, this can lead to a serious injury.

That's exactly what happened to me about seven years ago. I was working on a bag in a hotel gym while traveling for business. I was tired and my mind was on client issues. My bad! I wasn't fully focussed and thus didn't catch the slight move in the trajectory of the bag, and bam, I twisted my wrist. Since I work at full speed and power on the bag, the impact was significant, and it literally took me about six months of rehab to feel fully recovered and be able to train again at normal speed. That's a big loss of time and improvement opportunity for a split-second loss of focus, but that's how important focus is.

When I train, I deliberately take a few seconds to practice some rituals to make sure I'm fully focussed on the session coming up. Besides improving my ability to focus while performing, it serves as a wonderful mental health moment. Since I'm fully focussed on training, my mind stops thinking about everything on my to-do list and whatever needs my urgent attention. So I get an hour of mind-refreshing rest, and when I get back to the outside world, my energy and intensity are restored, and my performance soars.

I've taught this skill to my ATP tennis players, and it's made a huge difference in their performance. The ability to stay focussed on the present moment is such a powerful tool for competitive athletes. When they don't develop this capacity, this is what it looks like.

Several years ago, I started working with a player in the top 50. The first tournament I attended after agreeing to work together was Wimbledon. I watched his first round match and saw how lack of focus made him lose a winnable match. Here's how it played out.

My player won the first set and started serving the first game of the second set. He was slightly more relaxed after winning the first set than he should have been. This was his first loss of focus. At the same time, his opponent was more aggressive, because he had lost the first set and knew he needed to establish himself or the match dynamic would work against him. I call this the *wounded animal* reaction, and all my players learn to look out for it. Since my client had lost focus, the opponent broke his serve. No big deal, in and of itself, but my client then began to *time travel* as I explained in the previous chapter.

His focus was on the errors of that first game of the second set, and so his attention was dispersed, just like the martial artist pushing on the wall. That loss of focus meant he had less mental resources to focus on the next point. When the opponent started serving, my client had part of his mental strength and focus still living in the past. Since his focus had been dispersed between the past (the previous game) and the present, his skills and ability to respond were reduced. His mind was still thinking about the last game as the ball flew past him on his opponent's serve. He then moved to the other side of the court for the next serve, while he berated himself thinking about the previous game, and now, the point he'd just lost also. Of course, now his focus was even more dispersed, and the second point ended similarly to the first one. This dynamic went on and on as each mistake caused another loss of focus. When this happens to my clients, as I mentioned before, I call it *hemorrhaging*. Their *focus wound*, as it were, is just gushing energy and draining them. The opponent just rolled right over him with little resistance in the second set, and the dynamic continued until he lost in four sets.

After the match, I explained the principle of focus, and we worked on the skill over the next few months. He eventually learnt to focus one point at a time, no matter what had occurred before, and his performance improved, jumping significantly in the rankings.

The example of my client is a good reminder of why Zen masters have been teaching the value of staying present for centuries. Firstly, it's the only thing that is real. What do I mean by that? Well, as I mentioned when we looked at mitigating fear, the past is gone, and no amount of thinking about it will change that fact, and the future is really just one of a number of multiple possible futures. Focusing on the past or future robs us of focus and energy in the *now*, which is really the only place you can impact the future. What you do *today* is what will most impact your future. Now, that doesn't mean that you shouldn't learn from the past and foresee possible challenges in the future. It's wise to adapt your actions and decisions based on wisdom gained from past lessons and to consider potential future variables, but that's very different than living in the future or past. In fact, you take those learnings and apply them in the only place you can—the present.

Thomas M. Sterner, in his wonderful book, *The Practicing Mind,* describes the flow-like state that is achieved when the mind is still and completely in the present:

> ". . .the practicing mind is quiet. It lives in the present and has laser-like, pinpoint focus and accuracy. It obeys our precise directions, and all our energy moves through it. Because of this, we are calm and completely free of anxiety. We are where we should be at that moment, doing what we should be doing and completely aware of what we are experiencing. There is no wasted motion, physically or mentally."

By the way, people will often say to me something along the lines of: *I can't help it; that's just the way I am. I worry about the future.* Well, that's BS. The reality is that it's the neural pathway you've become comfortable with and hardwired into your system. The bad news is that you've done it so often, it's very entrenched and very automatic. The good news is that you can always rewire your reactions and the stories you tell yourself, but you need to begin by gaining awareness.

If you honestly evaluate how worry and stress can impact your future, you'll find that it has never helped anyone improve a situation or avoid a potential outcome they feared. Once you've analyzed the situation and decided on the best course of action, there comes a point where you can no longer influence the outcome, and regardless of how much you worry, you won't change any external factors. The only thing you will achieve if you continue to worry is to wear yourself out, become exhausted, and have less fresh ideas to face whatever situation finally materializes.

II. Focus on eliminating multitasking

We mentioned above how dispersing your energy reduces your power. I can't think of a better example of that in our modern society than the popular myth of multitasking. First off, let's be clear: multitasking, meaning doing several things in parallel, is a myth. You can't actually do two things at the exact same time. For example, try counting to 100 and saying your ABCs at the same time. You can't! What you can do, at best, is to *alternate* quickly between one and the other, but you can't think, or say for that matter, *"one"* at the same instant you think *"A."*

When you multitask, you're in effect spreading your energy across several tasks, and switching your focus quickly between them. In addition to the loss of performance due to the dispersed energy that we mentioned, you have an additional cost derived from the effect of connection and disconnection. The connection/disconnection effect is basically the loss in momentum from stopping, changing activities, refocussing, then getting into a rhythm. Metaphorically, it's similar to the energetic cost of repeatedly running in one direction, coming to a full stop, and then running in the opposite direction again. With simple, rote tasks, you will notice that disconnection costs less. Since you can count, and you know the alphabet without having to concentrate much, you can switch between them without too much disconnection effect—although even there, you will find yourself thinking, *Where was I in the counting or the alphabet before I switched?*

When you get into more complex and demanding tasks that require all your energy and focus, you really start to notice the connection/disconnection effect. Have you ever noticed that, when you sit down to start working on something complex or creative, it takes you a while to get into the groove? Once you manage to hit *cruising speed,* if you stop or get interrupted, you'll notice when you get back to the task, you need time to fully focus, remember where you were, and basically recover the rhythm you were performing at before the interruption. This is true for purely cognitive tasks and for physical tasks that require concentration.

If you're working on perfecting a specific technique for your craft, such as your forehand in tennis or a spinning kick in martial arts, you'll be focusing on the process cues you need to refine and improve the technique. If, while doing this, you are forced to switch between techniques, you'll find you're less likely to remember the cues and your learning curve will be slower and less permanent. That's why you'll see pros repeat a certain technique, for example 100 inside-outside forehands, in a row, so they can focus on perfecting that part of the process. Once you have that, you can work on transitioning from one technique to the next with minimum loss of efficiency, but you will always have a *cost* of change or connection/disconnection.

It's no wonder, if you look at the modern workplace, that productivity is generally way below what it could be. Team members are constantly changing from one meeting or discussion to another, and they are being interrupted when trying to do deep work by calls or emails that pop onto their desktop, breaking the flow of concentration and generating a cost in terms of lost productivity due to the connection/disconnection effect. Simply focusing on one task, during a period of time—say 20-40 minutes—will drive performance exponentially higher.

Productivity expert Cal Newport, who is an associate professor at Georgetown University, and author of the best selling book, *Deep Work*, believes that the future will be run by those who know how to go deep into their work, stating,

> "Depth will become increasingly rare and therefore increasingly valuable."

Newport offers an equation he calls *The Law of Productivity*, where focus is a key variable:

High Quality Work = (Time Spent) X (Intensity of Focus)

One last thought on multitasking. According to a Harvard study, people spend almost 47% percent of their waking hours thinking about something other than what they're doing. These types of findings reinforce my conviction that there is a lot of room to improve performance in most organizations.

III. Focus on aligning decisions with your priorities

The third type of focus that is essential for optimal performance is the focus of decisions and priorities. One of the ways the best in the world drive their performance is by focussing their decisions and actions on a very specific set of priorities—and saying no to anything that does not directly take them closer to their mission. We discussed this when speaking of *standards* in the *Mindset* block.

This may sound extreme, but if you have a very ambitious goal, such as becoming the best you can be in your craft, you need to focus on those activities that take you closer to your goal, and say no to the rest, no matter how enticing or appealing they may appear in the short term. Another way of looking at it is that top performers focus on decisions that often signify delayed gratification but contribute to a specific, ambitious mission. We saw in a previous chapter the story of how Kobe Bryant explained the off-season training contract he signed with himself. This seemingly absurd activity provided focus and avoided splurging willpower or energy on deciding what he was going to do or not do on any given training day. It was in the plan, and there was no room for not carrying through with the plan. This is a world class example of ruthless focus that drove exceptional performance.

As you've seen throughout the rest of this book, I'm a huge believer in the value of objective data to keep yourself honest about how focussed you really are on your goals. An exercise I have been doing for years, and I suggest you take the time to do, is what I call a *diary audit*. Just follow these three simple steps:

1. Take a blank sheet of paper and draw a table with three columns. In the first column, write a list of key activities you spend your time on during a typical day. You can choose the correct level of detail in your particular case, but the key is that you include all those that are essential to achieving your goal, as well as those that you know you do, such as sleep and eat. Therefore, if learning is fundamental to achieving your goal, write it down on the list. For an athlete, the *training* category may be detailed into more specific items such as stretching, strength development, or perfecting technique.
2. In the second column, insert the average hours you spend every day in each category, making sure that the sum equals

24 hours. To get a good and true picture of how you really spend your time, I suggest doing this exercise with your diary in front of you. Make sure you find the approximate time you spend on an average day. You're looking for an order of magnitude, but make sure it's accurate, even if it's not exact to the minute.

3. Finally, divide the hours you spend on each activity by 24 hours, and you will know what percentage of your life you devote to each of the categories you have identified as important. Here's where many eyebrows go up. This simple exercise gives you a realistic picture of how much time you are actually dedicating to the things that will drive you closer to your goal, and how much time you are not using optimally. The impact is magnified when you realize that, if you were honest about the time you spend in a typical day, what you have before you is a miniature model of your life planning and your priorities. If you say mental skills training is essential for you, but you only spend a half hour a week on it, that works out to about 4-5 minutes a day (depending on how many days you divide by) and averages 0.3% of your total time. You then either recognize that this activity is not essential for you, or you need to sharpen your focus and program more time for that activity. Likewise, if you are a CEO and decide that speaking to the team to understand their temperature and insights is something important, make sure the real time you spend on this represents a percentage of your day that you would not be embarrassed to share with the team.

I once heard Arnold Schwarzenegger explain a similar concept in a keynote speech. He said he allocated six hours for sleeping. Someone asked,

"What if you need to sleep 8 hours?"

Schwarzenegger's response was legendary:

"Then sleep faster."

IV. Focus on your ideal level of activation

Every performer has days when everything seems to flow and days where they struggle to perform at their best. That's just part of being human. Now here's where the greats differentiate themselves. When they're not having their best day, top performers focus on a very specific part of their performance and try to get that right as a way to get back into flow.

Instead of trying to do the advanced stuff that blows competitors away, when elite performers are struggling to find their ideal rhythm, they focus on process cues, and not on the scoreboard. One important tool I teach players when they need to find stability and consistency in their performances is managing what I call a performer's *ideal level of activation*. Each individual—and this applies across the board to top performers in any field, including business leaders—has a specific level of activation at which they perform optimally. It's not always a case of more is better. In fact, some clutch performers give their best when they are below a certain threshold. There is no right or wrong level, only levels that adapt better to one person's personality and style of execution.

The level of activation that works for one person may not work for another. Here are a few examples of equally legendary performers who need to operate in different ranges to perform optimally.

Rafael Nadal is notorious for his high-energy, high-intensity style. He will jump up and down before a match, and he plays at a very high level of activation. He also increases his intensity level as he plays more matches. Nadal is known for wearing opponents down with his extremely high level of activation over long matches. By contrast, Nadal's main rival, Roger Federer, was a player who clearly played better when he was slightly more relaxed. Somewhere between 80% to 90% of maximum activation was his sweet spot, and this is where he played his own magical brand of tennis. As opposed to Nadal, he seemed to play better when he'd had less match play and came in fresher. Both are legendary players, but each had a very different *ideal level of activation*, and the key is that neither one would have performed as well if they tried to mimic the level of activation of his rival.

Another example of excellence at different *ideal levels of activation* can be seen in legendary quarterbacks Joe Montana and Tom Brady. Teammates have declared in interviews that Brady played best when he was angry, and one former Patriots player, Julian Edelman, even insinuated in a recent interview that long-time Patriots Head Coach Bill Belichick would sometimes berate Brady to spark that higher level of activation. Joe Montana, on the other hand, was known as *Cool Joe,* because even in the highest pressure moments, he remained at a lower *ideal level of activation.* A famous anecdote that illustrates this occurred in Super Bowl XXII, when the 49ers were trailing the Cincinnati Bengals and had time for only one more drive. Knowing the game was on the line, and sensing the tension in the huddle, before calling a play, Montana said,

"Hey, look behind the end zone, it's [actor] John Candy."

That line brought the tension of the rest of the team down just enough to free up their maximum potential, and Montana went on to lead his team down the field and throw the game-winning touchdown to John Taylor with 34 seconds remaining. Montana later admitted that, in pressure moments like those, he focussed on enjoying the game and pretending he was a child playing in the park, acting out his childhood fantasies of being in the Super Bowl and driving for the game-winning drive. *Cool Joe* knew how to manage an *ideal level of activation* to get the most out of himself and his team.

Coaching Case File: How level of activation improved a player's performance

An ATP player I worked with was in the top 100, with potential to rise higher, but was not managing to level up. After working together for a while on how to manage pressure, we identified that he had very powerful shots, but he tended to get too excited and commit too many errors, even when he wasn't in high-pressure moments of the match. He was giving away free points, not just in critical games or set points, but during the entire match. When we reviewed recent matches on video and calculated the sum of those points, it was clear that he had to fix this, or he'd struggle against consistent and experienced players.

I explained the concept of *ideal level of activation,* and he agreed to explore it with me. We scanned other players and found which style and identity felt right for him. It's not always a case of more is better. Remember, there is no right or wrong level, only levels that adapt better to one person's personality and style of execution.

We worked to refine his identity as an extremely powerful being, who needed to unleash only 80-90% of his power. He would not let his opponents *contaminate* his game and make him hit harder (as had occurred in the past). We burnt in his mind that he was so strong that he could match pace with any player while staying at 90% power. This allowed him to keep a cool head and view the match strategically, while pressuring his opponents with his pace. As we progressed, he began applying that identity in tight match situations and found he could pressure rivals into committing mistakes while he felt he was working within a safe zone of activation where he did not need to take unadvisable risks or push his power to the max.

This worked so well for him that we began asking, *"What else would someone who has power and knows how to manage his level of activation be able to do?"* and he discovered he had room for improvement in other parts of his game where he clearly held too much physical tension. We worked on serve mechanics, and explosive relaxation improved his serve speed, resulting in much greater power. We combined this with breathing techniques I showed him, and when he was in high-pressure moments, he'd use diaphragm breathing to relax, then use that 90% power and improved serve to blast opponents. This greater power from a slightly lower level of activation gave him a new weapon that allowed him to assert his identity as a powerful player, who unleashed his potential in a controlled manner. That year he reached his first ATP 500 final and achieved his highest career ranking.

Coaching Case File: How a corporate team used focus to launch a new business unit

One of my large corporate clients had grown very rapidly over the past few years and found themselves needing to drive innovation of new products and services outside their core offering. The problem was that, every time they started exploring something new, some *urgent* matter in the core business would take them off track. Their focus was continually dispersed, and as you've learnt, that resulted in little power to move anything significant forward. The CEO was increasingly frustrated and needed diversification to appease market analysts.

I suggested creating a special group that we would separate from the business and see if focus could change the results. The CEO gave me the mandate, and I launched a 6-month pilot with a group of 25 people from across the business, from sales to operations. We first created an environment that would allow them to focus without getting distracted. We moved them to a different location, outside the main offices, to avoid them getting *hijacked* at the coffee machine by someone in the core business that needed help. We also set strict rules around use of emails, messaging apps, and even phones. Participants were allowed to check email for 30 minutes at the start of the day and then at the end of the day again. Their accounts generated automatic messages advising emailers that they may take 24 to 48 hours to respond.

Participants were also forbidden from working on tasks from their normal job while in the task force, to eliminate multitasking. At the beginning, they felt a lot of anxiety about not being able to respond, but after a week or two, they unanimously shared that being able to focus on one clear task made them feel much more productive, and also refreshed and energized. We set targets for the teams around a series of goals, including defining the value proposition in this new service offering, identifying competition, and developing a sales plan.

Within six months the group was considered one of the top three strategic players in the new niche and was being invited to the biggest tenders in the market, several of which they won. The model was so successful that, after the pilot period, the Chief Revenue Officer reorganized his team around similar business units. This was the ultimate recognition that the focus had made a huge impact in performance.

We Will "Rice": Communication As a Performance Driver (From One to Many)

The single biggest problem in communication is the illusion that it has taken place.

George Bernard Shaw
(*Nobel Prize-winning playwright*)

WHAT'S THE BIG DEAL?

Imagine if you had the answer to world peace. I bet you'd be extremely excited to share it with world leaders and anyone who would listen, knowing that as soon as they implemented your idea, the suffering of millions would end. Can you feel the excitement and positive energy just by imagining it? Now imagine that you suddenly lost all your ability to communicate, verbally, in writing, or by any other fashion, and you were unable to share your brilliant insight with anyone. How frustrating would that be? It would be enough to drive you insane.

The point of the above simulation is to highlight that you can have all the talent, brilliance, and skill in the world, but none of it means anything if you are not a world class communicator. Most people are not world class. Not even close. Effective communication skills are one of the glaring gaps in most businesses and sports organizations. In fact, the title of this chapter comes from a written communication I accidentally saw years ago where what was meant to be an inspirational message turned into a meme, because the person misspelled the word *rise* as *rice* instead. Despite the fun we can have by pointing out that spelling mistakes can happen—after all, we're all human *beans* [pun intended]—the underlying message is dead serious. Effective communication skills are near the top of my list of severely undervalued and underutilized performance levers.

One reason language is such a powerful performance tool is because, I believe, ultimately, leadership is a transfer of belief and contagious conviction. Great leaders are great communicators and powerful storytellers, and they rally teams around a passion-driven mission. To do that, you need to understand the impact your words can have, both positive and negative, and become a master of choosing and using language capable of helping others get *unstuck* and inspiring them to discover new limits of what's possible.

Moreover, the tools in this block have been about exceptional execution, or *Mojo*. To transfer and implement those tools across an organization requires an exceptional ability to communicate and align ideas, expectations, and priorities. Without elite communication skills, you can never aspire to maximizing the performance of a team or an organization and generating synergies amongst its members.

If you've never thought that communication could be so powerful, strap yourself in, because you're about to gain access to a performance driver that will open up a whole new world of potential for you, your team, and your entire organization.

Why is language so powerful?

Let's start by laying the groundwork. Language is so powerful because it implicitly conveys our beliefs, opinions, and evaluations, even when we don't mean to do so.

Let's do a little experiment so you can experience and deeply understand what I mean by this. Imagine your child comes home with a bad grade on a test (if you don't have a child, imagine you have one or think of a younger sibling or simply someone you are mentoring). Here are two different reactions you could have. Let me know if you notice a difference in how they might make you feel.

Reaction #1: *See, this is what happens when you're lazy and don't study.*

What is your child hearing when you say this? You are affirming that your child *is* lazy. This is an evaluation of their character or identity. Secondly, you are stating with no room for doubt that your child didn't study and didn't try. There is no room there for the possibility that they *did* study, but need to learn how to study more effectively, or how to transfer that knowledge to test situations. These words will make your child feel shame and sadness because they disappointed you, and will probably negatively impact their feelings of self-worth.

Is that what you really want to achieve? I doubt it. We might try to justify it by saying that children have to learn to be responsible. That's the hands-off, crappy manager approach of *it's your problem; you need to fix it.* Try taking a performance-mentoring approach, and let's change your response to something like the following.

Reaction #2: *How do you feel about this? Why do you think you didn't get a better grade? Do you need to understand the material better? Do you* *think if you'd prepared differently, you would have had a better result? Would you like to explore new ways to study to see if that helps?*

Let's break down this second reaction and see what it can produce:

Asking *how do you feel?* is a game-changer because, before berating or evaluating your child, you're opening a dialogue to share how they feel. This allows your child to share their feelings of frustration or confusion or guilt, or whatever. By starting like this, you're opening up a dialogue, instead of passing a definitive sentence. And most importantly, you're acting like a great leader and saying, *I'm going to help you because we're in this together.*

Why do you think you didn't get a good grade? Here you're allowing your child to feel in control of the analysis. You might be surprised to find that your child probably already has an idea of what needs to change or improve, but even if they don't, you've established a dynamic where you're going to work it out together. Not you vs. them, but together as a team.

The rest of the questions help your child explore possible reasons for the result. Study habits, content knowledge, and understanding are all areas to explore, plus any your child may also identify. Can you imagine the difference of impact that you have on your child, who sees you as a role model and authority figure, and whose opinion is important? We need to think about how we communicate, especially when we feel frustrated, to ensure that the result is building a stronger base, not planting the seeds of self-doubt and a negative self-image that may stay with someone over the long term.

Deciphering Rules:
a fundamental skill they never teach you

One of the most valuable and effective communication tools I've ever learnt is the concept of *deciphering rules*. The best way to explain this concept requires a quick explanation of the neuroscience of how we store knowledge in our brains. As we go through life, the bulk of our knowledge is stored not as pure facts, but as what are referred to as *causal explanations*. We try to link new data to similar ideas that are familiar to us. Thinking is, basically, bringing two concepts together in a relationship.

We form concepts when the synapses in our brains link neurons in specific patterns. In essence, our brains tell stories to help us understand what's happening and how to respond. The relevant implication is the following: most of the things we know aren't facts; they are the stories we tell ourselves about those concepts. In other words, what we *know* is not absolute truth but rather opinions, assumptions, and interpretations.

As a result, since the brain—specifically the left hemisphere—is wired to find explanations for concepts, and it finds safety in the familiar, it relies on the existing neural connections that have always worked before. This means that, when we give meaning to events and concepts, it is the unconscious that is loading your conscious mind with thoughts and emotions that are presented as facts, but in reality they are just hypotheses.

Here's the *so what*! Since facts aren't facts, but rather interpretations each person believes, there is no way to know exactly what specific words, actions, or ideas mean to another person. In this context, *rules* are similar to what we discussed in the chapter about *Masters of Meaning,* where we learnt that nothing has a fixed meaning. Each person attributes a personalized meaning based on their experiences, paradigms, and the influence of their environments, especially in childhood years. The challenge when communicating, then, is understanding how other people will interpret your words or ideas.

In this sense, the Golden Rule, although very well-intentioned, is not the best advice. The Golden Rule advocates treating others as you would like to be treated yourself, but what you need to do is treat people as *they* wish to be treated. The problem is that no one ever teaches us *how* to identify and understand how others interpret actions and words. The art of understanding what others value and how events make them feel is, in essence, the skill of *deciphering rules.*

Let me draw out how this can lead to significant communication issues and damage relationships with an example almost anyone can relate to: *deciphering rules* in a marriage or similar sentimental relationship. If my wife and I have not established a dynamic to share what we need and how different things make us feel, we could easily find ourselves in the following situation. Imagine that one of my wife's internal rules is that, when she feels upset about something, her definition of *being loved and supported* is being left alone. In her mind, for whatever reason, be it upbringing, previous experiences, or whatever (in fact, the why doesn't matter), this is what she believes love looks like when your partner is angry or distressed. Of course, we have never discussed this. It just seems incredibly obvious to her that this is the correct way to act.

I, on the other hand, may strongly feel that *being loved and supported* when I'm angry or sad looks very differently. I expect my partner to be very attentive, very loving and present, both emotionally and physically. Sit on the couch and hold my hand. Tell me how much you love me. Just make sure I know you are there for me. Like my wife, I've never thought to break this down for her. I just consider it the only reasonable way to act.

So you can see where this is going, right? When one of us is very upset, the probability is that the other person will, out of the immense love and commitment we feel for each other, try to show the sad partner love and support *as we would like to receive it!* But, instead of helping, our actions will only serve to further upset the other person. The worst part is that we won't understand why, so the partner trying to give the support and love will give some meaning or explanation to our significant other's rejection of our sincere and loving support. This can generate yet another misunderstanding if, for example, I (mistakenly) interpret that she doesn't want my support because she no longer loves me. My reaction to that interpretation may generate another reaction in her, and things can quickly spiral out of control. All because we don't know how to communicate clearly and deeply.

This type of blind spot about another person's rules occurs many times a day, at different levels. We stack mistaken meaning on top of erroneous interpretation and end up building a story that we believe. As you saw when we talked about how the brain stores data, we will store this story as absolute truth, although it is nothing more than opinion, assumptions, and interpretations based on imperfect data and filtered through our own personal biases, many of which we are not even aware of. Can you now truly appreciate how much of a superpower it is to be a master communicator? Imagine how you could drive performance if you could avoid these mistaken dynamics in a company or on a professional sports team.

I can read your mind....NOT!

One of the things I see often that sabotages effective and productive communication is the terrible habit of thinking that you know what others are thinking and what their intentions really are. Here's a bucket of cold water. No matter how smart you are, or how well you think you know the other person, you never really know, with certainty, what the other person is thinking. What you are doing is taking a guess, more or less informed and educated, on what you think is going on in their thoughts and emotions, but in reality, you have nothing concrete to affirm what another person's intention is.

So here's a rule to live by: *never judge intention, rather base your feedback on behaviors.* When you do this, you change the dynamic from an emotional, aggressive statement like this . . .

"You did that to make me feel stupid."

. . . to one where you share your *rules* and how you feel, and invite the other person to open a dialogue, similar to the following:

"When you do that, I'm sure it's not your intention, but I want to let you know that it makes me feel that you consider me stupid or inferior."

What you will find—and it's a surprisingly consistent outcome when people start using this principle—is that the other person will usually be surprised that their comment made you feel that way. And, if they have an interest in strengthening the relationship, they will try to explain what their true intention was and explore with you ways to communicate without making you feel attacked or insulted.

A good tool to keep you from jumping to false conclusions is to always try to find two or three other potential explanations or *meanings* for the other person's behavior. So, for example, if you are the coach of a team, and a player seems to be giving a half-hearted effort, instead of berating them and implying that they are lazy, not interested or not committed to the team, ask yourself what else could be behind the behaviors. Could they feel ill? Could they have a serious personal problem at home? Could they feel unmotivated by something that you said or did the day before? Each of those reasons will make you feel differently towards the player, and as a result, you will react differently, and even your tone and body language will be different.

This sounds too simple to be effective, but if you try it, you will find it a game-changer. When you start by setting the premise that you don't have certainty on anything the other person is thinking, feeling, or going through, you approach communication in a much more empathetic and constructive way. Likewise, set limits and don't allow anyone to stick you with an intention they imagined is behind your actions. When this happens, I always stop people in their tracks, politely but firmly, stating,

> "No, you can't go there. You have no idea what my intention was. Only I know that, so if you want to know, ask, but you can't inform me of why I did something because you don't know."

It may often happen, when there are strong emotions stirring within someone, that they do not know themselves why they do certain things, and opening the dialogue may help them realize how some of their hidden biases are influencing their behavior, opening the path to build a new, more constructive dynamic going forward. You'll see an example of this in one of the cases I've included at the end of this chapter.

Small details make a huge difference: be deliberate when you speak

When speaking about how to practice, and the evolution of your craft as you strive for mastery, a consistent theme has been that elite performers focus on and optimize small details that make huge differences. These details are key to helping produce world-class performances. It's the difference between the poetry of Mikhail Baryshnikov and a lesser dancer or the brilliance of Roger Federer vs. other ATP pros who are good, but not legendary.

The same is true when you communicate. The best of the best not only focus on *deciphering rules,* but they are also meticulous in the words they choose, the order in which they communicate, as well as their tone, body language, and overall energy. All these things change how your message is received, and great leaders don't leave to chance how others will interpret what they want to communicate.

If you want an easy example to illustrate how word choice and delivery affect the dynamic of an interaction, try this. Tell someone who is nervous to "relax." Depending on how and when it's said, and the dynamic between the two people, the reaction can be completely different. Imagine you are nervous about something and discussing it with your partner. *Relax* can sound reassuring if your partner says,

"Relax, you've got this under control."

However, it can sound patronizing if the same partner says,

"Just relax. You're getting irrational."

Same word, very different interpretation, that leads to different emotions and a whole different dynamic.

One powerful application of language in driving performance comes from the power of aligning expectations. People tend to be lax about how precise their language is when trying to explain what they expect from others. In high-performance environments, this is a huge risk factor, because, if there is not crystal clarity about what success looks like and what is expected from each member of the team, then you leave room for individual, and misaligned, interpretations. Think of this in the context of an organization like the Navy SEALs. They leave no room for error or interpretation about what each member of a team must do and what success looks like, because if they did, someone might end up dead.

You don't need to be risking your life, however, for clear expectations to be essential.

In sports, if a coach says something like,

"I need you to work harder,"

this actually provides no real clues as to *what* do I need to work, and what does *working harder* mean in practical terms?

Instead the coach could say something like,

> "I need you to work with the strength coach to improve your explosive speed and stamina. Then you need to spend extra time with assistant coach X reviewing the playbook and strategy for each game. I'd expect at least an extra hour a day from you."

This provides very clear direction and the player can know what they have to do. Generic and ambiguous instructions like *work harder* leave the door open to a frustrated player who is deeply committed and tries their hardest, but does not work on the things the coach wants and expects, thus both parties end up unhappy and frustrated.

Another example, this time in business, would be a manager saying during a performance review to a team member,

"You need to show more initiative."

When I hear this, I advise the person to respond,

"What would it look like if I had more initiative? What things would I have to do to show more initiative? How can we measure this so I know if I'm advancing?"

This response will usually show if the manager is genuinely interested and qualified, or just throwing down smoke bombs because they think it's their job to criticize so that people will magically improve their performance and *try harder.* If the manager is a leader, they will be able to break it down in an actionable fashion, like this,

"For example, I want you to suggest five new accounts per month that we should be targeting, including this analysis [shares outline that will guide the team member] on each one."

That's an actionable step that later can be measured and leaves no room for confusion. It's also genuinely helpful for the person receiving the feedback, instead of just being disheartening and frustrating.

I can't overemphasize this! If you apply language to align expectations with your team, you'll find performance will shoot up.

Also, always ask and listen. I mean, *really* listen, not the modern version of listening which is remaining quiet, thinking of what you will respond until the other person stops talking. I mean listen deeply, and ask sincere, probing questions.

Other useful communication tools

Here are some additional techniques that I find very useful when using language to drive performance.

Ask better questions to get better answers

Einstein said that, if he had an hour to solve a problem, he'd spend 55 minutes defining the *right* problem. All too often we focus on the wrong thing, which makes solving the issue almost impossible.

To make this tangible, imagine a tennis player struggling to improve a part of their game. A poor-quality question would sound like this:

"Why is my second serve so shitty?"

Phrasing it like this leads to an internal dialogue like the following:

"Why is your second serve shitty? Because you're not good enough to play at this level. You've never been a big server and your first coach told you that you'd never have a real serve."

If the question is poorly-phrased, as in this example, it opens up the door for you to focus on a whole host of reasons that basically convince you that you'll never fix this, and you should just accept it. You're not feeding your brain a question that drives a productive answer, so what you get is an excuse that lets you off the hook. After all, it's not your fault that you've never had a natural ability to do this, right? Wrong. That's victim mode and will never take you anywhere positive.

A much better question that this player could ask themselves is:

"What do I need to do to take my second serve to world class?"

Now you have question that leads you directly to clear action steps, such as:

"I can seek out an expert serve coach to improve my technique. I can also plan and dedicate 10 extra hours a week just to practicing my second serve with what I learn from the coach. Additionally, I can study film of my second serve and compare vs. the best servers on tour to see what I can learn. Also, I'm going to work on unique variables that I can improve now such as serve placement, spin, etc."

Can you see how the quality of the question you asked changes the energy and dynamic and creates a space where you can actually start to solve issues, instead of wallowing in self-pity?

Keep asking "why"

This is a great technique to get to the root cause of what's driving someone's behaviors. Often people will give you a more superficial response, so the idea is to continue to ask *why* until you get to the root cause. Let's see this with the example of a person who does not want to speak in public at work. The conversation could sound like this:

Manager: *Why don't you want to speak in public?*

Team member: *I don't think I'm credible.*

Manager: *Why don't you feel credible?*

Team member: *I don't have as much experience in the company as others.*

Manager: *Why does that make you not credible to talk about the subject where you are an expert? You have worked many years in this field elsewhere.*

Team member: *That was in my native country, and here I'll be speaking to an international group.*

Manager: *Why does that matter?*

Team member: *I don't think I can get my ideas across properly.*

Manager: *Why do you feel you won't be able to get your ideas across?*

Team member: *Well, English is my second language. I have a strong accent and limited vocabulary.*

As you can see, the issue this person has is not about standing in front of peers, nor about the technical content of their speech, but rather an insecurity about language skills. This would allow the manager to help drive solutions both in the long term (e.g. hiring a personal language tutor) and in the short term (e.g. structuring the presentation format in a way that allows the speaker to follow notes and have a more fluent speaker on hand to help with clarification questions). Without the cycle of *why* questions, the manager would not have understood the root cause and would not have been able to influence performance.

Two from Teager

Two specific tools that I learnt from a fellow named David Teager (may he rest in peace), who was one of the founders of United Research, which later was integrated into Gemini Consulting, was to use specific language when posing questions. Teager taught us how to use the following two phrases that I've found surprisingly useful over the years. When trying to engage in dialogue in a way that does not generate a sense of conflict and opens up the creative faculties of the brain, use the phrases *I wish I knew* ... and *how to...*

Let's see how this works. Imagine you're in a heated argument with a colleague or teammate. You seem to be going in circles. The other person is saying something along the lines of, *You're not giving me what I need* or *That's not up to the level I expect.* Using *I wish I knew* helps break the cycle. For example, you could say,

> "I really want to solve this, but I think I'm missing something. **I wish I knew** how to meet your expectations. Can you help me define what I need to do differently and what that output would look like?"

You've just changed the dynamic and set the stage indicating that you want to provide what they need, and have asked them to help you understand what it is and what you need to do to satisfy them.

Here's another example, this time using the *how to* tool. Say your team is struggling with a rival who seems to be beating you to market. The team is saying things like *We're just too slow* or *We're getting killed because we have heavy bureaucratic processes.* You can change the dynamic by saying,

> "Okay, here's the problem to solve: I want to know **how to** cut our go to market time by 40%."

People will initially balk and return to all the reasons that you can't. Here's where the question is so powerful because you can redirect energy:

> "Listen again to the question. I asked you to give me ideas on **how to** cut our go to market time by 40%. Don't tell me why

we can't. I know you've invested a lot in consolidating the list of reasons why we can't. The only thing you can answer is *how can we* do this? What would need to be true? Even if it seems impossible, I'm asking you to think outside of the box."

With this phrase, you will change the focus from the *barriers* to the *opportunities* and the actions you need to take to drive those opportunities. Humans tend to get stuck on the reasons why they can't, and miss all the ways they can.

In summary, language can be an incredibly powerful foundational tool, and you should invest time and effort in improving your communication skills, because the quality of your questions determines the quality of your information. The quality of your information directly affects the quality of your decisions, and the quality of your decisions influences your chances of success. Thus, great leaders are passionate and strategic communicators and great storytellers that rally teams around a passion-driven mission.

Foundational skills that require communication excellence

I believe there are a series of foundational skills all humans who interact with others should learn, and many of these require strong communication skills. A partial list of what I help clients implement in their organization are teams that have at least the following skills:

Real communication skills: These include active listening, rephrasing, understanding rules/empathy, and managing expectations.

Innovation: We saw above how language can help free teams from limiting paradigms. Communication allows us to model ideas and ways of working that allow for cross-fertilization across industries or disciplines.

Psychological safety: With the rising awareness of the importance of mental wellbeing in athletes and employees, how can this *not* be a key skill to develop? Optimal performance requires an environment where feedback is sought out and errors are not just tolerated, but provoked, because you are pushing people to develop skills outside their current level through *Deliberate Practice*.

I believe that, looking forward, we need to change the way we think about skills development, be that in schooling, companies, or sports teams. The result will not only be much better performance, but a social system that helps develop everyone's unique talents and contributions.

Communication advice from Mike Smith, former head coach of the Atlanta Falcons

There are, and have been, many amazing coaches in professional sports history. What makes them special is unique to each one, but one of the common traits they share is that they inspire and raise the performance of the individuals and teams they lead. Although he may not have the list of trophies that other coaches have amassed, I find Mike Smith has one skill at which he is one of the best: effective, empowering communication.

I want to share a very brief summary of the key points I've picked up from Mike's use of communication in his leadership philosophy, because I think any CEO or coach should use this as a checklist to see if they're covering these essential points. I've complemented Mike's model with my own insights wherever I thought that might increase clarity and understanding.

First off, although mission is defined by top leadership, Mike reminds us that culture needs to be built all the way from the locker room up to the boardroom. To do this, communication of the vision, mission, and values frequently—and at all levels—is an essential ingredient. I would add that you need to communicate not just what the values are, but how each team member can personify them, and then regularly monitor that everyone—including and especially top leaders— is walking the talk.

When choosing and shaping your team, Mike suggests having as many optimistic and contagiously enthusiastic communicators of the mission as possible. Weed out toxic, negative people. You can't afford to have those energy drains disperse your momentum if you're aiming to be world-class. Remember what we discussed about the power of focussed energy. I'd add here a mention to my official title in my company, GOLD Results. On my business cards and email signature, I have the title *CEO* crossed out, and below my title is *Chief Passion Officer.* I do this because it reminds everyone that this is my key function. My job is to rally a team of ridiculously talented individuals around a common mission and infuse them with the same intense passion I feel. Then, I need to provide them all the support I can to unleash their unique skills, and get out of the way so they can shine and take us places I alone could not.

As far as guidelines on communication activities, Mike suggests communicating daily, both at an individual level and in groups. He reminds us that, if there is a void in communication, it gets filled with fear and negativity. Communicating is not just *emitting;* it's fundamentally about listening and understanding, so ask questions

THE OPTIMAL PERFORMANCE FORMULA

and truly listen deeply. If you don't listen, you won't have an accurate feeling of your team's morale and temperature.

Communicate with the intention to connect! Slow down and break bread with your team members, because relationships take time and effort. You can't pretend to be a tight group if you don't invest enough time and energy together. This involves sincere caring for the team and their wellbeing. Value each team member as a person, not a number. Be a transformational leader instead of a transactional one.

In addition to the great insights from Mike Smith, I'd add how important it is to create a culture of psychological safety where people can truly speak out and give and share feedback in a way that is positive and builds up the team, as opposed to being a weapon for team members to attack each other. Hold standards high and make sure each person understands that they are responsible for holding others to a higher standard, no matter what their role in the team or their level of seniority. Leadership is defined by how you act, not what your title says.

Coaching Case File: How deciphering rules helped improve a player's performance

I worked with a tennis player who seemed to just stop trying at the end of tough matches. His coach and team couldn't understand it and felt frustrated because everyone believed the player could have won many of the matches if he'd continued to fight until the end. After one match at a major tournament, the tennis coach stormed out, furious after the player threw the fifth set, and asked me to speak with him. Here's how the dialogue went (notice the use of the *why* technique):

Me: *What happened out there in the fifth set? You were battling and staying neck and neck, then you seemed to just drop your level. WHY did you change how you were playing in that last set?*

Player: *I don't know. I just lost focus and felt like I wanted to get out of there as fast as possible.*

Me: *WHY did you want to get off the court so fast?*

Player: *I just didn't feel right. I wasn't able to create separation from my rival. It was really tight the whole time.*

Me: *WHY is that a problem? As long as you hold serve, you're technically tied. Why did that make you feel "not right"?*

Player: *Because if I can't get an advantage, then he might get a lucky break and take the set and match.*

Me: *And WHY is that so bad? That's the nature of the game. You give your best and forget about the score, which you can't control. If you stop trying, you don't even give yourself a chance. WHY is it better to just stop like you did?*

Player. *I don't know. I guess it's less risky.*

Me: *WHY do you say that? How is it less risky?*

Player: *If I stop trying, then I'm just seen as an immature kid, but if I try and lose, then I'm a failure.*

BINGO! That last statement allowed me to finally get to the core of what was behind the behavior. Then I was able to start working with the player to examine and fix these mistaken beliefs and replace them with more empowering ones that drove improvement in his performance in tight matches.

Coaching Case File:
How word choice affected dynamics
under pressure in a corporate client

One very large multinational client asked my team to improve the performance of an important high-profile project. The internal person leading the project for their company was struggling with the complexity of a multi-country, cross-functional program that had over 100 active stakeholders and participants. On one occasion, there was a critical process being carried out over the weekend that one of my team members was coordinating. The process was programmed to start at 8:30 and the client reached out at about 8:45 to ask,

"How's the process going? Did everything start on time?"

The team was on top of it, so the person who responded *meant to say* ,

"I haven't checked in the last five minutes, but I know it started on time and should be running smoothly, but let me check and confirm where we are."

What this person actually said was,

"I don't know. Let me check."

What the client interpreted from that response is that the team had *not* been there and no one was following up to make sure things got done. The person who gave that response did not think how it might give the impression that no one was controlling the process. Can you see how the power of words changed the feeling completely? It may just sound nuanced, but to the listener, it's a completely different response. Great communicators not only think of how they *say* things, but also try to have empathy regarding how the listener, with their specific background and circumstances, will *hear* and *interpret* the answer. If your listener is under pressure, as was the case with this client, they may be more prone to jump to negative conclusions.

I worked with the team on how they needed to communicate, not just in terms of how they chose their words, but we also deciphered the client's unspoken rule that was something like: *If everything is under control, then the team should proactively update me before I have to ask. If no one is updating me, then no one is making sure things are on track.* Notice, this is one person's individual interpretation, formed from previous experiences and the meaning they gave to those events. Another person may have a different rule and assume, *If I don't hear anything from the team, it means everything's under control.*

Once we deciphered this client's rule, we set up a schedule of giving periodic updates, with carefully-crafted messages to ensure no misunderstandings. The rest of the project proceeded like clockwork, and the client was very satisfied. This is a great example of how communication skills are key levers of performance and should be required foundational skills in any organization.

FINAL THOUGHTS

What Now?

Throughout this book, I've shared the key elements of my personal toolbox in a way that you can go back and reference as you advance along your journey.

The next step, however, is yours.

You need to decide if all the effort necessary to implement *The Optimal Performance Formula* is worth it for you. I hope your answer is a resounding *yes*, and that these insights have helped increase the passion burning inside you to achieve what few dare to even try.

If you take away one idea, I hope it's this. All the science and the real-life stories I shared should bring you to one, unequivocal conclusion. Your limits are not defined by your luck in the genetic lottery, nor by the challenges you've found along the way. The most important factors that will determine how far you go along your mastery journey are how hard you work and how you leverage the tools that you now have in your hands to dissolve the obstacles you'll encounter along the way.

As you've seen, prodigies don't exist. What creates elite performers are unstoppable souls burning with the passion to make their mission a reality, despite what others see, believe or can comprehend.

Don't ever give up on your dreams. The world needs more unreasonable dreamers.

I'm rooting for you!
Adolfo

Resources

To continue supporting organizations, athletes, and individuals from all walks of life in their quest for optimal performance, I founded GOLD Results. On our web page, there's a section with free resources that may be of use to you.

www.gold-results.com

Recommended Reading

The following is a list of wonderful books I've enjoyed that will enable you to delve deeper into varied performance subjects and scientific research I've summarized in this book.

Accelerating Excellence:
The Principles that Drive Elite Performance
James King

Atomic Habits
James Clear

Be Like Water: *Practical Wisdom from the Martial Arts*
Joseph Cardillo

Be Your Future Self Now:
The Science of Intentional Transformation
Benjamin P. Hardy

Beyond Grit:
Ten Powerful Practices to Gain the High-Performance Edge
Cindra Kamphoff

Champion's Mind: *How Great Athletes Think, Train, and Thrive*
James A. Afremow and Jim Craig

Competent is Not an Option: Build an Elite Leadership Team
Following the Talent Development Game Plan of Sports Champions
Art Turock

Discipline Equals Freedom: Field Manual
Jocko Willink

Elite Minds: How Winners Think Differently to Create a Competitive
Edge and Maximize Success
Stan Beecham

Fear Less: How to Win at Life Without Losing Yourself
Pippa Grange

Finding Your Zone: Ten Core Lessons for Achieving Peak
Performance in Sports and Life
Michael Lardon and David Leadbetter

Flow: The Psychology of Optimal Experience
Mihaly Csikszentmihalyi

Flow in Sports: The Keys to Optimal Experiences and Performances
Mihaly Csikszentmihalyi and Susan Jackson

Grit: The Power of Passion and Perseverance
Angela Duckworth

High Performance Culture in Sports:
The Playbook for Program Excellence
Michael Allen, Phillip Ragain, Mike Allen, and Ron Ragain

Immunity to Change: How to Overcome It and Unlock the Potential in Yourself and Your Organization
Robert Kegan and Lisa Laskow Lahey

INNER EXCELLENCE: Train Your Mind for Extraordinary Performance and the Best Possible Life
Jim Murphy

Inside Sport Psychology
Costas I. Karageorghis and Peter Terry

Learn, Improve, Master:
How to Develop Any Skill and Excel at It
Nick Velasquez

Legacy
James Kerr

Mastery: The Keys to Success and Long-Term Fulfillment
George Leonard

Mind Gym: An Athlete's Guide to Inner Excellence
Gary Mack

Mind Your Mindset:
The Science That Shows Success Starts with Your Thinking
Michael Hyatt and Megan Hyatt Miller

Peak: Secrets from the New Science of Expertise
Anders Ericsson and Robert Pool

Peak Performance: Elevate Your Game, Avoid Burnout, and Thrive with the New Science of Success
Brad Stulberg and Steve Magness

Performing Under Pressure:
The Science of Doing Your Best When It Matters Most
Hendrie Weisinger and J. P. Pawliw-Fry

Powerful: Building a Culture of Freedom and Responsibility
Patty McCord

Primed to Perform: How to Build the Highest Performing Cultures Through the Science of Total Motivation
Neel Doshi and Lindsay McGregor

Psycho-Cybernetics
Maxwell Maltz

Raise Your Game:
High-Performance Secrets from the Best of the Best
Alan Stein Jr. and Jon Sternfeld

Rare Breed:
A Guide to Success for the Defiant, Dangerous, and Different
Sunny Bonnell and Ashleigh Hansberger

Relentless: From Good to Great to Unstoppable
Tim S. Grover

Shift Your Mind:
9 Mental Shifts to Thrive in Preparation and Performance
Brian Levenson

Stillpower: Excellence with Ease in Sports and Life
Garret Kramer

The Art of Impossible: A Peak Performance Primer
Steven Kotler

The Captain Class:
The Hidden Force Behind the World's Greatest Teams
Sam Walker

The Culture System:
A Proven Process for Creating an Extraordinary Team Culture
J.P. Nerbun

The Obstacle Is the Way:
The Timeless Art of Turning Trials into Triumph
Ryan Holiday

The Mindful Athlete: Secrets to Pure Performance
George Mumford, Phil Jackson

The Score Takes Care of Itself: My Philosophy of Leadership
Bill Walsh, Steve Jamison, and Craig Walsh

The Practicing Mind: Developing Focus and Discipline in Your Life
Thomas M. Sterner

The Sport Psych Handbook
Shane Murphy

The Standard: WINNING Every Day at YOUR Highest Level
Ben Newman

The Winning Mindset: What Sport Can Teach Us About
Great Leadership
Damian Hughes

There's No Plan B for Your A-Game:
Be the Best in the World at What You Do
Bo Eason

Thinking in Bets: Making Smarter Decisions When You Don't
Have All the Facts
Annie Duke

Unleash the Warrior Within: Develop the Focus, Discipline,
Confidence, and Courage You Need to Achieve Unlimited Goals
Richard J. Machowicz

Unlocked: Embrace Your Greatness, Find the Flow, Discover Success
George Mumford

What Business Can Learn From Sport Psychology:
Ten Lessons for Peak Professional Performance
Martin Turner, Jamie Barker

Why The Best Are The Best:
25 Powerful Words That Impact, Inspire, And Define Champions
Kevin Eastman

Win In The Dark: Some think you shine under the bright lights, the
bright lights only reveal your work in the dark
Joshua Medcalf and Lucas Jadin

Winning:*The Unforgiving Race to Greatness*
Tim S. Grover

With Winning in Mind
Lanny R. Bassham

WOLFPACK:
How to Come Together, Unleash Our Power and Change the Game
Abby Wambach

You Win in the Locker Room First*:*
The 7 C's to Build a Winning Team in Business, Sports, and Life
Jon Gordon, Mike Smith

177 Mental Toughness Secrets of the World Class*:*
The Thought Processes, Habits and Philosophies of the Great Ones
Steve Siebold

About the Author

Adolfo Gómez Sánchez has dedicated over three decades to studying and modeling what drives optimal performance. His mission is to mentor professional athletes, people leading multinational corporations, and other top performers to fulfill their maximum potential.

His insatiable quest to decode performance has led him to complement his Graduate Degree from Yale University with an unending study of the growing body of scientific research on performance. His academic training is paired with 30 years of experience in the trenches as a competitive athlete and performance mentor to C-Suite executives, professional athletes, and performance artists. A fundamental factor in Adolfo's optimal performance journey is his lifelong passion for training, teaching, and competing across five different martial arts, including a stay in Japan to train with legendary teachers.

He has applied his skills in business as CEO leading up to 300 people, and has led post-merger integrations, transformations, and turn-arounds, implementing performance tools and techniques across four continents and dozens of countries.

The result of his journey is a blueprint for performance he calls *The Optimal Performance Formula* that he leverages to help clients consistently prove that ...

"Impossible just means that no one has done it . . . YET!"